PENGUIN BOOKS
A BETTER INDIA: A BETTER WORLD

N.R. Narayana Murthy is the Founder-Chairman of Infosys Technologies Limited, a global software consulting company headquartered in Bangalore, India. He serves on the boards of Unilever, HSBC, NDTV, Ford Foundation and the UN Foundation. He also serves on the boards of Cornell University, Wharton School, Singapore Management University, Indian School of Business, Hyderabad, Indian Institute of Information Technology, Bangalore and INSEAD.

The *Economist* ranked Narayana Murthy among the ten most-admired global business leaders in 2005. He topped the *Economic Times* list of India's most powerful CEOs for three consecutive years: 2004 to 2006. He has been awarded the Padma Vibhushan by the Government of India, the Légion d'honneur by the Government of France, and the CBE by the British government. He is the first Indian winner of Ernst and Young's World Entrepreneur of the Year award and the Max Schmidheiny Liberty prize, and has appeared in the rankings of businessmen and innovators published by *India Today*, *Business Standard*, *Forbes*, *BusinessWeek*, *Time*, CNN, *Fortune* and *Financial Times*.

PRAISE FOR THE BOOK

'Narayana Murthy is a role model for millions of Indians. An iconic figure in the country, he is widely respected and looked up to not only for his business leadership but also for his ethics and personal conduct. He represents the face of the new, resurgent India to the world. I am sure this collection of his speeches will inform, inspire and guide many in the years to come'

—Manmohan Singh,
Prime Minister of India

'Narayana Murthy overcame many obstacles and demonstrated that it is possible to create a world-class, values-driven company in India. Through his vision and leadership Murthy sparked a wave of innovation and entrepreneurship that changed the way we view ourselves and how the world views India. In ░░░░░░░░ ░░n of his speeches, he delivers a timely mes░░ ░░░░░░░░░░ance of values and leadership in b░░░

                                                            ░ates,
C░   ░tion

A BETTER INDIA
A BETTER WORLD

N R Narayana Murthy

PENGUIN BOOKS

PENGUIN BOOKS
Published by the Penguin Group
Penguin Books India Pvt. Ltd, 11 Community Centre, Panchsheel Park,
New Delhi 110 017, India
Penguin Group (USA) Inc., 375 Hudson Street, New York, New York 10014, USA
Penguin Group (Canada), 90 Eglinton Avenue East, Suite 700, Toronto,
Ontario, M4P 2Y3, Canada (a division of Pearson Penguin Canada Inc.)
Penguin Books Ltd, 80 Strand, London WC2R 0RL, England
Penguin Ireland, 25 St Stephen's Green, Dublin 2, Ireland
(a division of Penguin Books Ltd)
Penguin Group (Australia), 250 Camberwell Road, Camberwell,
Victoria 3124, Australia (a division of Pearson Australia Group Pty Ltd)
Penguin Group (NZ), 67 Apollo Drive, Rosedale, North Shore 0632,
New Zealand (a division of Pearson New Zealand Ltd)
Penguin Group (South Africa) (Pty) Ltd, 24 Sturdee Avenue, Rosebank,
Johannesburg 2196, South Africa

Penguin Books Ltd, Registered Offices: 80 Strand, London WC2R 0RL, England

First published in Allen Lane by Penguin Books India 2009
Published in Penguin Books 2010

Copyright © N.R. Narayana Murthy 2009

All rights reserved

10 9 8 7 6

ISBN 9780143068570

Typeset in Californian FB by SÜRYA, New Delhi
Printed at Gopsons Papers Ltd, Noida

To
Akshata,
Rohan,
young Infoscions,
and the youth in India and the world,
with confidence that you will create a better India
and a better world

Contents

Acknowledgements   ix
Introduction   xii

PART I: ADDRESS TO STUDENTS

Learning from Experience   3
The Indian of the Twenty-first Century   9
Succeeding in the Contemporary World   18
Succeeding in a Globalized Corporation   23
The Need for Excellence   29
The Legal Professional in the Era of Globalization   33
A Case for a More Open Trade Regime in India   37
The Role of Religion in Education   42

PART II: VALUES

What Can We Learn from the West?   47
The Role of Discipline in Accelerating National Development   55
How Can We Stop Corruption in India?   66
In Praise of Secularism   72
Time for Chak De, India!   76
My Empowered India   78

PART III: IMPORTANT NATIONAL ISSUES

Lessons from the Economic Reforms of 1991   83
Population and Economic Development in India   93
A Framework for Urban Planning in Modern India   101

The Eight Visions that Changed the Face of India   112
Software Enterprises: The Temples of New India   116

PART IV: EDUCATION

What Would I Do if I Were the Principal   129
   of a Secondary School?
A Framework for Reforms in Higher Education in India   132
The Unfinished Agenda   149

PART V: LEADERSHIP CHALLENGES

On Leadership: Lessons from the Infosys Journey   157
A Leadership Mindset for a Resurgent India   166

PART VI: CORPORATE AND PUBLIC GOVERNANCE

Good Corporate Governance: A Checklist or a Mindset?   173
Corporate Governance and its Relevance to India   185
Corporate Governance: A Practitioner's Viewpoint   193
A New Model for Effective Public Governance   201

PART VII: CORPORATE SOCIAL RESPONSIBILITY AND PHILANTHROPY

Compassionate Capitalism   211
The Travails of Philanthropy in India   219

PART VIII: ENTREPRENEURSHIP

Reflections of an Entrepreneur   229
On Entrepreneurship   238

PART IX: GLOBALIZATION

Do We Need a Flat World?   247
Making Globalization Work for India   257
Transforming Emerging Economies and   270
   Leaving Behind Legacies

PART X: INFOSYS

The Importance of Respect for a Corporation   281
The Journey So Far   285
On Reaching Adulthood   288

Acknowledgements

First of all, I must thank my son, Rohan, for persuading me to put my speeches into a book. Despite his eighteen-hour-a-day work schedule as a doctoral student, he called me very often during the last three years and was relentless in his arguments for why this should be done. His encouragement and kind words lifted my spirits on the rare difficult days, and enhanced my enthusiasm on normal days. My daughter Akshata and wife Sudha have both been enthusiastic supporters in this project, for which I am immensely grateful. I must also thank the other two most important women in my life—my mother and mother-in-law. They have been constant sources of encouragement.

Several organizations—universities, corporations, publications and associations—in India and abroad invited me to deliver these lectures and write these articles. I am grateful to them. My colleagues and former colleagues—K.G. Lakshminarayanan, Devi Pabreja, Joseph Alenchery, Sudarshan N. Murthy and Sandeep Raju—have contributed immensely to producing these speeches through their research and by preparing the drafts for these speeches. These speeches would not have had the same value without their hard work and commitment. I am extremely grateful to these wonderful people—it has been a privilege to work with them. Prof. Jitendra Vir Singh, Professor of Strategy at Wharton School and Dean of Nanyang Business School in Singapore, added lustre to a few of my speeches with his powerful ideas and language. I am very grateful to him. It is difficult to find another secretary like A.G. Panduranga. I am lucky he works with me. Without his commitment to secretarial support, this book would not have seen the light of day. I am grateful to him for his help.

My experiment in using entrepreneurship as an instrument to create jobs and address the problem of poverty in India started out as an idea during my stay in France in the seventies and became a reality through Infosys. In addition, Infosys has been a wonderful platform on which I've been able to experiment several of my ideas, beliefs and convictions on innovation, values and leadership. The Infosys journey of twenty-seven years has made me what I am, taught me several important lessons, and has given me tremendous prestige and wealth. An average person like me would be nothing without this powerful platform. Infosys would not have been successful without its wonderful co-founders and key early-adopters—N.S. Raghavan, Kris Gopalakrishnan, Nandan Nilekani, K. Dinesh, Ashok Aurora, Shibulal, Mohandas Pai, Srinath Batni, V. Balakrishnan, Late G.R. Nayak, Ramadas Kamath, Phaneesh Murthy, Sharad Hegde, Colonel Krishna, Eshan Joshi, Muralikrishna, D.N. Prahlad, Pravin Rao, A.S. Krishnamurthy, Vinayak Pai, Binod, Subu Goparaju, Suresh Kamath, Malliga, Ramachandrappa, the families of the co-founders and the key early-adopters, our current and past independent directors, and many more whom I have not mentioned by name. I am grateful to these people and to the hundred-thousand-plus Infoscians for providing me such an impactful opportunity.

In many ways, Infosys could not have been a success but for the extraordinary learning experience I had while running the software group at Patni Computer Systems (PCS) at Mumbai. I am grateful to Ashok Patni, his brothers Gajendra and Naren Patni, Suresh Manek, Harish Tandon, Ghanshyam Gupta, Jamshyd Mehta and other colleagues at PCS for the exciting time I had there.

I would not be where I am but for the affection of my late father, my late father-in-law, brothers, sisters, brothers-in-law, sisters-in-law, nephews and nieces from my side and Sudha's. I thank them all.

My ideas on society, the nation and the world have also been influenced by my discussions with several elders, teachers, bosses, friends, colleagues, students and relatives in India and abroad.

I am amazed at the professionalism of Udayan Mitra, Publishing Director, Allen Lane at Penguin India. My need for high quality and on-time completion of anything I do is not easy to satisfy in Indian conditions. He has managed to achieve both with his commitment, hard work and patience. It has been a pleasure and a great learning experience working with him. I am also indebted to Mike Bryan, the CEO of Penguin India, and Heather Adams, Consulting Editor at Penguin India, who have both been enthusiastic partners in this project. I would also like to thank Hemali Sodhi, General Manager, Marketing and Anantha Padmanabhan, Vice President, Sales at Penguin India for all their help.

I am grateful to Dr Manmohan Singh, our prime minister, and to William Henry Gates III, Chairman of the Board, Microsoft Corporation, for their kind words about me and the book. I am grateful to my friend Ravi Venkatesan, Chairman of Microsoft India, for his help in obtaining the endorsement from William Henry Gates III.

Numerous books, videos, URLs, articles and research publications have given me ideas for my speeches. Wherever possible, I have mentioned the specific source(s) and author(s). I thank all these publications, owners of URLs, and authors of books and articles.

I am at my best when I work with youngsters. It has been a privilege to work with over 130,000 young Infoscions through this journey. I thank them for bringing so much joy to me.

Introduction

We are passing through exhilarating times. Notwithstanding the Mumbai tragedy, India is on an exceptional ride towards betterment. When I travel, I see confidence everywhere around me. For the first time in the last three hundred years, we have received the respect of almost every major country. In the recent past, we have had several notable achievements. We have created a globally competitive software industry. Many of our companies and entrepreneurs have found a place in global rankings. Our scientists and engineers have sent a space vehicle to the moon. We have leveraged satellite technology to bring the power of television to nearly every village in India. Thanks to indigenous telecom technology, the villages of Assam and Kerala are just a phone call away from Delhi. We have built huge dams and bridges; we have become self-sufficient in food; we have made progress in primary education and health care; and we have built world-class educational institutions. Our surgeons and physicians tackle the most complicated medical problems in our hospitals. Our journalists and TV show anchors have kept our governments, companies, institutions and citizens on their toes, thanks to their commitment to the truth. A small number of patriotic, honest and competent politicians and bureaucrats make us wish for more of their type for this country. The non-resident Indians have distinguished themselves in whatever society they have chosen to live in. Their contributions to science, technology, commerce and medicine have lifted the image of India. Our soldiers and officers make huge sacrifices to keep us safe.

Sachin Tendulkar has become the batsman with the highest runs and the highest number of centuries in both Test and one-day cricket. Viswanathan Anand has become the world chess champion again. Saina Nehwal has won the world junior badminton championship. Abhinav Bindra won the first individual gold medal for India in the Olympics. A.R. Rahman, Gulzar and Resul Pookkutty have just won Oscars, bringing glory to India on the international entertainment scene. All of them have done the country proud.

Our GDP growth rate has been one of the highest in the world for the past several years. Our foreign exchange reserves have been bountiful. Today, India sends the largest number of students to the USA for university education. Despite the recent global financial crisis, our government and industry leaders are confident that we will continue our outstanding economic progress.

However, all these achievements have been shared only by a section of Indians. We are far from the dreams of Mahatma Gandhi, Jawaharlal Nehru and Rajendra Prasad of creating an India where every Indian will be provided with the wherewithal to develop and rise to his/her fullest stature, and where poverty, ill health and ignorance will have vanished. More than 300 million Indians still do not have freedom from hunger, illiteracy and disease.

We have some work to do to achieve the goals of a free nation famously articulated in his 'four freedoms' speech by US President Franklin D. Roosevelt—freedom of speech and expression, freedom of religion, freedom from want, and freedom from fear. The enigma of India is that our progress in higher education and in science and technology has not been sufficient to take 350 million Indians out of illiteracy. It is difficult to imagine that 318 million people in the country do not have access to safe drinking water and 250 million people do not have access to basic medical care. Why should 630 million people not have access to acceptable sanitation facilities even in 2009? When you see world-class supermarkets and food chains in our towns, and when our urban youngsters gloat over the choice of toppings on their pizzas, why should 51 per cent of the children in the country be undernourished? When India is among the largest producers of engineers and scientists in the world, why should 52 per cent of the primary schools have only one teacher for every two classes? When our politicians and bureaucrats live in huge houses in Lutyens' Delhi and the state capitals, our corporate leaders splurge money on mansions, yachts and planes, and our urban youth revel in their latest sport shoes, why should 300 million Indians live on hardly Rs 545 per month, barely sufficient to manage two meals a day, with little or no money left for schooling, clothes, shelter and medicine?

These questions have been troubling me right from that day when I spent a lonely, hungry, cold and introspective twenty-one hours in the guard's compartment on a freight train going from the historic city of Nis, in what was then Yugoslavia and is now Serbia, to Istanbul, way back in 1974. I have had some success in demonstrating the power of entrepreneurship in solving the problem of poverty through my experiment of creating Infosys. Yet, when I look at the big canvas of India, I often feel confused, agitated and powerless—but also motivated to find a solution to this problem.

It was pretty early in my deep introspection into the phenomenon of equitable economic progress in developing countries that I was fortunate to read three seminal books that have influenced my thinking deeply. They are: *The Protestant Ethic and the Spirit of Capitalism* by Max Weber; *My Experiments with Truth* by Mahatma Gandhi; and *Peau Noire, Masques Blancs (Black Skin, White Masks)* by Franz Fanon. In many ways, my entire philosophy of economic development is based on these three wonderful books. Many of my speeches are based on the lessons I have learned from them. Max Weber's book is a complex one. His thesis is about the importance of good values—hard work, honesty, austerity—and focus on entrepreneurship in bettering the life of an individual and society. While it appears very elementary today, it was not so for me in the early seventies. I had been brought up in an environment of hard work and good values. In my naiveté, I had assumed that all societies and nations were similar and did not include these factors in my analysis of why India was different from France. Therefore, Max Weber laid the foundation for my belief that decent and hard-working people with high aspirations make great nations, no matter what the odds are. This was the first piece of the development puzzle for me.

Mahatma Gandhi opened my eyes to the importance of good leadership in raising the aspirations of people, making them accept sacrifices to achieve a grand vision, and most importantly, in converting that vision into reality. Gandhi realized that trust in leaders is extremely important if the followers have to commit to sacrifices. He unleashed the most powerful instrument for gaining trust—leadership by example. He ate, dressed, travelled and lived like the poor. Maintaining Gandhi's simple style did pose lots of logistics and security problems. In one of her lighter moments, Sarojini Naidu, his compatriot in the freedom struggle, is reported to have said that it took a fortune to keep Gandhi in poverty. But walking the talk was extremely important to the Mahatma who understood the pulse of our people like no other Indian leader. The biggest lesson for me from Gandhi's book and life is the importance of leading by example. I realized fairly early that this was the second piece of the development puzzle.

I thought I understood the power of Weberian and Gandhian philosophies in the economic development of nations and societies. I had seen good values and good leadership, at least among the early group of our politicians and bureaucrats. However, I continued to be puzzled why my country was not making the kind of progress that seemed so natural. This is where Franz Fanon's book came in handy. His seminal book on the colonizer mindset of elites in a postcolonial society opened my eyes to the role of the bureaucracy and the elite in decelerating the progress of the poor and the disenfranchised. The colonial mindset of the 'dark elite in white masks' in a postcolonial society—the mindset that the ruled and the rulers have different sets of rights and responsibilities with a huge asymmetry in favour of the rulers—was indeed the third piece of the development puzzle. I see this attitude of the Indian elite every day in how they send their children to English medium schools while forcing the children of the poor into vernacular schools, extol the virtues of poverty while living in luxury, and glorify the rural life while they sit comfortably in cities.

Perhaps many readers may be surprised that the traditional ingredients of capital, material resources, technology and talent do not appear as pieces in this puzzle. I do accept that these four are important for economic progress. However, I rate these ingredients below the three I have listed earlier for two simple reasons. First, right from my primary school days, I have been taught that India has abundant material resources and developable talent. Second, I have seen many examples of countries, without one or more of these ingredients, design solutions to acquire them in plenty. Japan and Switzerland import vast amounts of material resources and produce world-class technology and other goods for export. Countries like China attract huge capital. In the recent past, India has designed appropriate policies to scale up foreign direct investment and portfolio investment several-fold. We have done pretty well in certain areas of technology. Open any newspaper or magazine, and you will see many articles on how countries like China, Singapore and South Korea have been able to move up the global rankings in advanced talent development. I am convinced that visionary leadership in India can easily overcome the shortage of capital, material resources, technology and talent.

When I returned to India in the mid-seventies, I was determined to conduct an experiment to demonstrate some of these beliefs of mine. I was toying with the idea of joining a political party and had even discussed this with my then friend and later my wife—Sudha. While Sudha was sympathetic to my idea, many others in my inner circle—friends as well as relatives—were, perhaps, not equally enthusiastic. I realized pretty quickly that I had to first validate some of my beliefs on a smaller canvas. That is when I decided to test the power of entrepreneurship in solving the problem of poverty in India. I started Softronics to develop software for the Indian market. Pretty early in this experiment, I realized that India was not yet ready to buy software, and that I had to focus on developed markets for any success. I was also not sure if I had sufficient expertise in handling sales, people, customers and finance. I closed Softronics and joined Patni Computer Systems (PCS) as the head of the software group in Mumbai. The PCS experience was a godsend. I had one of the finest bosses anybody could wish for—Ashok Patni, a brilliant, gentle and compassionate person. During my four years there, I learned a lot about the software business. I met a team of wonderful youngsters, six of whom joined me in my next venture—Infosys. I wanted the Infosys experiment to demonstrate to the Indian public and industry peers that there were virtues in compassionate capitalism; that it was possible to create wealth legally and ethically in India; that you could follow the finest principles of corporate governance here; that the democratization of wealth spurred high-growth, sustainable companies; and that value-based business leadership created goodwill for businesses even in our society. This experiment has entered adulthood now and demonstrated a certain level of accomplishment, thanks to the extraordinary colleagues of mine at Infosys.

In parallel, I continued to strengthen my belief that any large-scale success in the development of our country requires acceptance, by the people at large, of the three pillars of development—model citizenry and a good work ethic among people, particularly the youngsters; high-quality leadership by our elders: politicians, bureaucrats, corporate leaders, leaders in various professions, and influential thinkers in society; and, finally, eliminating the 'black skin–white mask' attitude of our elite so that they can relate to the reality that is India and seek solutions that provide equitable and inclusive growth (which has become a catchphrase now, thanks to the efforts of our prime minister Dr Manmohan Singh).

My discussions with several people, including then President A.P.J. Abdul Kalam, indicated that communication of good values by reputed people was an important first step in changing the mindset of youngsters. It was Prime Minister Atal Bihari Vajpayee who suggested the importance of selling India abroad and also of extending the scope of my speeches to include the global student audience. Before he became President, Dr Kalam had even toyed with the idea of using a caravan to travel around the country and speak to children, and I was to be his part-time ally. It was not to be since he became the President in 2002. Around this time, Dr Manmohan Singh, then a member of Parliament, read my Darbari Seth Memorial speech on secularism, and encouraged me to continue speaking to youngsters. Encouragement from such eminent people led to my decision to accept as many invitations as I could in India and abroad to speak to young people.

I believe that our challenges are to recognize the limitations and imperfections of our world as it is, think of a world as we want it to be, and make sacrifices and work hard to create such a world. Our ability and willingness to accept imperfections around us is the first step to removing them. The ability to summon enthusiasm and energy to work hard to reinvent a grand future without these imperfections, rather than behaving as if these problems do not exist and just saying we are the best country in the world, is positivism and optimism. Not recognizing our problems, behaving as if nothing has happened or that nothing can be done to improve our situation, and isolating ourselves from the troubled world of poverty and suffering are all signs of utter pessimism. That is why you will see me talking about the current state of affairs in the country and in the world in my speeches, offering solutions, and exhorting the youth to evaluate these solutions and act to create a better future for themselves, for the country and for the world. I exhort them to go beyond what they think is possible. Borrowing the words of George Bernard Shaw, Robert Kennedy best summed up this challenge when he said, 'Some men see things as they are and ask why; I dream of things that never were and say why not?' This is what great leadership is all about. The new generation of our leaders has to overcome the constraints of the context, the present mindset and the diffidence inherent in them to bring in change that will make this nation and this world a better place to live in. The US President Barack Obama expressed this well in his 'Yes, we can' slogan. My dream is to see a whole generation of youngsters who will embrace the slogan 'Yes, we will' and actually work hard to translate those wonderful ideas of change into reality. We cannot let the hard work and sacrifice of the founders of our nation go waste before our eyes.

I have selected thirty-eight speeches from the hundred and fifty I have given during the last few years for this book, eliminating duplication as far as possible. I have covered issues seminal to the future of India and the world. Some critical terms like globalization, leadership, inequality, corporate governance and values have been defined again and again in several speeches for the sake of completeness of the presentation.

I am a believer in the role of youth in building a great future for India. At Infosys, I surround myself with smart and trusted youngsters. In most strategic decisions, I insist on the participation of a critical mass of my young colleagues. I am a proponent of bringing younger people into leadership positions. Many people lament that today's youth have no values, are undisciplined and do not believe in hard work. I disagree with them. Most young people I see are better than what I was when I was their age. Therefore, it is appropriate that I start off this book with a series of lectures delivered to student audiences—undergraduate and graduate students in management[1], technology[2], business[3], design[4], law[5], foreign trade[6] and liberal arts[7] throughout the world. My speeches to students in India focus on the state of the country, the progress we have made, the challenges we have, the new mindset required, the importance of values in nation building and the need to leverage excellence in ideas and in execution to create an inclusive India and an inclusive world. Wherever necessary, I have emphasized the importance of executing ideas rather than just articulating. But somehow, in this country, it is fashionable to see ideas as an end in themselves without any focus on implementation. In fact, articulation is accomplishment enough for most of our intellectuals! This tendency to keep discussing an idea without making any progress towards implementation is sometimes taken to ridiculous levels. If my count is correct, we have had thirty-

---

[1]'Succeeding in the Contemporary World'—Convocation Address, INSEAD, Fontainebleau

[2]'The Indian of the Twenty-first Century'—Convocation Address, Indian Institute of Technology, Delhi

[3]'Succeeding in a Globalized Corporation'—Convocation Address, IESE Business School, Barcelona

[4]'The Need for Excellence'—Convocation Address, National Institute of Design, Ahmedabad

[5]'The Legal Professional in the Era of Globalization'—Convocation Address, National Law School of India University, Bangalore

[6]'A Case for a More Open Trade Regime in India'—Convocation Address, Indian Institute of Foreign Trade, New Delhi

[7]'The Role of Religion in Education'—Convocation Address, Punjab University, Chandigarh

three seminars on building a power station for Bangalore city over the last twenty-five years. Yet, there is still no power plant in Bangalore and we continue to suffer from blackouts.

I also believe that good leaders integrate the fifty-thousand-feet bird's-eye view of the world with the ground-level worm's eye view. They can articulate a great vision, get into the most intricate details of implementation of the vision, and implement the vision on time, within budget and with the requisite quality. I am convinced that a laser focus on implementation and the ability to get into details are the most urgent needs for the development of our country.

My speeches to international students focus on lessons I have learned from my entrepreneurship journey and in my life[8], the importance of emerging markets, corporate governance, and contemporary issues like global warming and restoring faith in capitalism.

My Weberian orientation leads me to believe that individually, we are what our culture is and what our values are. Culture is about our beliefs, our priorities in life, things that bring us joy and sorrow, how we spend our time and money, our concern for the less fortunate, and how we interact with each other. Values form the protocol for behaviour followed by each member of a community to enhance hope, confidence, enthusiasm and joy for every other member of the community. Values become extremely important in our quest for aggressive development, in our determination to redeem the pledge of our founding fathers, and in our desire to be recognized as a trustworthy and productive member of the global community. Therefore, in my lectures on values, I have spoken about hard work, discipline[9], teamwork[10], secularism[11], honesty[12], respecting contracts, putting the interest of society ahead of one's personal interest,

---

[8]'Learning from Experience'—Pre-commencement Lecture, Stern School of Business, New York University

[9]'The Role of Discipline in Accelerating National Development'—General K.M. Cariappa Lecture, New Delhi

[10]'Time for Chak De, India!'—Published in the *Times of India*

[11]'In Praise of Secularism'—Darbari Seth Memorial Lecture, New Delhi

[12]'How Can We Stop Corruption in India?'—Published in *Business Today*

openness to learn from others, the 'Chak De, India!' spirit, empowerment[13], and, finally, on building on the good aspects of our culture and learning from what is good in Western culture[14].

In my 2008 Malcolm Wiener Lecture at the Kennedy School[15], I spoke about the benefits of the 1991 economic reforms, the importance of continuing reforms both at the Central and the state levels, and the need for broadbasing these reforms for inclusive growth. I have also spoken about the need for our leaders to straddle the multiple worlds that constitute India—the rural and the urban, the educated and the not-so-well-educated, the rich and the poor. Thanks to excellent work by David Bloom, David Canning and Jaypee Sevilla, the concept of 'demographic dividend' has become a handy tool for our politicians, civil servants and intellectuals to ignore a serious issue confronting our country—population growth and readying our youth for nation building. Let us remember that no reforms can bring about inclusive growth unless our population growth is contained and our working-age population is made ready, through quality education, nutrition and health care, for participation in nation building. The advances we have made in our economy are being lost partly because of the high growth rates of our population. This is the theme of my A.D. Shroff Lecture on population[16].

Indian politicians have a dilemma. The economic energy is in urban areas while the electoral strength is in rural areas. Politicians who were seen as pro-urban were voted out by the electorate in the 2004 elections. However, the reality is that, all over the world, economic development has led inevitably to urbanization. Opportunities for economic growth are primarily in urban and semi-urban areas in the medium term. Therefore, we have to focus on improving the efficiency of our cities and towns so that we can enhance the economic growth to create better opportunities for our

---

[13]'My Empowered India'—Published in the *Indian Express*

[14]'What Can We Learn from the West?'—Lal Bahadur Shastri Memorial Lecture, New Delhi

[15]'Lessons from the Economic Reforms of 1991'—Malcolm Wiener Lecture, Harvard University

[16]'Population and Economic Development in India'—A.D. Shroff Memorial Lecture, Mumbai

urban and rural populations. This is the theme of my P.N. Haksar Lecture on urban planning[17].

It is clear to me that technology has a key role in improving the lives of our poor. There are many examples of technology-based progress towards poverty alleviation in India and elsewhere. Therefore, I have included a piece on the technologies that have made a tremendous difference to the poor in post-Independence India[18].

The Indian software industry has been an exemplar for Indian industry. The industry is still in its infancy. But, within a short period of twenty-odd years, it has created a large number of high quality, high disposable-income jobs; focussed on excellence in winning in global markets; earned the respect of customers in advanced countries; generated considerable net foreign exchange for the country; and, barring a few cases, followed the best principles of corporate governance. This industry has huge opportunities in the future and faces significant challenges in seizing those opportunities. This is the theme of my Jawaharlal Nehru Lecture on the Indian software industry[19].

It is a truism today that a nation that does not achieve full literacy and does not foster excellence in higher education and research cannot overcome poverty and become a world power. Higher education can be a boon only if there is a sound foundation of critical thinking, curiosity, active participation in the classroom, and a problem-solving orientation at the high school level. This is the theme of my lecture to high school principals[20]. Thanks to Jawaharlal Nehru's vision, India started out well in higher education, building a number of world-class institutions of higher learning in science, technology, medicine, law, design, architecture, management and liberal arts; attracting a large number of well-educated Indian faculty from advanced countries like the USA, UK, Australia, Germany and France;

---

[17]'A Framework for Urban Planning in Modern India'—P.N. Haksar Memorial Lecture, New Delhi

[18]'The Eight Visions that Changed the Face of India'—Published in *The Hindu*

[19]'Software Enterprises: The Temples of New India'—The twenty-third Jawaharlal Nehru Memorial Lecture, London

[20]'What Would I Do if I Were the Principal of a Secondary School?'—A lecture delivered at the Conclave of Principals of Bishop Cotton Group of Schools, Bangalore

and fostering an environment of interaction between researchers in India and abroad. Indira Gandhi too followed this tradition pretty well till 1980 when a few overzealous bureaucrats introduced unnecessary restrictions on the exchange of scholars between India and the outside world. Successive governments tightened their grip on higher educational institutions. This has resulted in excessive bureaucracy and rigidity in these institutions and a consequent loss of excellence. But all is not lost. Even now, we can look around us, learn from better performing institutions in India and abroad, and bring back the glory of our higher educational institutions. This is the theme of my K.C. Basu Lecture on higher education in India[21].

However, the agenda for highly accomplished universities, even in advanced countries like the USA, cannot end just with the students of these universities excelling in their chosen fields of expertise—science, technology, medicine, law and liberal arts. These universities have to get their alumni to carry the wonderful values they imbibed as students to the real world and make a difference. They have to become better human beings. They have to stand for a nobler purpose. They have to address the myriad problems that cripple the development of mankind as a whole. In other words, even the most advanced universities in the world have an unfinished agenda. This is the theme of my Cornell lecture[22].

I do not know of any community—a company, an institution or a nation—that has achieved success without a long journey of aspiration, hard work, commitment, focus, hope, confidence, humility and sacrifice. To rally people to commit to such a regime that is gruelling yet rewarding in the end requires great leaders—change agents—who have the courage to dream big and stand up for their beliefs, who have the power of creating a grand vision, and who can articulate that vision to a large mass of followers. These leaders have to create trust in their followers through leadership by example, instil hope and confidence in them about the future, make them feel enthusiastic and proud about being part of the journey, and convert

---

[21]'A Framework for Reforms for Higher Education in India'—The third K.C. Basu Memorial Lecture, Kolkata

[22]'The Unfinished Agenda'—A lecture delivered at the inauguration of Jeffrey Lehman as the president of Cornell University

that vision into reality through hard work and excellence in execution. Mahatma Gandhi, Lee Kuan Yew, Abraham Lincoln and Bill Gates are all good examples of such great leadership. The urgent need of the day is to create an environment for such leaders to emerge in large numbers in politics, business, academia and other areas. Unfortunately, today, there is a paucity of trustworthy leaders in developing countries, where there is a huge need for them. Likewise, in these days of complete loss of faith in leadership on Wall Street as well as on Main Street, it is extremely important for business leaders to rededicate themselves to the task of earning back the trust of the community. These are the themes of my Bloomberg lecture[23] and my piece on leadership in *Business Today*[24].

The last ten years have indeed tarnished the image of corporate leaders like never before. The actions of Enron, WorldCom, Permalat and a host of other companies across the globe as well as the recent one in India have relegated the Chief Executive Officers (CEOs) to the lowest rank among the trustworthy professions. No amount of rule-based governance prescriptions will enhance the ethical behaviour of corporate leaders. What is needed are: a change of values among corporate leaders; creating a set of principles and guidelines that will attract and empower high quality individuals as independent directors of the corporation; a set of systems, processes and incentives that will enhance fairness, transparency and accountability in the management of corporations; and an environment that measures success of corporate leaders by not just how much money they make but by how much respect they receive within their own corporations and communities. These are the themes of my Robert Maxon[25], C.D. Deshmukh[26] and Ranganathan[27] Lectures on corporate governance. Public governance

---

[23]'On Leadership: Lessons from the Infosys Journey'—A lecture delivered at the Bloomberg Leadership Conference, New York

[24]'A Leadership Mindset for a Resurgent India'—Published in *Business Today*

[25]'Good Corporate Governance: A Checklist or a Mindset?'—Robert P. Maxon Lecture, George Washington University, Washington DC

[26]'Corporate Governance and its Relevance to India'—C.D. Deshmukh Memorial Lecture, New Delhi

[27]'Corporate Governance: A Practitioner's Viewpoint'—Ranganathan Memorial Lecture, New Delhi

in emerging countries is another topic that has received tremendous attention in recent times. Corruption, nepotism, apathy, a colonial mindset, lack of transparency and accountability and lack of incentives have wreaked havoc on the implementation of public projects in India. It is necessary to design new models of governance that will attract the best talent, provide incentives, bring in fairness, transparency and accountability and accelerate development in emerging countries like India. This is the theme of my J.R.D. Tata Lecture on public governance[28].

The best index of a company's success is its longevity. Such longevity comes from living in harmony with the context—the society. Society contributes customers, employees and investors for a corporation. It contributes politicians and bureaucrats who frame policies that influence the success or failure of a corporation. Therefore, society is an important stakeholder for corporations. Long-term success of a corporation requires it to earn the goodwill of society by demonstrating social responsibility. This need for social responsibility has become even more essential in these days of scepticism about capitalism. The solution to raising trust in capitalism is to move towards compassionate capitalism which is capitalism with fairness, transparency and accountability, practised by leaders towards their stakeholders—customers, employees, vendor-partners, the government of the land and society. These are the themes of my lectures on corporate social responsibility[29] and compassionate capitalism[30].

France of the seventies was a unique country. It was the only Western, developed country that had a flourishing Communist party. My stay in Paris in the seventies was highly educational for me not just in my profession—computer science—but also in generating ideas on social and economic development. I had the opportunity to talk to lots of intellectuals, politicians and functionaries of the Right, the Centre and the Left. I studied, observed, collected data, and drew some conclusions on the basic instruments for economic development

---

[28]'A New Model for Effective Public Governance'—The fifth J.R.D. Tata Memorial Lecture, New Delhi

[29]'The Travails of Philanthropy in India'—Maulana Azad Memorial Lecture, New Delhi

[30]'Compassionate Capitalism'—A lecture delivered at the Global Brand Forum, Singapore

and alleviation of poverty in the world. My conclusion was that the only solution to the problem of poverty is the creation of jobs with good disposable incomes. Such a solution requires entrepreneurs who convert ideas into jobs and wealth. Just as there are only a few good surgeons, journalists, engineers, doctors and artists, there will only be a few successful entrepreneurs. These people are human and they need incentives to succeed just like everybody else. It is not the responsibility of governments to create jobs. However, it is the responsibility of governments everywhere to create a fair, transparent, speedy and incentivized environment for these entrepreneurs to succeed. My observations on the basic ingredients of entrepreneurship are: an idea whose value to the market can be expressed in a simple sentence, not a complex or compound one; a market that is ready to accept the idea and pay for it; a team that brings a mutually exclusive and collectively exhaustive set of skills, expertise, experience and wisdom to running a business; an enduring value system; and, of course, finance. These frameworks and the story of the journey of my entrepreneurship form the themes of my lectures at Wharton[31] and at the Madras Management Association[32].

Thanks to globalization, every country that can provide the best value for money in a product or a service in the global bazaar can improve not just the lives of its own people but also of many nations whose people use those products and services. International trade has been shown to benefit both the trading partners. But, these days, there is tremendous scepticism about the benefits of globalization in both advanced countries like the USA and in emerging countries like India. In my Dell Lecture[33], I talk about why globalization is a boon to advanced countries. In my Nani Palkhivala Lecture[34], I talk about what it will take for India to succeed in globalization. In my Stanford

---

[31]'Reflections of an Entrepreneur'—Commencement Lecture, Wharton School of Business, Philadelphia

[32]'On Entrepreneurship'—The fourteenth Anantharamakrishnan Memorial Lecture, Chennai

[33]'Do We Need a Flat World?'—The first Michael Dell Lecture, University of Texas, Austin

[34]'Making Globalization Work for India'—The fourth Nani Palkhivala Lecture, Mumbai

lecture[35], I explain to MBA students why, in a globalized world, emerging markets will become important both as producers and as consumers. I exhort them to seek opportunities in emerging markets, in general, and at the bottom of the pyramid in particular.

The last two speeches in the book were delivered on the occasion of Infosys reaching a billion dollars in revenue[36], and at the silver jubilee celebrations of the company[37]. Also included in the last section is an essay on my favourite topic—why respect is important for a corporation and how to achieve it[38].

I have deliberately kept my speeches simple in ideas and in expression. After all, the objective is to communicate powerful concepts to the youth from all over the country and the world in a simple way. It is very important to remember that a few million English-speaking Indians do not make up India. In fact, they are in a small minority. However, the reality is that English is the only link language for India and that most of us have been schooled in English. Even then, we must not forget that any transformation of India will require good ideas to stir the fertile minds of the children in the remotest villages of India, to give hope to the forgotten voices of the oppressed youth in the innards of our urban slums, and to bring out the best among the smart, hopeful and confident English-speaking children in the finest schools of our cities. The script for the new India will be written not just in the comfortable drawing rooms of the rich folks but also in the ghettos and slums of the poor, the hopeful and the disenfranchised. Those of us who realize this and act quickly will make this country a better place. This is what inclusive growth is all about.

Our challenge is well illustrated by the cover of the book. It is to bring hope and betterment to the millions of poor, uneducated, undernourished and disenfranchised rural and urban poor children

---

[35]'Transforming Emerging Economies and Leaving Behind Legacies'—'View from the Top', a lecture delivered at the Graduate School of Business, Stanford University

[36]'The Journey So Far'—A lecture delivered on the occasion of Infosys's Billion Dollar Day celebrations, Bangalore

[37]'On Reaching Adulthood'—A lecture delivered on the occasion of Infosys's twenty-fifth anniversary celebrations, Mysore

[38]'The Importance of Respect for a Corporation'—Published in *Businessworld*

so that they can indeed become like the well-fed, well-clothed, happy and confident urban school child on the cover. It is to bring the context, environment, facilities and opportunities taken for granted by the child on the cover to the poor urban and rural children. It is very important to understand that this is not a zero-sum game and that the betterment of poor children cannot be at the cost of the opportunities available to the children who are already privileged. This is why our politicians, bureaucrats and the elite have to straddle multiple worlds—the urban and the rural, the rich and the poor, the educated and the not-so-well-educated. They have to juxtapose the two realities of India to understand and appreciate the complexities and challenges of their task, and create appropriate policies that enhance the hope and confidence of these multiple worlds that make up India. If my lectures can communicate these huge challenges to the readers, I would have succeeded in my purpose for publishing this book.

These challenges will not be met by shibboleths and slogans but by the hard work of committed and value-based leaders and followers. It is extremely important for my generation of leaders to realize and act with the belief that our legacy will be written not in our words but in our actions. It will be written only by leaders who have the integrity of thought and action. It will be written by only those who have the self-confidence to recognize our problems, seek solutions from those that have good ideas and those that have solved them well, and are willing to work hard to implement such solutions.

I have tried to make each speech complete in itself even if it meant some repetition of important ideas. I have made an attempt to offer my own solution, right or wrong, to almost every problem I have discussed. They are not easy solutions. They call for tremendous discipline, sacrifice, patriotism and hard work. If we succeed in these solutions, the results will be stunning. Our lives will be worth living. We would have paid our dues to the future generations. Most importantly, we would have lived up to the hopes of our founding fathers. If these speeches can motivate at least a few thousand youngsters to accept these suggestions and make this country and the world a better place, then my job is done.

Happy reading.

PART I

ADDRESS TO STUDENTS

Learning from Experience

Today I am going to share with you some of my life lessons. I learned these lessons in the context of my early career struggles, under the influence of sometimes unplanned events which were the crucibles that tempered my character and reshaped my future.

I would like to first share with you some key events of my life, in the hope that these may help you understand my struggles and how unplanned events and chance encounters with influential people shaped my life and career. Later, I will share the deeper life lessons that I have learned. My sincere hope is that sharing these thoughts will help you see your own trials and tribulations for the hidden blessings they can be.

The first event occurred when I was a graduate student in Control Theory at Indian Institute of Technology (IIT), Kanpur. At breakfast on a bright Sunday morning in 1968, I met a famous computer scientist who was on sabbatical from a well-known US university. He was discussing exciting new developments in the field of computer science with a large group of students, explaining how such developments would alter our future. He was articulate, passionate and quite convincing. I was hooked. I went straight from breakfast to the library, read four or five papers he had suggested, and left the library determined to study computer science. When I look

Pre-commencement Lecture, Stern School of Business, New York University, 9 May 2007 back today at that pivotal meeting, I marvel at how one role model can alter the future of a young student for the better. This experience taught me that valuable advice can sometimes come from an unexpected source, and chance events can sometimes open new doors.

The next event that left an indelible mark on me occurred in 1974. The location: Nis, a border town between what was then Yugoslavia (now Serbia) and Bulgaria. I was hitchhiking from Paris back to Mysore, my hometown. By the time a kind driver dropped me at Nis railway station at 9 p.m. on a Saturday night, the restaurant was closed. So was the bank the next morning, and I could not eat because I had no local money. I slept on the railway platform until 8.30 p.m. on Sunday night, when the Sofia Express pulled in. The only passengers in my compartment were a girl and a boy. I struck up a conversation in French with the young girl. She talked about the travails of living in an Iron Curtain country. Suddenly, we were roughly interrupted by some policemen who, I later gathered, were summoned by the young man who thought we were criticizing the Communist government of Bulgaria. The girl was led away; my backpack and sleeping bag were confiscated. I was dragged along the platform into a small 8x8 ft room with a cold stone floor and a hole in one corner by way of toilet facilities. I was held in that bitterly cold room without food or water for over seventy-two hours. I had lost all hope of ever seeing the outside world again, when the door opened. I was dragged out unceremoniously, locked up in the guard's compartment on a departing freight train and told that I would be released twenty hours later upon reaching Istanbul. The guard's final words still ring in my ears: 'You are from a friendly country called India, and that is why we are letting you go!'

The journey to Istanbul was lonely, and I was starving. This long, lonely, cold journey forced me to deeply rethink my convictions about communism. Early on a dark Thursday morning, after being hungry for 108 hours, I was purged of any last vestiges of affinity for the Left. I concluded that entrepreneurship, resulting in large-scale job creation, was the only viable mechanism for eradicating poverty in societies. Deep in my heart, I always thank the Bulgarian guards for transforming me from a confused Leftist into a determined, compassionate capitalist! Inevitably, this sequence of events led to the eventual founding of Infosys in 1981.

While these first two events were rather fortuitous, the next two, both concerning the Infosys journey, were more planned and profoundly influenced my career trajectory.

On a chilly Saturday morning in winter 1990, five of the seven founders of Infosys met in our small office in a leafy Bangalore suburb. The decision at hand was the possible sale of Infosys for the enticing sum of $1 million. After nine years of toil in the then business-unfriendly India, we were quite happy at the prospect of seeing some money at last. I let my younger colleagues talk about their future plans. Discussions about the travails of our journey thus far and our future challenges went on for about four hours. I had not yet spoken a word.

Finally, it was my turn. I spoke of our journey from a small Mumbai apartment in 1981 that had been beset with many challenges, but also about how I believed we were at the darkest hour before the dawn. I then took an audacious step. If they were all bent upon selling the company, I said, I would buy out all my colleagues, though I did not have a cent in my pocket. There was a stunned silence in the room. My colleagues wondered aloud about my foolhardiness. But I remained silent. However, after an hour of my arguments, my colleagues changed their minds to my way of thinking. I urged them that if we wanted to create a great company, we should be optimistic and confident. We have more than lived up to our promise of that day. In the eighteen years since then, Infosys has grown to revenues in excess of $3 billion, a net income of more than $800 million and a market capitalization of more than $28 billion, 28,000 times richer than the offer of $1 million on that day. In the process, Infosys has created more than 70,000 well-paying jobs, 2,000-plus dollar millionaires and 20,000-plus rupee millionaires.

A final story: On a hot summer morning in 1995, a Fortune-10 corporation had sequestered all their Indian software vendors including Infosys in different rooms at the Taj Residency hotel in Bangalore so that the vendors could not communicate with one another. This customer's propensity for tough negotiations was well known. Our team was very nervous. First of all, with revenues of only around $5 million, we were minnows compared to the customer. Second, this customer contributed to 25 per cent of our revenues. The loss of this business would potentially devastate our recently listed company. Third, the customer's negotiation style was very aggressive. The customer team would go from room to room, get the best terms out of each vendor and then pit one vendor against the other. This went on for several rounds. Our various arguments why a fair price—one that allowed us to invest in good people, R&D, infrastructure, technology and training—was actually in their interest failed to cut any ice with the customer. By 5 p.m. on the last day, we had to make a decision right on the spot whether to accept the customer's terms or to walk out.

All eyes were on me as I mulled over the decision. I closed my eyes, and reflected upon our journey until then. Through many a tough call, we had always thought about the long-term interests of Infosys. I communicated clearly to the customer team that we could not accept their terms, since these could well lead us to letting them down later. But I promised a smooth, professional transition to a vendor of the customer's choice. This was a turning point for Infosys.

Subsequently, we created a Risk Mitigation Council which ensured that we would never again depend too much on any one client, technology, country, application area or key employee. The crisis was a blessing in disguise. Today, Infosys has a sound de-risking strategy that has stabilized its revenues and profits.

I want to share with you, next, the life lessons these events have taught me. I will begin with the importance of learning from experience. It is less important, I believe, where you start. It is more important how and what you learn. If the quality of the learning is high, the development gradient is steep, and, given time, you can find yourself in a previously unattainable place. I believe the Infosys story is living proof of this.

Learning from experience, however, can be complicated. It can be much more difficult to learn from success than from failure. If we fail, we think carefully about the precise cause. Success can indiscriminately reinforce all our prior actions.

A second theme concerns the power of chance events. As I think across a wide variety of settings in my life, I am struck by the incredible role played by the interplay of chance events with intentional choices. While the turning points themselves are indeed often fortuitous, how we respond to them is anything but so. It is this very quality of how we respond systematically to chance events that is crucial.

Of course, the mindset one works with is also quite critical. It matters greatly whether one believes that ability is inherent or that it can be developed. The former view, a fixed mindset, creates a tendency to avoid challenges, to ignore useful negative feedback and leads people to plateau early and not achieve their full potential. The latter view, a growth mindset, leads to a tendency to embrace challenges, to learn from criticism and enables people to reach ever-higher levels of achievement.

The fourth theme is a cornerstone of the Indian spiritual tradition: self-knowledge. Indeed, the highest form of knowledge, it is said, is self-knowledge. I believe this greater awareness and knowledge of oneself is what ultimately helps develop a more grounded belief in oneself, courage, determination, and, above all, humility—all qualities which enable one to wear one's success with dignity and grace.

Based on my life experiences, I can assert that it is this belief in learning from experience, a growth mindset, the power of chance events, and self-reflection that have helped me grow to the present. Back in the 1960s, the odds of my being where I am today would have been very small indeed. Yet, with every successive step, the odds kept changing in my favour, and these life lessons made all the difference.

I would like to end with some words of advice. Do you believe that your future is pre-ordained, and is already set? Or, do you believe that your future is yet to be written and that it will depend upon sometimes fortuitous events? Do you believe that these events can provide turning points to which you will respond with energy and enthusiasm? Do you believe that you will learn from these events and that you will reflect on your setbacks? Do you believe that you will examine your successes with even greater care? I hope you believe that the future will be shaped by several turning points with great learning opportunities. In fact, this is the path I have walked to much advantage.

A final word: when, one day, you have made your mark on the world, remember that, in the ultimate analysis, we are all mere temporary custodians of the wealth we generate, whether it be financial, intellectual, or emotional. The best use of all your wealth is to share it with those less fortunate.

I believe that we have all at some time eaten the fruit from trees that we did not plant. In the fullness of time, when it is our turn to give, we must in turn plant gardens that we may never eat the fruit of, which will benefit the generations to come. I believe this is our sacred responsibility, one that I hope you will shoulder in time.

Go forth and embrace your future with open arms, and enthusiastically pursue your own life journey of discovery!

The Indian of the Twenty-first Century

For me, there is no greater joy than being with the young and the learned. I am reminded of a Sanskrit sloka that glorifies the educated person:

Swagruhe poojyate jheshtha, swagraame poojyate prabhuhu
Swadeshe poojyate raja, vidwan sarvatra poojyate
(The eldest is respected in his house, the headman in his village
A king is respected in his country, but the learned everywhere)

As you graduate from an educational institution and become responsible members of a larger society, it is worthwhile to ponder over what the purpose of all these years of education has been and how you can use it to make a difference to society. Progress is based on dreams and requires change. Change requires learning. Education is about learning to learn. Education is therefore the main instrument a nation has to achieve progress. Being educated means you are assuming responsibility in society—responsibility to show fairness to the less fortunate, to create a future that posterity can be proud of, and to fulfil the promise that freedom brought us. It is about raising one's confidence to think of a worthy dream and the ability to translate that dream to reality by high-performance action. It is about opening up one's mind to accept new ideas, evaluate them and use

Convocation Address, Indian Institute of Technology, New Delhi, 9 August 2001 them for progress. You must be grateful to your parents, teachers and the country for providing you with this instrument.

It is appropriate that you consider an important issue at this time. And that is, has India made sufficient progress since Independence? Can we be happy about this progress? Have we kept up with the pace of progress the rest of the world has seen? Have we achieved sustainable progress? Have we fulfilled the dreams of our founding fathers who wanted an India where every individual would be free and provided with the wherewithal to develop and rise to his/her fullest stature? Can we dream of an India where poverty, ill health and ignorance will have vanished?

The numbers say it all, when it comes to what we have yet to achieve. We are a nation of one billion people with just 28 per cent living in urban areas; an average person earns only Rs 1,498 a month (our per-capita GDP is one of the lowest in the world); only 54 per cent of our people are literate; the average life expectancy is only 61 years; the country has an HDI (Human Development Index) of 127 out of 175 nations in the world; 318 million people do not have access to safe drinking water; 250 million people do not have access to basic medical care; 630 million people do not have sanitation facilities; 51 per cent of children are undernourished; and half our primary schools have only one teacher for every two classes! I can go on and on with these statistics. Our politicians have brought the country to a deplorable state in the fifty-plus years of independence.

Let me complete the picture. Corruption is everywhere. Development has slowed down; India has the highest reservation percentage in the world and has become the only country where merit is of secondary importance. Chauvinism based on caste, religion, region and language has become the norm rather than the exception. We have created an election system where there is actually an incentive for our politicians to keep our people poor, helpless and illiterate. The chasm between the haves and the have-nots has been increasing. Unlike in China, population control has been more or less abandoned. Educated engineers and scientists are deserting India in a hurry. Misguided and misunderstood notions of socialism and meaningless slogans have become the staple diet of our political masters. Of course, there are exceptions amongst our politicians, but these are rare indeed.

If you have the benefit of quality education, you are among the few blessed ones in such an India. You have to thank society, your parents and your teachers because an average child is entitled to only Rs 600 per year for primary education.

Today, we have political freedom but not economic freedom—the freedom from hunger, disease and illiteracy. I believe that achieving economic freedom is the responsibility of this generation. It is our charter to transform this society, fulfilling the dream of Mahatma Gandhi of wiping the tears from the eyes of every poor child. Can we do it? My answer is an unequivocal yes. Do you know why I am so confident? It is because I believe that a plausible impossibility is better than a convincing possibility. Further, I have tremendous confidence in the power of youth, in the energy, confidence, determination and enthusiasm that every one of our young citizens possesses in abundance. But it is a mammoth task and requires that you do some hard thinking, indulge in some introspection and decide to do what previous generations have not done.

To achieve these goals, we must create a civilized society—a society where everybody has equal opportunity to better his or her life; where every child has food, shelter, health care and education; a society where duties come before rights; where each generation makes sacrifices to make life better for the next generation.

Bringing about such change, and eradicating poverty, however, requires a new mindset for the twenty-first century—one that makes us determined to make this society better. C.K. Prahalad once told me, 'Being a developing country is just a mindset.' I entirely agree with him. In fact, when I went to France in the early seventies, the 'mindset' was the first difference I noticed between a developed nation and a developing one. In France, everybody acted as if it was their job to discuss, debate and quickly act on improving public facilities. In India, we discuss, debate and behave as if the improvement of any public facility is not our task, and consequently, do not act at all. You have to change this mindset to one of identifying with all public causes, and act quickly to resolve any problems in the public domain. To do this, every individual has to give back to society, in some form or other, more than what he or she has received from it. That is how countries achieve progress. Every hardworking, sincere and honest citizen—teachers, politicians, bureaucrats, military personnel, professionals, administrative staff and janitors, just to name a few—has an important role in this task. Nobody is too small. However, the educated ones amongst us who have benefited from the sacrifice of our less fortunate brethren have a greater opportunity and responsibility to contribute than them. Educated Indians who embrace the twenty-first-century mindset will have to follow a few canonical attributes. Let me talk a little bit about these.

First, we need high aspirations. Aspirations energize us to overcome limitations posed by the context we are in. They engender and sustain hope, the main fuel for progress. They help us achieve miracles. Mahatma Gandhi's aspiration for an independent India is the reason why you and I can walk as free people today. It is not an exaggeration to say aspirations build civilizations. You must therefore raise your aspirations high in whatever you do.

Cynicism has no role in the task of building our nation. Cynicism takes away energy and enthusiasm which we require in plenty if we have to realize our dream.

Seek opportunities in areas that are outside government control. That is where the big opportunities lie and where merit will be recognized and rewarded. That is where quality jobs can be created in your quest to solve the problem of poverty.

Confidence is extremely important for progress. Openness is a sign of such self-confidence. Hence, the ability to accept, evaluate, adapt and adopt new ideas is what will separate the successful from the not-so-successful. We have to shun any thoughts and ideas that take us towards jingoism, chauvinism and parochialism. In this age of the interconnected global village, no nation desiring economic progress should isolate itself from the outside world. Nations that did so in the fifties and sixties have realized the futility of such isolation, reversed the trend successfully and benefited from the resultant openness. It is time that we overcame the East India Company syndrome and benefited from the best practices of nations that have solved their economic problems ahead of us. After all, to be the best, we have to benchmark with the best in the world. Anything short of this will not get us to the top. This requires a lot of discipline and hard work.

Thanks to our colonization of over a thousand years, people are mistrusted and oppressed in our society. We are a society where the interest of the government is deemed more important than the interest of the people; where the jobs of a few thousand people in public sector institutions are held more sacrosanct than the millions of consumers that these institutions are expected to serve; where an Indian multinational feels less trusted by its own government than by governments abroad; and where bureaucrats assume they know more about running world-class educational institutions than the finest intellectuals in those institutions.

Unfortunately, even after fifty years of independence, we have not overcome the legacy of our erstwhile rulers who themselves have changed rapidly in the meantime. We have to recognize that public sector interest is not public interest and that the interest of the government is not the interest of the people. One demonstration of this understanding would be the proactive removal of all monopolies the government runs. Government monopolies all over the world invariably create an asymmetry between the benefits to government officials and the people. It is difficult for me to understand why, for example, our government has still retained licensing in education while it has disbanded most industrial licensing. Over a period of ten to twenty years, the government should gradually get out of all activities other than defence, external affairs, home and macroeconomic policies, and should become just a regulator in all areas of commerce.

Our elite continue to behave like people with brown skin and a white mask, as Franz Fanon described in his famous book on postcolonial societies. You must change this mindset, else you will always see yourself and society around you in opposition to each other.

Another bane of our thousand-year-long enslavement is apathy. The main reason why India is still very backward is our unwillingness to take proactive action even when the solution to the problem is staring us in the face. We escape from the responsibility to solve our problems by blaming destiny. Let us remember the words of Prophet Mohammed who said, 'God changeth not what is in a people until they change what is in themselves.' My own experience with people from all walks of life confirms this thesis. We have become a nation that is good in rhetoric but poor in action. You have to downplay rhetoric and focus on action.

You must believe in and act according to the principle that putting public interest ahead of private interest in the short term will be better for your private concerns in the long run. Simply put, this means putting the interest of a public institution—country, state, city, college or company—ahead of an individual's interest in any transaction. In fact, the behaviour of our corrupt politicians, bureaucrats and corporate leaders can be traced to an utter disregard for this vital principle.

Ego, vanity and contempt for other people have clouded our minds for thousands of years and impeded our progress. Humility is scarce in this country. Even Al Berouni, the famous Persian writer, who visited India during the eleventh century and met many Indian pundits, remarked on this tendency. It is time we realized that India is at the bottom rung of economically successful nations, accepted the fact, made an effort to respect peoples better than us for their achievements, learned from them and improved our own economic status.

No society that has shunned merit has succeeded in solving its problems. While reservation in admission to schools and financial assistance for economically weaker sections of society for a certain period of time is desirable, there are grave doubts whether such economic backwardness should be determined by caste, as is done today in India. It is ironical that people now see sustenance of backwardness as an instrument for progress rather than hard work, intelligence and honesty. Thus, we have become perhaps the only nation in the world where people fight to be called backward! You have a responsibility to debate this issue and work to create a climate of opinion where people aspire to economic progress the right way.

We have adopted an economic model where the government has taken on the responsibility to create and sustain jobs without any regard for efficiency and accountability. The result is underemployment, inefficiency, insubordination, demoralization of people with merit and value destruction in the economy. There have been, in recent times, some discussions on dismantling this model. But it takes vision, courage and rapid action to carry out this creative destruction. You must encourage leaders who have taken on this task, and lend a hand in disseminating the positives of such an initiative to the masses.

You must remember that the only way to solve poverty in this country is to create more jobs. This requires entrepreneurship. We already have too many people employed at very low wages in the agricultural sector. Hence, you have to create jobs in the manufacturing and service sectors. Our governments, since they have little or no accountability to the people, are not likely to create any more jobs. Thus, we need more and more entrepreneurs. We need more engineers, scientists, bureaucrats and politicians who have a mindset to encourage entrepreneurship. There must be a concerted effort to create new jobs.

The reason for the lack of progress in many developing nations is not the paucity of resources but the lack of management talent and professionalism. Being professional and effective in our work helps us optimally utilize our resources—human talent, raw materials, domestic and foreign investment and infrastructure, just to name a few. This is because a professional individual owes allegiance to his profession and not to any organization or person. Accordingly, he does not let personal relations interfere with his professional dealings. He is fair and unbiased and starts every transaction on a zero base, without bringing in any baggage from prior transactions. He makes objective decisions, and believes in the principle, 'In God I trust; everyone else must bring data to the table.' Thus, everyone in the organization, no matter how high or low in the hierarchy, will have an equal opportunity to convince him on any issue. Consequently, everyone will be confident and enthusiastic in dealing with him.*

---

*Whenever I use 'he', I mean both male and female professionals. At Infosys, our female managers are great examples of professionalism.

You also have a duty to lead by example in work ethic, honesty, following the rule of law and contract, and charity. In modern times, the best example of such leadership was set by Mahatma Gandhi, the father of our nation. In every act of his, he walked the talk and practised the precept. No wonder he had the trust, confidence and support of every Indian in his objective to achieve India's independence through non-violence.

In my opinion, the Indian professional, unlike his/her Western counterpart, is rather stingy when it comes to charity. Unless you can give back to your school or college at least a small part of your life's earnings, it is difficult to strengthen these institutions for the sake of future generations. Further, the reputation of the Indian professional is very poor in living up to contractual obligations. In fact, a large majority of professionals who received financial assistance either from the government or from educational institutions for studies abroad have gone back on their contractual commitments in a manner that they or their children cannot be proud of. A hundred per cent compliance with contracts is the only way to help future generations benefit from financial initiatives that help worthy and needy students.

Create excellence in whatever you do. By connecting these islands of excellence, you can create a critical mass for your revolution to change society.

Remember that reality is, finally, something you actively create. Reality in India means corruption, dirty roads, pollution, and no power. Reality in Singapore means clean roads, no pollution, enough power, good airports etc. It is your task to define and create our new reality.

The future for India lies in you. I have no doubt that you will become useful citizens of this society, or for that matter whichever society you choose to live in.

Let me close with another Sanskrit sloka that is at the heart of what I said and believe.

Ahimsa prathamam pushpam, pushpam indriya nigraham
Sarvabhoota daya pushpam, kshama pushpam visheshata
Shanti dhyana pushpa tataivacha, sathyam ashthavidam pushpam
Vishnum praseedham kareth

(Non-violence, controlling the desires, kindness to all, forgiveness, peace, meditation, charity and truth are the eight flowers that please the Lord)

Indeed, these attributes characterize the ideal Indian of the twenty-first century.

Succeeding in the Contemporary World

It is always nice to be in Paris, my favourite city. My mind goes back to that wintry day thirty-seven years ago when I landed at Orly with barely fifty francs in my pocket, hardly a word of French on my lips, yet full of excitement that I was in the land of the student revolution of 1968, the land of my favourite mathematician, Laplace, and my favourite actress, Brigitte Bardot. The French people were courteous and most welcoming whether it was the garcon at a bistro, my professors at the Alliance Française, my colleagues in the office or even the committed functionaries of the French Communist party with whom I had the privilege of having long discussions on communism. Somehow, even today, this city retains the freshness, excitement and vitality that I felt during my stay in the seventies.

Graduation day is an important event in one's life. It is a day when you step out of the open, collegial and intellectually stimulating environment of the citadel of learning into the real world full of contradictions, astounding possibilities and tough challenges. The world that you will excel in as professionals is so different from the one that I stepped into when I was your age forty years ago, thanks to three important recent phenomena: globalization, global warming and laissez-faire capitalism. I will spend some time explaining why these are seminal themes that will change the shape of this world and discussing what your role is in such a world.

Commencement Address, INSEAD, Fontainebleau, 18 December 2008

What is globalization? I will define it at two levels. At the macro level, it is about frictionless flow of capital, services, goods and labour across the globe. It is also about global sharing of ideas, knowledge and culture. It is about creating a shared concern and a plan to fight global issues like poverty, AIDS, terrorism and global warming. At the microeconomic or firm level, it is about sourcing capital from where it is cheapest, sourcing talent from where it is best available, producing where it is most efficient and selling where the markets are, without being constrained by national boundaries. Infosys, IBM and Adidas are all good examples of globalization at the firm level.

What are the implications of globalization for you, the corporate leaders of the future? First, corporations worldwide will face tremendous competition since innovation can come from anywhere in the world—developed as well as developing countries. With globalization, success today has become essentially about how fast you can develop new ideas, implement them, and gain competitive advantage in the marketplace, so that you can create a better company, society, country and world. Hence, your focus on talent, innovation and reducing time-to-market and cost-to-market will have to increase by an order of magnitude. You will be required to make quick decisions based on confidence and conviction. In such an environment, I believe that the only unchanging attributes of a successful corporation will be openness to new ideas, meritocracy, speed, innovation and excellence in execution. Your challenge is to create a mindset that embraces these attributes.

You will have to create an environment of tolerance and respect for multi-culturalism in your corporations. Emphasizing universal values—honesty, decency, hard work, tolerance and courtesy, seeking what is good in each of us, and de-emphasizing differences—will be essential to make these multicultural teams work at their best. You will have to learn to appreciate the aspirations of professionals from multiple cultures. You will have to instil a mindset of openness to learn from other cultures while retaining the good aspects in ours.

Second, in this flat world, every nation that has something to contribute to the global bazaar can improve the lives of not just its own people but people throughout the globe—the rich and the poor, the urban and the rural, the powerful and the weak, the educated and the not-so-educated. The developing countries, in particular, present global leaders with unprecedented opportunity. In fact, currently, more than half of the world's GDP (measured at purchasing power parity) is accounted for by developing countries. The consumer base in developing countries is consequently becoming significant, thanks to their fast-growing economies, higher disposable incomes and demographic differences, with countries like China and India having a large number of consumers in the under-thirty age category. Thus, you have to stop thinking of just the 'rich' customers of developed economies. You will have to lead in the creation of products and services that suit the pockets of the 2 billion poor people at the bottom of the pyramid. While the per-unit revenue and per-unit profit may be small, given the large number of such consumers in developing countries, your corporations can make a tidy sum of profit. But to do that, you will have to understand and act according to the consumer preferences of these countries.

Generally, the emerging economies (EEs) were either colonized in the past or were under despots or Communist rule. In other words, capitalism was not practised there till recently and there is a deep suspicion of capitalism, foreign companies and individuals. Hence, your success requires you to create trust in these societies. In every decision you make, ask if it makes your company and the country better. If in doubt, choose the country's interest, since your company cannot succeed unless the country succeeds. Such a policy is a sure way to create profitable and enduring businesses in EEs. Unilever is a wonderful example of this principle.

Now, let me turn my attention to the second phenomenon—global warming. One of the consequences of globalization is the legitimate desire of countries like China and India to upgrade the quality of life of their citizens by providing facilities like cars, electricity and housing. These require enormous amounts of energy and result in increased carbon emissions in an already burdened planet. Such carbon emissions have been increasing at a high rate over the last thirty-five years, thanks to the rise of developed countries. There is conclusive evidence that such emissions have resulted in the rise of air and ocean temperatures, melting of polar ice-caps and rising of sea levels worldwide. Such trends will lead to ecosystem destabilization, reduction in the availability of water and food, and the onset of diseases on an unprecedented scale. The solution is not to force developing nations to forgo what the developed world has enjoyed for over a century. It is to come together as one planet and use innovation in technology to produce alternate energy solutions and reduction of carbon emissions. The awareness of the impact of climate change has been raised, thanks to the untiring efforts of the Intergovernmental Panel on Climate Change (IPCC), its wonderful chairman Dr R.K. Pachauri, and former US Vice President Al Gore. However, a significant part of the work remains to be done by future business and political leaders. This is where your contribution will become important. Focus on reducing energy and water consumption in personal life, building energy-neutral buildings and creating energy-efficient manufacturing processes. Help your consumers and your supply chain reduce energy and water consumption through your products, services and vendor-partners. After all, this is the only planet we have. Conduct yourself as if you have borrowed it from the next generation. Remember that you will have to give it back to them in good shape.

That brings me to my third theme—laissez-faire capitalism, yet another consequence of globalization. It is now clear that either communism has been given up as an unviable ideology or been replaced in practice by state-directed capitalism. Unfortunately, the greed of several corporate leaders, the meltdown of Wall Street, the increasing differences between the salaries of CEOs and ordinary workers, and the unbelievable severance compensation paid to failed CEOs have called into question whether capitalism is indeed a solution for the benefit of all, or if it is an instrument for a few cunning people to hoodwink a large mass of gullible middle-class and poor people. Never before in the history of capitalism have so few people brought so much misery to so many. The recent debate in the US Congress illustrates this sentiment well. Several well-known commentators have opined that the recent $4 trillion bailout of the global economy is a strong testimony to the new adage, 'If you borrow $100, it is your responsibility to repay. If a corporation borrows $100 billion, it is the government's responsibility to worry.' This bailout has started a debate on whether the current form of laissez-faire capitalism is sustainable without the fundamental socialistic instrument of state support.

I believe that no amount of legislation and regulation will solve the problem of greed and save capitalism. The only way you can save capitalism and bring it back to its shining glory is by conducting yourselves as decent, honest, fair, diligent and socially conscious business leaders. In every action of yours, you have to ask how it will make the lowest level worker in your corporation and the poorest person in your society better. You have to learn to put the interest of the community—your corporation, your society, your nation and this planet—before your own interest. That is why, in my company—Infosys—we practice the adage: 'The softest pillow is a clear conscience.'

To succeed in these days of globalization, global warming and laissez-faire capitalism, every worker in your corporation will have to accept tremendous sacrifices in the short term and hope that goodness will, indeed, succeed in the long term and make life better for every one of them. Converting hope into reality requires that leaders become trustworthy. It is my belief that leading from the front and leading by example are the only instruments for gaining the trust of your colleagues. To create such a lasting legacy of decent leadership, just ask the question, 'What can I do so that people will miss me if I disappear tomorrow?'

I urge you all to set a new standard for corporate leadership through leadership by example. Demonstrating decency, fairness, honesty, transparency and accountability as leaders will indeed revive capitalism and make this world richer, happier, greener and safer than the one you inherited.

Succeeding in a Globalized Corporation

As you leave the portals of this great institution known for preparing leaders of international business, you know that your education here has prepared you to cross national borders seamlessly, adapt to new cultures quickly, create goodwill with host nations effortlessly, and use your education to add value to those societies and make your corporations stronger. Such an education is rare and precious. My experience in Paris in the early 1970s, when I was utterly unprepared to benefit from the wonderful French culture, is a good example of why institutions like this are precious. While it was exciting to be in Paris in the seventies, it was frustrating not just for me but for my extremely kind and understanding friends in Paris because I was not clued into the culture.

What are your challenges as a citizen of the world? You have to be adaptive in the office and outside. You have to accept that there is more to history than 'Western triumphalism' and that new history is being created in Asia and elsewhere. You have to throw out the traditional mindset that Asian success is a zero-sum game played with the West. You have to accept that we live in a flat world where new ideas and products could come from anywhere. You have to be in the vanguard of the effort to create a fair, equitable, peaceful, green and happy planet. You have to unlearn traditional rules of international business and quickly learn the rules of the globalized corporation. I

Convocation Address, IESE Business School, Barcelona, 9 May 2008

define globalization as sourcing capital from where it is cheapest, sourcing talent from where it is best available, producing where it is most cost-effective and selling where the markets are, without being constrained by national boundaries. Infosys, which leverages the abundant technical manpower in India and China to produce software for Western corporations, is a good example of a globalized corporation. In the past, it was always outdated Western ideas, products and services that found markets in developing nations. Today, the economic success of China and India and the rapid rise of emerging countries have changed most of our assumptions on markets, talent and capital flows. You will have unique challenges as a leader and manager as well. As a leader you will have to decide on an objective that is laudable, exciting and aspirational. And you will have to be a global manager—a management professional whose aspiration transcends national boundaries, who benchmarks performance on a global scale, and who is comfortable in dealing with many cultures.

It is generally accepted that the success of a corporation is determined by innovating and executing good ideas to become more and more relevant to customers. Innovation comes from the power of the mind, a mind that is happy, energetic and enthusiastic. Such power also comes from the quality of people in a corporation. That is why we at Infosys believe that the market capitalization of the company is zero when the last of our employees has gone home in the evening, no matter what it was during the working day. Show me a successful corporation, and I will show you a happy, hopeful, confident, enthusiastic and energetic set of people right from the chairman to the janitor. Show me a successful manager, and I will show you an inclusive team with every member seeing a rainbow and confident of catching a part of it. Teamwork has only grown more important today—we live in a complex world that requires multiple competencies and hard work to succeed. However, no individual possesses either the skills or the stamina to handle every aspect of a task. Hence, teamwork is crucial. A manager must enhance the confidence, enthusiasm, energy and hopes of his team members. Creating such a team, transcending biases of nationalities, races, religious beliefs and classes, and embracing both multi-culturalism and diversity is your big challenge. After all, it is such teams that convert plausibly-impossible goals to convincingly-possible ones.

What should you do to create such a team? Tolerance and respect for other cultures and beliefs in the team is a must for its members to become comfortable about their identity. Every member must be an inclusive traveller towards a grand vision and must see a benefit in moving towards that vision. There cannot be two classes of citizens in a team if they are to be productive and happy. Emphasizing universal values—honesty, decency, hard work, tolerance and courtesy, seeking what is good in each of us, and de-emphasizing our differences—helps us to seek a common cause and work together. We will be better human beings if we are open-minded about learning from other cultures while retaining the good in our own.

Innovations and new ideas thrive in an environment that encourages open debate, discussion and participation by everybody in the team. Such an environment thrives when people are confident that their ideas will be evaluated using data and facts, and that personal biases will have no place in teamwork. That is why we at Infosys believe in the adage, 'In God we trust, everybody else brings data to the table.' In fact, this was the first lesson I learnt thirty-seven years ago from my teacher, Prof Krishnayya.

No matter how good an idea is, it has no value unless other people understand it, embrace it as their own and help you implement it. Hence, communication is crucial to the success of a manager. Given that we are to work in multicultural teams, we have to use universally understood, simple but powerful words and metaphors to communicate with people across the globe. Though English will continue to play a major role as a common business language globally, it is essential to understand and appreciate local languages. We live in an age when the only constant is change and learnability is the only instrument you have to handle fast-paced change. Learnability is the ability of an individual to constantly and quickly learn new ideas and unlearn outdated ideas, be they technical or managerial. It is also about a mindset that is open to new ideas, new people, new cultures and new paradigms, all factors necessary for the success of a global leader.

Confident people attract good talent, and generosity is a sign of such confidence. A successful manager is unfailingly generous and shares the credit for his achievements with every one of his team members. He follows the adage, 'Praise in public and criticize in private.' In fact, fostering such self-esteem is extremely important for individuals to contribute ideas and add value to a team effectively. Self-esteem flourishes when discussions can be held in an environment of civility and courtesy to everybody. That is why we at Infosys believe in the adage, 'You can disagree with me as long as you are not disagreeable.'

Remember that performance is all-important in a global environment. Performance leads to recognition, recognition leads to respect, and respect leads to power. If we want to become a powerful nation, the only instrument we have is performance, achieved through hard work, smartness, excellence and integrity.

Creating trust in host societies is extremely important in order to succeed there. To do this, you will have to demonstrate your commitment to the best principles of corporate governance in every action of yours. Corporate governance is focussed on maximizing shareholder value while ensuring fairness to all the stakeholders—customers, investors, employees, vendor-partners, the government of the land and society at large. In these days of free-flowing global capital, the ability to attract capital requires that corporations adhere to the best global standards of corporate governance. The foundation of our corporate governance philosophy at Infosys is the adage, 'The softest pillow is a clear conscience.' We also believe that it is good practice to under-promise and over-deliver. Further, it is best to deliver bad news to the stakeholders proactively and at the earliest. This creates goodwill with stakeholders. They fully understand that there will, inevitably, be ups and downs in every business. What they value, however, is for managements to level with them at all times. This belief of ours derives strength from the adage, 'When in doubt, disclose.'

One of my strongest beliefs is that corporations have an important duty to contribute to society. While, on average, tremendous progress has been made in enhancing the economic well-being of people, the chasm between the haves and the have-nots of the world has unfortunately widened, especially in the developing world. Goodwill from society is extremely important. After all, society contributes customers, employees and investors, and, through political leaders and bureaucrats, creates policies that impact your corporation. No corporation can sustain its progress unless it makes a difference to society. In all your decisions, put the interest of the host society first and then your corporation. Such a policy has always succeeded for entrepreneurs.

I want to repeat a few words of advice that I often use when I address the youth of the world because these ideas are an integral part of my life's experience and my beliefs.

- First, I want to emphasize the importance of being trustworthy in all your dealings.
- Second, fear is natural but you should not let your actions be governed by it. Just as fear may sometimes be the hidden voice of your intuition pointing out what your rational mind may not yet have seen, it is also sometimes an invitation to explore a new part of yourself and the world.
- Third, a supportive family is the bedrock upon which satisfying lives and careers are built. Create a support system for yourself with people who will rejoice in your success and be there for you during your moments of dilemma, self-doubt and moral conflicts. With this rock-like support behind you, you can endure almost anything in your career.
- Fourth, excellence in work leads to excellence in life and vice-versa. Unless you are a happy person at home, you cannot be a happy person in the office. Success in life is when others' eyes light up when you walk into a room, and your eyes light up when you are with other people. Enjoy life. Share jokes with your colleagues and family. Take your work seriously but not yourself!
- Fifth, learn how to manage yourself, especially your feelings, in a way that respects the dignity of others and yourself.
- Finally, live your life and lead your career in a way that makes a difference to your society. When, one day, you have made

your mark on the world, remember that, in the ultimate analysis, we are all mere temporary custodians of the wealth we generate, whether it be financial, intellectual or emotional. The best use of all your wealth is to share it with those less fortunate.

It is on such foundations that great leaders and organizations flourish.

Go forth and embrace your future with open arms, and enthusiastically pursue your own life journey of discovery!

The Need for Excellence

In many ways, graduation day signifies that you have joined the ranks of adults. You are now entitled to a lifetime of paying taxes and innumerable kinds of bills! The good news is that the opportunities before you are also endless. Your illustrious institution has equipped you to realize your dreams—the future is now yours to choose.

During your stay here, you may have visited the Sabarmati Ashram nearby, and been inspired by that place. I want to ask you a fundamental question that was evident in many of Mahatma Gandhi's speeches. Why is it that India does not boast of any product of international class and international recognition? We do have many successes including a vibrant democracy, a free press and an independent judiciary. We have the third largest pool of world-class scientists and engineers, and have gained self-sufficiency in foodgrains as well as in building dams, rockets and satellites. However, there is no single field where we can confidently say, 'We are the best in the world.'

You should ponder over this question since design plays a crucial role in the success of any product, be it ceramics, manufactured goods or software applications. In fact, I believe that the long-term success of a technology is dependent on how quickly it becomes user-

Convocation Address, National Institute of Design, Ahmedabad, 11 December 2001

friendly. Let me take the example of Information Technology (IT). In the past, we were more concerned with optimal use of hardware rather than with user-friendliness and ease of software development. Today's computers have 66,000 times the computing power, at the same cost, of the computers built in 1975. Thus, improvements in computing power over the years have led to increasing the emphasis on effectiveness and ease of use for the customer. This industry has realized that delivering effective solutions requires addressing the human aspects of the solutions. In fact, Graphical User Interfaces (GUIs) have become the industry norm. The ongoing convergence of IT and consumer electronics portends the emergence of even more user-friendly and intelligent goods. Therefore, design will continue to play an important role in this technology-driven world.

Let me briefly talk about the reasons behind India's poor performance in creating world-class products and services and what we can do about it.

A crucial factor for success has always been excellence—whether it is in business, sports or arts. We have not paid enough attention to excellence. Perhaps an important reason for this was the command and control economy that existed till recently. In those times, there was no incentive for improvement as the Licence Raj ensured protection for incumbents.

Political considerations forced successive governments to cling on to misguided notions of socialism. Luxury was looked down upon. It was politically more correct to provide basic accommodation rather than to construct an impressive building. This, by itself, could be excused as part of the travails of development with its emphasis on quantity rather than quality. However, what was disturbing was the creation of a mindset that equated high quality with exorbitant costs. Thus, the government felt reasonably justified in delivering substandard goods and services to its citizens. This sapped our confidence in our ability to provide world-class goods and services to our people.

Success in independent India was then due to whom you knew rather than what you could do. The pervasive bureaucracy led to widespread suspicion of any non-governmental initiative. The use of the 'tender' process for awarding contracts purely based on cost rather than credentials became widespread.

Another misguided notion was the belief that consumer goods are, at best, a necessary evil. The Mahalanobis model emphasized capital goods vis-à-vis consumer goods. The socialist system introduced many other vices into the country. Perhaps the most important of these was the lack of accountability. People who ran governments and public sector institutions were accountable to no one but themselves.

Fortunately, the old mindset is changing for the better. The liberalization of the Indian economy in the early 1990s has brought in a new context and forced this change. Indian companies have started dreaming of competing with the best in the world. In fact, it was liberalization that laid the foundation for the success of the Indian software industry.

The forces of globalization and technology are reshaping our world. Global trade now accounts for nearly 25 per cent of the world's GDP. Privatization has become a global phenomenon with more than a hundred countries pursuing the privatization agenda. The Internet has grown to reach more than 450 million users. The mapping of the human genome will possibly lead to the development of new categories of drugs and improve the quality of our lives. These are fundamental forces at work. In fact, the world you are stepping into is vastly different from the one that we lived in even ten years ago.

In these times, you will be competing with the best in the world. The task before you is no doubt arduous. Years of protectionism have sapped Indian companies of their creativity and emphasis on excellence. However, you must strive hard to mould the view among decision-makers that India is synonymous with not just competitive costs but also high quality. Indian companies are increasingly establishing their presence in the global markets. They are your natural allies. As they build the brand of India Inc., you must be there to assist them in doing so.

Pursue excellence. Aim high and dream big. Make excellence in execution your core belief. Remember, excellence can be acquired only by relentless training, frank feedback and constant self-improvement. Such excellence can prosper only in an environment where it is recognized and rewarded. Strive to create such an environment at your workplace.

Your dreams and your enthusiasm are of utmost importance. As you step into the real world, remain young at heart and be open to new ideas. Never accept the status quo. Endeavour to be the best in the world in whatever you choose to be. Remember the words of Harold Taylor: 'The roots of true achievement lie in the will to become the best that you can become.'

Finally, remember that words mean nothing unless backed by actions. Henry Ford often said, 'You cannot build a reputation on what you are going to do.' Therefore, build your reputation with your achievements. The nation needs you.

The Legal Professional in the Era of Globalization

Today marks a milestone from where you continue your quest for more knowledge. In many ways, it signifies that you have arrived in the real world, one that is changing at a very rapid pace, thanks to the forces of globalization and technology. Over the past twenty years, the growth of world trade has averaged 6 per cent a year, twice as much as the growth in the economic output of the world. We clearly live in an interconnected world where the happenings on the NASDAQ find an echo in the Mumbai Stock Exchange.

In this new environment, legal professionals have a tremendous responsibility in making India competitive, because law, among other things, is an instrument of change. You have the opportunity to assume key responsibilities as administrators, legislators, lawyers, judges and legal advisors and usher in transformational change.

Let me give an example. The most important factor in the success of the Indian software industry in the 1990s was the liberalization of our economy. Liberalization helped us by reducing friction from government agencies to business and by improving the velocity of decision-making in our own board rooms. Lawyers in the Central government played a seminal part in the reforms agenda by quickly casting the new set of rules in a modern legal framework. They acted according to the advice of the French writer Antoine de Saint-

Convocation Address, National Law School of India University, Bangalore, 11 August 2002

Exupery who said, 'As for the future, your task is not to foresee but to enable it.' It is your continued responsibility to help Indian businesses face the challenges of globalization by revamping our archaic bankruptcy laws, labour laws and laws in industries that have not yet been touched by reforms. As a country that hopes to leverage the power of global capital to create jobs for citizens, India has to be at the forefront of creating a modern, business-friendly, fair and fast-response justice system.

The work of legal professionals in these days of globalization transcends local jurisdictions and national boundaries. Businesses are constantly looking out for international opportunities. Hence, legal professionals have to make it easy for Indian businesses to establish their presence in remote corners of the world. It is necessary for our legal professionals to be fully aware of the uniqueness of legal systems in the most important markets of the world—the G-7 countries and the developed world. Thus, courses in International Law become very important. Law schools in developed nations have been responding to globalization by introducing new courses in International and Comparative Law. In fact, the most visible change in the law school curricula in the USA during the last decade has been in this area. Indian law schools should follow this trend and enable our students to think globally.

Just as global markets are becoming increasingly integrated, so are legal services. India is a signatory to the General Agreement on Trade in Services (GATS). From 2005 onwards, our service sector is open for competition from international service providers. Hence, legal professionals in India must be prepared to face competition from foreign law firms. This is best done if Indian legal professionals adopt the best global practices and create a culture of legal excellence. A global mindset is a necessary condition for global excellence. The 1999 Bologna Declaration requires universities in Europe to adopt a common standard for legal education to provide mobility of lawyers in the countries of the European Union. Such a mindset would emerge in India if our law universities encourage academic exchanges and research with international law universities. Otherwise, our students will move on to law schools abroad. Law schools at Harvard and Stanford universities have been steadily accelerating the enrolment of foreign faculty and students.

Today's information age is sometimes called the golden age of Intellectual Property (IP) law. IP rights are critical to continued investments in research and technological innovation. The leading law schools in the developed world have incorporated changes in their curricula to bring focus on IP law. For instance, Stanford Law School has a course on 'High Technology and IP Law' that covers cyber laws, telecommunication laws and laws governing other high-technology industries. Our legal professionals have to be trained in such courses if we want them to be successful in negotiations between Indian hi-tech companies and their Western counterparts.

Alumni in our law schools also have to be trained from time to time on advances in law practices. This is where the Continuing Legal Education (CLE) mechanism becomes important to keep your alumni and other lawyers up to date. In fact, I would suggest that such continuing education be made mandatory for renewing bar licences.

Today's professionals cannot survive without keeping pace with technological developments. Use of technology reduces delays in administration of justice, helps lawyers and judges prepare for arguments and judgments, and provides legal assistants with quick research on case laws. Such use of technology improves reuse of knowledge, improves productivity and reduces cost and time spent on cases. Thus, IT skills will become one of the core competencies required of any legal professional.

There is a huge gap between the demand and supply of judges in India. The Indian court system has just twelve to thirteen judges for every million people whereas in the United States that ratio is well over 100 for a million people. If our legal system has to deliver justice on time, we have to bridge this gap. One way is to increase the intake of law students at institutes such as the National Law School. The National Law School system should create more and more such schools throughout the country.

Law is a fundamental social institution. The affirmative action laws and the anti-trust laws are examples of how the legal system regulates and influences the social environment. In these days of civil society activism, human rights issues assume great significance. Countries with a poor human rights record are not considered conducive for economic investments. Issues related to labour standards and child labour have also come into focus. Sweatshop conditions in several industries such as apparel and footwear have been of concern the world over. Competent lawyers with a conscience have to fight against such abuses and ensure fairness in society. Law schools in developed nations have increased their focus on such courses. For instance, Harvard Law School has a programme called the Human Rights Programme (HRP) where students carry out a range of activities that provide a critical understanding of human rights. India cannot afford to be left behind in this area.

As you step into your work life, remember that ethical behaviour is the foundation for sustainable success. Corporate governance is crucial for the success of any corporation. As legal advisors to corporations, you must endeavour to adopt transparent and ethical practices in all your transactions. In every legal advice that you provide, remember that societal interest comes before the interest of your employer.

Your education enables you to influence and change the social and legal framework of the country. Your degree is a testimony that you have learned the nuances of law and that you are ready to take charge of your future. Let us dream together of making our country a better place. Dream big and aim at the plausibly impossible changes. Keep as your watchword what Eleanor Roosevelt once said: 'The future belongs to those who believe in the beauty of their dreams.'

A Case for a More Open Trade Regime in India

India, today, is one of the fastest growing economies in the world. But our nation of a billion people is still far from achieving many of its goals. Twenty-five per cent of India's population is poor and 39 per cent is illiterate. We rank 127th in the world on the Human Development Index.

A key contributor to poverty in India is the overdependence of the population on agriculture. Today, 65 per cent of the Indian population depends on agriculture while the share of this sector in our country's GDP is a low 22 per cent. Consequently, the sector has an excess supply of labour. The average value added per agricultural worker in India is 27 per cent of the value of a non-agricultural worker.

Clearly, a dynamic industry sector can significantly reduce India's overdependence on agriculture, and reduce poverty. China, for example, pulls 1 per cent of its people out of agriculture every year and puts them into its booming construction and manufacturing sectors. That has been possible since China has a sound export market. On the other hand, Indian industry relies heavily on the domestic market for growth. This is not good for several reasons. The purchasing power of the bulk of the Indian population is low. India's rural population has a per capita income of approximately Rs 11,000

Convocation Address, Indian Institute of Foreign Trade, New Delhi, 17 April 2005

per year or a little over Rs 30 a day. Monthly per capita expenditure in rural areas is Rs 554, and in urban areas Rs 1,022. Thus, disposable income in India is low. This means India must look towards exports to drive the growth of our industries and for the creation of jobs.

Exports have been key to economic growth in most countries. It is generally agreed that countries with a strong export focus, and driven by a free trade policy, had the highest GDP growth between 1990 and 2000. The top fifth of countries ranked by freedom of trade and export growth averaged an annual per-capita GDP growth of 2 per cent, while the bottom fifth saw annual GDP per-capita grow at a mere 0.2 per cent during that period. In the 1990s, the economies of East Asia saw exports of both goods and services grow to 30 per cent of GDP—twice the 1980 ratio—and their GDP growth rate averaged more than 10 per cent a year in the same period.

Recently, growth in Indian exports has been robust. Exports touched an all-time high figure of $79 billion in 2004, growing at a rate of 23 per cent. However, the economist Raghuram Rajan has noted that on the International Monetary Fund's trade restrictiveness index, India still has a score of eight on ten, placing it amongst the most restrictive countries in the world. India's total foreign trade in 2004 was less than 1 per cent of the global total. Today, China's exports of goods and services are six times that of India's. In 2003, the increase in China's imports and exports alone was larger than India's total exports and imports.

India must embrace a greater openness to trade. In today's era of globalization, characterized by falling geographic and regulatory barriers, India cannot ignore the world market. It is wise to remember Peter Drucker's words that there is no distance in today's world economy and that everything is 'local'. This is where you have a significant role to play. You are the future leaders who will help shape our trade and export policies and put India on the global map. Your education enables you to influence our politicians to make the right decisions for economic growth.

The World Bank estimates that India can grow at double-digit rates with the right trade reforms and competition-friendly policies. It is clear that India faces its moment of truth. There is an important question we must answer unambiguously. That is, will we seize the opportunities before us and become a key player on the global stage? If the answer is in the affirmative, we must create a sense of urgency for reforms.

Successive Indian governments have had a historical ambivalence towards exports and openness in trade. Let me tell you an amusing story. Sometime in the eighties, an Indian prime minister suggested to the commerce secretary that they coin the slogan 'export or perish' to bring exports to the front burner. The commerce secretary replied, 'Sir, let us not take any such risky decision. I am afraid this country will decide to perish.' This ambivalence continues even today. In fact, India holds the record of filing the maximum number of anti-dumping cases under the WTO between 1995 and 2003.

Clearly, we have to make some difficult choices—choices which may be unpopular but are necessary to drive reform. You will be part of the effort to make this country more open to trade. To work past opposition in taking such tough but unpopular decisions, you must have the courage of conviction. Be honest and true to your profession. Act fearlessly. Let me recall the words of Samuel Johnson who said, 'If you don't have courage, you may not have an opportunity to use any of your other virtues.'

For India to play a central role in world trade, Indian industry must be able to compete globally. Consequently, India must, first and foremost, encourage competition by opening up industry to foreign investment. This is the key to achieving global labour and capital productivity standards across Indian industry.

Let me give some examples. Foreign Direct Investment (FDI) in the IT, automotive and Business Process Outsourcing (BPO) sectors acted as a spur to domestic industries in India, forcing them to innovate. The impact of foreign investment on India's automotive sector, for instance, is a data point. Between 1992 and 2001, productivity grew by a staggering 256 per cent, and employment in the industry rose by 11 per cent.

The *Economist* has observed that the Indian economy is often portrayed as an elephant—big, lumbering and slow off the mark. To become a strong global competitor, we must change this perception.

We have to create powerful international brands that are recognized the world over to create a new image of India.

India's business climate is highly restrictive. According to a World Bank study, it takes eighty-nine days to open a business in India, 425 days to enforce a business contract, and ten years to close down a business! India's inflexible labour laws discourage investment and job-creation. When the global steel magnate Lakshmi Mittal was asked why he left India to seek his fortunes in Indonesia, he said, 'I found a free atmosphere there.' We must enable Indian entrepreneurs across sectors to build a global empire without having to leave home.

If you work in the corporate sector, you must become evangelists for reforms and for implementing international trade practices. There is a mindset of resistance towards facing foreign competition in India. An Indian cabinet minister once remarked that Indian businesses often appeal to the government to open up all sectors to more reforms and competition, except their own sector!

To be the best, Indian corporations have to benchmark with the best in the world. Anything short of this will not get you to the top. Benchmarking on a global scale is the only way to compete internationally. To do so, companies need an export orientation. You must be willing to take advantage of sales opportunities no matter where they arise; to use the cheapest resources no matter where they are available; to hire the best people no matter where they are from; and to face the fiercest competition no matter what its origin is. This is globalization.

Today, global capital is free to move wherever it finds a hospitable environment. Our professionals have globally-valued skills and have global opportunities. Our customers have access to the best global companies to buy products and services from. This is where adhering to the finest principles of corporate governance comes in handy. Unless our corporations follow the highest degree of fairness, transparency and accountability, they are unlikely to attract the best customers, employees and investors.

Put the interest of the nation ahead of your own interest. This will lead to your own betterment in the long run. Work hard to create a climate of opinion that prefers long-term growth ahead of short-term benefits. As educated citizens in a civilized society, this is an important principle you must follow.

Some of you will work in the government, and some in the private sector. As future leaders, it is your responsibility to bring about positive change. To become a change agent, you have to develop a new mindset characterized by self-confidence, openness, fairness, humility, global benchmarking and meritocracy. Be proactive in problem-solving. Embrace meritocracy to create a high-performance culture. Be willing to take risks. Do not rationalize failure; it renders people apathetic and justifies inaction. Remember that it is 'better to light a candle than to curse the darkness'.

Above all, embrace high aspirations. Aspirations energize us to overcome the limitations posed by context. In fact, sociologists assert that a collective positive spirit is critical for explosive growth in a country. As future leaders, you must raise aspirations among your team, and create confidence that India can, indeed, become a global power. If we can do this, a billion Indians will be the winners.

Let us together dream of making our country a better place. I urge you to go forward, and explore the realm of what is plausibly-impossible. Ask 'why not?' instead of 'why?'. Embrace a life of meaning and of excellence. Remember the words of Abraham Lincoln: 'It is not the years in your life that count, it is the life in your years.'

The Role of Religion in Education

I want to talk about something that is critical for a successful life as well as a successful career. 'All your scholarship would be in vain if at the same time you do not build your character and attain mastery over your thoughts and your actions,' Mahatma Gandhi often said.

As we enter the twenty-first century, I am reminded of the famous words of Albert Einstein that science without religion is lame, and religion without science is blind. In fact, as the influence of technology on our lives increases, the social and human aspect of our lives become all the more important.

The founding fathers of independent India wanted a nation where every religion would flourish and every voice would be heard. Thus, India has, very rightly, adopted secularism as its credo. The concept of secularism generally means that religion is an individual's private matter and that it has no place in any public transaction between individuals or between the state and the individual. This philosophy has tremendous merit. However, our education system has consistently downplayed religion. Consequently, we do not know much about other religions because people do not speak openly about them. Such ignorance leads to suspicion and mistrust. In fact, such suspicion and mistrust have resulted in attacks by people professing one religious pursuit on people practising other religions.

Convocation Address, Punjab University, Chandigarh, 28 December 2001

We cannot let this continue. The heritage of this country is too precious to be left to goons and illiterates to destroy it in their bigotry and hatred.

Religion plays an important role in our lives by shaping our values and our interactions with the world. It is part of our history and our culture. Importantly, religious beliefs manifest themselves in ethical questions and disputes, not only within nations and communities but sometimes even within organizations. As you go on to become the leaders of this country and the world, an understanding of the religious beliefs of your colleagues will be of vital importance.

We operate today in a globalized world. We interact with people of different cultures and different religions. Today, success requires that you be part of a highly motivated, collaborative and competent team spread across the world. Such high-energy units operate as unified teams and transcend barriers imposed by nationality, race and religious belief. Thus, it is important that we understand and appreciate the religious beliefs, convictions and practices of our colleagues.

It is important to accept and appreciate that India is a pluralistic society. Historically, India has suffered due to poor teamwork. Good teamwork requires leveraging the strength of the diversity in our thoughts and beliefs. To realize this strength, we have to demonstrate respect and tolerance towards the opinions and beliefs of others while holding on to the good things in us. In fact, we have tried to inculcate this philosophy in Infosys. The motto for workplace interactions at Infosys has always been, 'You can disagree with me as long as you are not disagreeable.'

For me, secularism is about respecting every religion and appreciating the positive aspects of each faith. 'Religion consists not of mere talk. He who looks on all alike and he who considers all to be equal is the truly religious,' says the Adi Granth. In fact, every religion teaches man to be good and has its positive aspects, be it the quest for knowledge of Hinduism, the tolerance of Sikhism, the sacrifice embodied by Christianity, the brotherhood of Islam, or the compassion of Buddhism.

If we are to teach tolerance to our children, they must know and appreciate the views of other people. This has been very well expressed by Mahatma Gandhi who said, 'I do not want my house to be walled in on all sides and my windows to be stuffed. I want the cultures of all the lands to be blown about my house as freely as possible.' Moreover, a free and frank debate helps in dispelling preconceived notions about different religions. In how many homes in India do parents encourage such a debate? Unless we participate in such an exercise it is difficult to embrace tolerance. Our education system must take a lead in this regard.

Consequently, teaching in schools and colleges must encompass all major religions, with the syllabi updated to include such discussions. This teaching must be started at the elementary school stage rather than being restricted to higher education. However, precautions must be taken in introducing religious education in schools. It is important that parents are reassured that when their children study different religions they are only learning the noble aspects of these religions and are not being forced to follow them. We have to sensitize our teachers as well. Teacher training must include exposure to all major faiths. Unfortunately, in India, despite having institutions of excellence such as the IITs and the IIMs, we have not created a single high-quality institute for training teachers.

Importantly, tolerance can be demonstrated only by those who have well-grounded convictions and confidence based on proven, unbiased data and facts. This is another reason why we have to encourage discussions in our primary schools on the ideas of various religions. If we do, our children will grow up to be the confident, open-minded, tolerant and pluralistic people that this country badly needs to solve the enormous challenges we face. In essence, we need uniters and not dividers.

You are set towards a bright future. There will be many times when your values will be tested. You will come out with flying colours, thanks to your education and your upbringing. When you get on with your life, be proud of your beliefs, and at the same time respect the beliefs, views and opinions of others. Remember that all religions and countries have something good to offer. It is for us to seek it out.

PART II

VALUES

What Can We Learn from the West?

I am going to focus on an important topic on which I have pondered for years—the role of Western values in contemporary Indian society. Coming from a company that is built on strong values, the topic is close to my heart. Moreover, an organization is representative of its society and some of the lessons I have learnt in running my company are applicable in the national context as well.

The word 'community' joins two Latin words: *com* ('together' or 'with') and *unus* ('one'). A community, then, is both one and many. It is a unified multitude and not a mere group of people. The Vedas say, 'Man can live individually but can survive only collectively.' Hence, the challenge is to form a progressive community by balancing the interests of the individual and that of society. To address this challenge, we have to develop a value system where people accept modest sacrifices for the common good.

What is a value system? It is the protocol for behaviour that enhances the trust, confidence and commitment of the members of a community. This goes beyond the domain of legality. It is about decent and desirable behaviour. It translates to putting the community's interests ahead of your own. Thus, our collective survival and progress is predicated on sound values.

There are two pillars of the value system—loyalty to the family and loyalty to the community. One should not be in isolation of the

Lal Bahadur Shastri Memorial Lecture, New Delhi, 2 October 2002

other because successful societies are those which combine both harmoniously. However, Indian society has, for over a thousand years, put loyalty to the family ahead of loyalty to society. On the other hand, the West has a much greater focus on loyalty to society than to the family. By combining the good in both these societies, I believe we can arrive at a desirable solution. It is in this context that I will discuss the role of Western values in contemporary Indian society.

Some of you might think that most of what I am discussing here are actually age-old Indian values and not Western values. However, I live in the present and not in a bygone era and I have seen these values practised primarily in the West and not in India. That is the reason for the title of this piece. I would be happy as long as we practise these values, whether we call them Western or old Indian values.

As an Indian, I am proud to be part of a culture which has deep-rooted family values. We have tremendous loyalty to the family. Parents make enormous sacrifices for their children. They support them until they can stand on their own feet. At the same time, children consider it their duty to take care of aged parents. We believe in the sayings 'matru devo bhava' (mother is God) and 'pitru devo bhava' (father is God). Brothers and sisters are encouraged to make sacrifices for each other and the eldest brother or sister is respected by the other siblings. Marriage is held to be a sacred union. Husband and wife are expected to live together for life. In joint families, the entire family works towards the welfare of the family. There is so much love and affection in our family life.

This is the essence of Indian values and one of our key strengths. Our families act as critical support mechanisms for us. In fact, the credit for the success of Infosys goes as much to the founders as to their families for supporting them through tough times.

Unfortunately, our attitude towards family life is not reflected in our attitude towards the community. From littering the streets to corruption to violating contractual obligations, we are apathetic to the community good. In the West, individuals understand that their loyalty to society is as important as their loyalty to their families.

They care more for society than we do. They generally sacrifice more for society than us. The result is a better quality of public and community life.

I will talk about some of the lessons that we, Indians, can learn from the West and add them to our own wonderful values so that we can make ours a better society.

In the West, there is respect for the community. Parks free of litter, clean streets, public toilets free of graffiti, these are examples of a society that respects the community and its spaces. On the other hand, in India, we keep our houses clean and water our gardens every day but when we go to a public park, we do not think twice before littering the place.

Corruption, as we see it manifested in India, is another example of putting the interest of oneself, and at best that of one's family, above that of society. Society is relatively free of corruption in the West. For instance, it is very difficult to bribe a police officer to avoid a speeding ticket abroad. This is because individuals there realize the cost to society of putting personal interest ahead of societal interest. But in India, corruption, tax evasion, cheating and bribery have eaten into our vitals. Contractors bribe officials and construct low-quality roads and bridges. The result is that society gets a substandard road, thanks to less money spent on the road. The same story is true in purchase of defence equipment, in obtaining licences and in recruiting for government positions, to cite just a few examples. Unfortunately, this behaviour has become so pervasive that it is condoned by almost everyone.

Apathy in addressing community matters has held us back from making progress which is otherwise within our reach. We see serious problems around us but do not try to solve them. We behave as if the problems do not exist or as if they belong to someone else. On the other hand, in the West, people approach societal problems proactively. There are several examples of our apathetic attitude. For instance, all of us are aware of the problem of drought in India. More than forty years ago, Dr K.L. Rao, an irrigation expert, suggested the creation of a water grid connecting all the rivers in north and south India to solve this problem. Unfortunately, nothing has been done about this. The story of power shortage in Bangalore is another instance. In 1983, it was decided that a power plant would be built to meet Bangalore's power requirements. Unfortunately, we have still not started it. The Milan subway in Bombay has been in a deplorable state for the last four decades, and no action has been taken. Considering the frequent travel required in the software industry, five years ago I had suggested the introduction of a 240-page passport. This would eliminate frequent visits to the passport office. In fact, we were ready to pay for it. I am yet to hear from the Ministry of External Affairs on this.

We Indians would do well to remember Thomas Hunter's words that idleness travels very slowly and poverty soon overtakes it. What could be the reason for our apathy? We were ruled by foreigners for over a thousand years. So, we have always believed that public or societal issues belong to some foreign ruler and that we have no responsibility to solve them. We have got used to just executing someone else's orders. 'We are what we repeatedly do,' said Aristotle. Having waited for some foreigner to tell us what to do over the last thousand years, the decision-makers in our society are not used to taking decisions on their own. They look to somebody else to take their decisions for them. Unfortunately, there is nobody to look up to, and this is our tragedy.

Our intellectual arrogance has also not helped our society. I have travelled extensively and, in my experience, have not come across another society where people are as contemptuous of better societies as we are, with as little progress as we have achieved. Let us remember that arrogance breeds hypocrisy. No other society boasts so much about the past as we do, with as little current accomplishment. This is not a new phenomenon but is at least a thousand years old. Al Berouni, the famous Middle Eastern logician and traveller of the tenth century who spent about thirty years in India, referred to this trait among Indians. According to him, during his visit, most Indian pundits considered it below their dignity even to hold arguments with him. In fact, on a few occasions when a pundit was willing to listen to him and found his arguments to be very sound, he invariably asked Berouni which Indian pundit had taught him these smart things!

The most important attribute of a progressive society is respect for others who have accomplished more than they themselves have, and the willingness to learn from them. Contrary to this, our leaders make us believe that other societies do not know anything worth emulating. At the same time, every day in the media you will find numerous claims from our leaders that ours is the greatest nation in the world. These people would do well to remember Thomas Carlyle's words that the greatest of faults is to be conscious of none.

If we have to make progress, we have to change this attitude, listen to people who have performed better than us, learn from them, and perform better than them. We continue to rationalize our failures. No other society has mastered this trait as well as we have. Obviously, this is an excuse to justify our incompetence, corruption and apathy. This attitude has to change. It is best to remember Sir Josiah Stamp who said, 'It is easy to dodge our responsibilities but we cannot dodge the consequences of dodging our responsibilities.'

Another important trait which we Indians should learn from the West is accountability. In the West, irrespective of your position, you are held accountable for what you do. In India, the more 'important' you are, the less answerable you are. For instance, a senior politician once declared that he 'forgot' to file his tax returns for ten consecutive years—and got away with it! There are over 100 loss-making public sector units (Central) in India. I have not seen action taken for bad performance against any minister or bureaucrat or a top manager of these organizations.

Dignity of labour is another integral part of the Western value system. In the West, people are proud of their job, no matter what it is. On the other hand, in India, we tend to look down on people who do jobs that require physical work or involve disciplined execution and accountability. Everybody in India wants to be a thinker and not a doer, for doing anything requires action and that is looked down upon. I have met many engineers, fresh from college, who only want to do cutting-edge work and not work that is of relevance to business and the country. We have not realized that it is as important and dignified to keep an office clean as it is to run the company well. Unless every person in the organization gives his or her best, the organization will not succeed. We need a mindset that reveres everyone who puts in honest work.

Indians become intimate even without being friendly. They ask favours of strangers without any hesitation. The other day, while I was travelling from Bangalore to Mantralaya, I met a fellow traveller on the train. Hardly five minutes into the conversation, he requested me to speak to his MD about removing him from the bottom 10 per cent list in his company for disciplinary action. I was reminded of what Rudyard Kipling once said, 'A westerner can be friendly without being intimate while an easterner tends to be intimate without being friendly.'

Yet another lesson to be learnt from the West is about their professionalism in dealings. The common good being more important than personal equations, people in the West do not let personal relations interfere with their professional dealings. For instance, they do not hesitate to give honest feedback about incompetent work to a colleague even if he/she is a personal friend. In India, we tend to view work interactions from a personal perspective. One important aspect of professionalism is implementing meritocracy. Meritocracy is not letting personal preferences or prejudices affect our evaluation of an individual's performance. As we increasingly start to benchmark ourselves with global standards, we have to embrace meritocracy. We are the most 'thin-skinned' society in the world. We see insults where none are meant. This may well be because we were not free for most of the last thousand years.

Another important aspect of professionalism is punctuality and respecting other people's time. In the West, punctuality is an important criterion in all transactions. But Indian Standard Time somehow seems to be always running late. Deadlines are typically not met. How many public projects are completed on time? The disheartening aspect is that we have accepted this as the norm rather than the exception. In India, coming late to a meeting is a sign of importance. The higher you are in the hierarchy, the later you are supposed to come to any meeting! Of course, if you are a VVIP, then you need not come to the meeting at all, even if you had agreed to attend it!

In the West, right from a very young age, parents teach their children to be independent in thinking. Thus, they grow up to be strong, confident individuals. In our culture, you are not supposed to think differently from your bosses and elders. Teachers in most schools and colleges do not like students who ask questions. I have seen people who are otherwise bright, refusing to show independence in thinking and preferring to be told what to do by their boss. We need to overcome this attitude if we have to succeed globally.

In the West, contractual obligations are seldom dishonoured. Enforceability of legal rights and contracts is the most important factor in enhancing the credibility of a nation that intends to do business globally. In India, we consider our marriage vows sacred. However, we do not extend the same line of thinking to the public domain. For instance, India had an unfavourable contract with Enron. Instead of punishing the people responsible for negotiating this, we reneged on the contract. It would have been all right if we had gone back on the contract because Enron was involved in illegal activities. But we went back on the contract much before we came to know about the illegal activities at Enron. I have given recommendations to several students for the national scholarship for higher studies in US universities. Most of them have not returned to India, even though contractually they were obliged to spend five years in India after completing their degree. In fact, according to a professor at a reputed US university, the maximum default rate for student loans is among Indians; all of these students pass with flying colours and land lucrative jobs, but they refuse to pay back their loans. Their action has made it difficult now for students from India to obtain loans. We have got to change this attitude.

We Indians do not display intellectual honesty either. For example, our political leaders use mobile phones to tell journalists at the other end of the line that they do not believe in technology! If we want our youngsters to progress, such hypocrisy must be stopped. We are well aware of our rights as citizens. Nevertheless, we often fail to acknowledge the duties that come with our rights. Let us remember US President Dwight Eisenhower's words that people who value their privileges above their principles soon lose both.

We have to remember that most of our fundamental social problems grow out of a lack of commitment to the common good. Henry Beecher said, 'Culture is that which helps us to work for the betterment of all.' I do believe that we can make significant progress by retaining our good values and by assimilating these Western values into our own culture.

Most of the lacunae in our behaviour come from greed, lack of self-confidence, lack of confidence in the nation and lack of respect for society. It is best to remember Mahatma Gandhi's words that there is enough in this world for everyone's need but not enough for everyone's greed. Let us work towards a society where we would do unto others what we would have others do unto us. Let us become responsible citizens and make our country a great place to live. 'Responsibility is the price of greatness,' said Winston Churchill. We have to extend our family values beyond the boundaries of our home.

Let us work towards the maximum welfare for the maximum people: *samasta jananam sukhino bhavantu*. Let us conduct ourselves as great citizens rather than just as good people, so that we can serve as good examples for the next generation.

The Role of Discipline in Accelerating National Development

The armed forces of India have stood for the most precious attribute that we in India lack today—discipline. In whatever sphere we operate, we see glaring examples of violation of basic discipline umpteen times a day. It is, therefore, appropriate that I talk about the role of discipline in accelerating national development.

First, let me talk a little bit about where we stand today with regard to national development. Since the reforms in 1991, India's GDP has grown at an average of 6 per cent a year, thus making India one of the fastest growing developing countries in the world. Poverty in the country has fallen from over 34 per cent at the beginning of the 1990s to below 26 per cent in 2003. Based on purchasing power parity, India is the fourth largest economy in the world, after the USA, China and Japan. A Goldman Sachs study suggests that economic growth in India can exceed China's by 2015. It estimates that India can overtake Britain in 2022 and Japan in 2032 to become the third-biggest economy in the world, after China and the USA.

I would define a country as developed if it has provided the ingredients for 'quality of life' for every one of its citizens: education, health care, nutrition, shelter, clean environment, opportunities to get ahead in life, and, most importantly, a confidence that the current generation of citizens is doing everything to make their country a

General K.M. Cariappa Lecture, New Delhi, 3 December 2005

better society for future citizens. Development is a state of mind. It creates a mindset of equity, fairness, hope, confidence, a can-do spirit. A developed nation creates and implements policies that engender an equitable and sustainable future for all its citizens.

Let us look at where we are today from this perspective. The vision outlined by the Indian government in 1956 of a poverty-free India, with full employment in twenty-five years, by 1981, still eludes us. India is ranked 127th among 177 countries on the Human Development Index; 260 million Indians are below the poverty line— a poverty line defined not by global standards but as defined by India itself. Adult illiteracy is at 39 per cent—over 300 million people in India are illiterate, the largest mass of illiterates in the world. Over 25 million children in the country are out of school. Malnourishment strikes half of all Indian children, and India accounts for one out of every five child deaths in the world every year. Unemployment in India is estimated at around 10 per cent. India will add 325 million people to the working population by 2016. This demographic would be a boon if we could provide gainful employment to the youth. Or, it could be a curse if they are idle and despondent. To bring these youths into the mainstream, India has to create 10 million jobs a year in the next five years. However, the economy has been adding only around a million new jobs a year at most.

Clearly, India faces significant immediate challenges in economic development. Can we overcome these challenges? I believe we can, since the odds are in our favour. For the first time since the Industrial Revolution, India has been recognized as a global contributor in a field—that is the hi-tech field. Today, Indians are known as dynamic entrepreneurs and the country is becoming an increasingly hot destination for foreign investment. There is enormous goodwill for the country in international capital markets. Well-known journalists like Thomas Friedman have been gushing about India. We must seize this short window of opportunity to achieve rapid economic growth.

However, every euphoric conversation about India ends in a whimper with questions like: Why is there so much corruption in your country? Why can't you have better infrastructure? Why can't you have a more responsive bureaucracy? Why can't you implement universal primary education and solve the problem of illiteracy? Why do you still have child labour? Somehow, it is difficult to reconcile India, a country with a rich, ancient civilization and a modern hi-tech capability, with such questions.

Why are we unable to make good on the promise that a small section of us—politicians, bureaucrats, corporate leaders, academicians, artists, military people, to name just a few—have kindled? There are several ingredients for national development—natural resources, human resources, leadership and, finally, discipline. There is no doubt at all that we are not short of natural resources. We are in the list of top ten countries in the world in almost every natural resource. In any case, countries with low natural resources like Japan, Switzerland and, most recently, Singapore, have shown that lack of natural resources is not a constraint for development. Surely, India, a nation of a billion people with the second largest pool of scientific talent in the world, should not complain of the lack of human resources. India, indeed, has a reasonable cadre of competent leaders. Our current prime minister, himself an extraordinary person by any global standard, has assembled a fine team around him. We have had globally respected leaders in bureaucracy, the corporate world, the military, academia and arts, just to name a few fields. Yet, somehow, these leaders, with all the capable human resources and valuable natural resources at their disposal, have not been able to resolve the basic problem of poverty in this country.

That brings me to the last ingredient—discipline. The utter lack of discipline exhibited by our people is rendering these other three powerful factors ineffective for fast-paced economic growth. We see umpteen examples of undisciplined behaviour around us every day. What is even sadder is that this behaviour has become the norm even among the powerful and the elite.

Discipline is about complying with the agreed protocols, norms, desirable practices, regulations and the laws of the land designed to improve the performance of individuals and societies. Discipline is the bedrock of individual development, community development, and national development. Most progress results from the combined effort of goal-oriented teams working in harmony. In other words, if each member of the team demonstrates that he or she follows the agreed protocol for behaviour of the team, then every member of the team realizes that no person is deriving undue advantage from their work. In such teams, the ingredients for success—trust, confidence, pride, hope, energy, enthusiasm and aspirations—will be high. Achievements of such teams will be extraordinary. Every goal will be met ahead of time. In fact, two great examples for the role of discipline in achieving wonders are the resurgence of Japan and Germany from near-destruction after World War II. The transformation of countries like Singapore and South Korea from third world countries to first world countries in our own lifetime is yet another example of the power of discipline.

Economic development is about raising the productivity of people. The more developed a nation, the higher is its per-capita GDP. Productivity comes from speed, innovation and excellence in execution. It is about continuously identifying better ideas and executing them better and faster. Such an effort requires discipline. Almost without exception, every developed nation has better discipline than a developing country.

A disciplined, united workforce brings strong productivity growth which in turn drives economic growth in a country. Michael Porter has spoken of 'the competitive advantage of a well-disciplined workforce' that enabled Singapore to drive labour productivity growth by 4.1 per cent annually between 1970 and 1993, compared to a growth of 1.3 per cent in the USA and 1.94 per cent in the UK during the same period. It helped Singapore surpass Britain in per-capita income four decades after it gained independence from that country.

I will now focus on discipline in time management, in thought and in action. Discipline in thought is about objectivity, about using data and facts for arguments, and about supporting an idea purely based on its merits. Discipline in action is about doing the right thing without being influenced by money, power or any form of self-interest.

Development requires leveraging human resources, the most precious of all resources. A developed society places the highest premium on effective time utilization of its people. There is a direct correlation between the rate of growth of a nation, and the effective time utilization by its people. Japan's rapid growth in the 1960s and 1970s was driven by large increases in productivity made by Japan's workforce. During this period, the value added per hour in Japan was $11.30, compared to $3.20 in the USA. The labour productivity in India is, on average, an abysmal 10 per cent of the US levels. The productivity of a Chinese worker is estimated to be 30 per cent to 180 per cent higher than that of an Indian worker, depending on the sector. Agricultural productivity in India is one-third of the European and half of the US levels.

Given that governments in developing countries play a large role in national development, discipline in time management by the government is vital. Unfortunately, this is an area where the government in India is lax. Approvals that take less than three months elsewhere take three to five years in India. Officials rarely come to office on time. Parliament sessions are routinely disrupted and adjourned over trivial disputes. A single hour of parliamentary work costs Indian taxpayers around Rs 17 lakh, and a parliamentary session costs over Rs 1.5 crore a day. Public officials in India view coming late to meetings and events as a sign of importance rather than as a sign of inefficiency. Recently, a chief minister cancelled his meeting with an Australian premier who had come to sign a sister-city agreement with the capital of the state. The Australian premier just could not understand this behaviour.

I believe that lack of discipline in thought, or intellectual dishonesty, is the second most inhibiting factor to fast-paced development. Most leaders in developing countries like India act contrary to what they understand is the right thing to do. Political leaders must practice discipline in making intellectually honest choices for economic growth. Making economic decisions as a result of political compulsions can significantly impact long-term growth in the country. There are many instances when policies propounded by a political party while in power are opposed by the same party when it is in the opposition. The other day, I had a very progressive chief minister visit me along with his finance minister. I asked him why he opposed the introduction of Value Added Tax (VAT). He could not give me a valid reason and left the argument to his finance minister. The finance minister first said VAT was not good for his state. When I explained the benefits of VAT to his state with examples, his answer was that his party did not like it. The same party, incidentally, had introduced VAT when it was in power at the Centre!

Successful economic decisions require discipline of thought or objectivity to focus on outcomes and results in investments. I recall a vivid example of the lack of such focus in a presentation made on rural housing investments to the State Planning Board of Karnataka in the early nineties. My questions on the outcomes and results were dismissed as coming from a troublemaker. On the other hand, in China, the pay and promotion of government officials are strongly linked to growth outcomes in their respective provinces. Officials are held to growth targets of 7 per cent per annum, and have to demonstrate progress every quarter in building infrastructure, lowering crime levels and so on.

In India, discipline in thought resulting in objective decisions has largely been compromised by a focus on caste and religion. This has made our political system a zero-sum game where parties are driven by narrow interests rather than by a focus on public interest. Debates and discussions in legislatures end up being motivated by party considerations rather than by a concern for progress. Such apathy among political leaders towards the interests of the community has significantly affected government policy. Consequently, there is little incentive for legislators to exercise a disciplined effort towards economic development and growth. Instead, they focus on appeasing and addressing the interests of their vote banks. For example, governments in India prefer to dole out subsidies to support groups rather than bring about overall development and growth in the country. Today, subsidies in our country stand at an alarming 14 per cent of India's GDP.

Lack of discipline in honest action leading to corruption is another inhibitor to our progress. Corruption is not just a moral issue but also a powerful inhibitor to economic progress in a poor country like India. Most economists observe that corruption thrives when politicians and bureaucrats espouse the choice of unnecessary and unviable public projects, inflated costs, and selection of incompetent contractors. Those politicians who proclaim their commitment to improve the lot of the poor would do well to remember that it is really the poor that suffer most in a corrupt country. Generally, most mega-projects are intended to bring health care, education and nutrition to the poor. As a result, as Dr Bimal Jalan notes, large-scale corruption results in spurious drugs, ill-built schools, absent and unqualified teachers and low-quality food stuff, and affects primarily the poor. The middle class and the rich do not depend on such services. Hence, corruption worsens inequality in an already unequal society. Also, corruption affects the small enterprises most because they cannot afford the increased costs that come from it. On the other hand, larger enterprises, with some exceptions, take advantage of ineffective, venal systems to create monopolies or increase their market share, thereby improving their profitability. Hence, every politician who espouses the cause of the underdog and the poor must embrace discipline and fight corruption.

Economists have demonstrated that corruption reduces growth rate and productivity, discourages investment, enhances fiscal drain and debilitates the confidence of people in the economy as a whole, thus creating a negative spiral. A well-known development economist has shown that a 50 per cent reduction in corruption in a highly corrupt country has the potential to increase the GDP growth rate by 1.5 per cent. Researchers have also showed that corruption reduces the ratio of investment to national income. If we had controlled our corruption, India would have had a GDP growth rate of 8 per cent during the eighties and the nineties rather than the 6.5 per cent that we achieved.

A disciplined approach to the execution of tasks and projects is essential to bridge a country's goals with actual outcomes from its development efforts. It is discipline in execution which enabled China to build a futuristic city in the Pudong district of Shanghai from what was farmland just a decade ago. Delhi's world-standard metro rail is another good example of discipline in execution. On the other hand, we see hundreds of examples where a project that would be completed in six months elsewhere in the world ends up with a multi-year, below-par quality execution in India.

Corruption and indiscipline have led to a complete demoralization of a rare group of honest, dynamic and daring officials in India. Today, honest, dynamic and visionary bureaucrats and politicians get punished and relegated to inconsequential jobs when they take tough decisions in the interest of the people or implement much-needed reforms in governance. The death of Satyendra Dubey of the National Highway Authority for his attempts to expose corruption in the organization, and the murder of S. Manjunath of IndianOil for trying to address corruption in the company's distribution system indicate how little honesty and discipline are valued in our public institutions. The youth of our country has lost faith in our public institutions and our government. The veteran politician Somnath Chatterjee once remarked how, when he asked a bright young girl what she wanted to pursue as a career, she answered, 'Anything except politics.'

I have demonstrated the need for discipline in three key areas—in human resources and time management, in thought, and in execution. Now let me turn to possible solutions for these problems.

Indiscipline has become all-pervasive. Today, our youth is disillusioned about the conduct of elders—politicians, bureaucrats and corporate leaders. They have been losing faith in our democracy and in our election system. They have been losing confidence in honesty, decency and hard work, and in the values that our forefathers espoused at the time of our independence. Thus, it is the need of the hour to implement tough decisions and policies that will instil a sense of discipline among India's politicians, bureaucrats, corporate leaders and society at large. Quick and drastic action has to be taken.

Role models are important to bring about big and lasting changes. Most societies have progressed because they have had generations of role models who demonstrated good behaviour and discipline. Unfortunately, we do not have many role models in contemporary India. For all our modernity, we live in a feudal society. Here, leaders are larger-than-life personalities. People watch every action of their leaders and imitate them. Thus, leadership by example has a very powerful role in making our society more disciplined. If a couple of generations of leaders follow the finest principles of discipline, then this will become the established norm. Let us remember the words of

Mahatma Gandhi who said, 'Be the change you want to see in others.' We have to encourage role models of good behaviour among ordinary citizens, right from their early years in school. We have to create such role models among bureaucrats as well.

Future Satyendra Dubeys and Manjunaths should not die. To achieve this, a whistleblower council, consisting of eminent men and women, should be instituted to investigate any complaints by whistleblowers. Such councils must have the power to take swift action to punish the guilty and protect whistleblowers. The council should be outside the purview of the state legislatures and be accountable only to the Parliament. No accused politician or official must be allowed to hold office until proven innocent.

Swift and harsh punishment to violators of discipline is the next best option. In fact, this is how developed countries like Singapore have ensured discipline. In a developed country, tax evasion or corruption is usually punished harshly, no matter who the culprit is. On the other hand, in India, the elite rarely get punished, no matter what their crime is. Let a few functions start on time even if the VIP has not come. You will soon see the VIPs arriving on time. Let us apply the laws uniformly across all sections of the citizenry.

Improving transparency towards discipline violations by the powerful and the elite will discourage such violations. This is where the media has an important role to play. We have to strengthen the Right to Information Act by not providing a safety net for the elite and powerful to hide behind.

Another factor contributing to indiscipline in India's political institutions is our deeply-flawed election system dominated by the politics of caste, religion and power. We have to create an election system that does not encourage corruption. We would do well to remember the words of the former prime minister Atal Bihari Vajpayee who said, 'Every MP who is elected to the Lok Sabha begins his career by making a false statement—the statement of account of his election expenses.' Such acts of fraud will have to be swiftly punished.

We must be open to learning from countries which have done better than us. This is the fastest path to progress. Unfortunately, because of our colonial past, we shy away from learning from advanced countries. This complex has to be overcome if we have to make decent progress.

We have to reduce bureaucracy and simplify procedures if we want our people to be more disciplined in following the rule of law. Remember that Tacitus said, as early as AD 55, 'The more corrupt the state, the more numerous the laws.' Today, simple procedures which take a day in developed countries take months in India. Procuring a business licence or permit in India, for example, requires approximately twenty steps which take, on average, 270 days to complete! An Indian manager spends, on average, 15 per cent of his time dealing with bureaucratic procedures. It is estimated that such myriad rules impede Indian GDP growth by 2.3 per cent a year. Government officials in India must be held to strict achievement targets. Pay must be linked to performance, and to the completion of time-bound projects and government programmes.

Today, improved regulations in corporate governance, stringent listing guidelines and increased competition for global capital have created incentives for better behaviour and greater discipline among our corporate leaders. Reforms have introduced competition and a greater focus on discipline across industry sectors in India. For example, McKinsey estimates that the introduction of reforms in India's auto sector drove productivity in the industry up by 400 per cent in five years. However, in many key industry sectors, we still have to move from profit paradigms based on government-directed policy to those based on a disciplined approach to markets. To instil discipline among our corporations, we must promote policies that create an open, competitive market across industries. Let us remember Adam Smith's words, 'The real and effectual discipline exercised over a businessman is that of the market and his customers.'

Today, we face what the sociologist Christopher Kingston calls the 'briber's dilemma' in combating corruption in our economic, political and social systems. Citizens have to mutually agree to 'collective action' to reform these systems. But such collective action is a difficult process in a society with a fractured sense of public good. Transparency International has noted that collective action efforts in India have been sporadic, localized and short-lived, and have not acquired the character of a larger movement. Consequently, Indians have accepted indiscipline as a 'fact of life', and as part of the fabric of all our institutions.

Clearly, India requires a cadre of leaders who will lead by example in their honesty, accountability, discipline and commitment to change. It is such leaders, who, by creating the possibility and hopes for change in our institutions, will foster an enthusiasm for reform. As the French writer Alexis de Toqueville observed, 'The inevitable becomes intolerable, the moment it is no longer perceived to be inevitable.'

Let us remember that our political parties elected the finest people as prime ministers in both the NDA and the UPA governments—Shri Vajpayee and Dr Manmohan Singh. By this act, our political leaders proved that merit is valued, and that this country rewards honest people. To me, this is the most important message that could be sent out to youngsters, and for this, I am grateful to the coalition partners in these two governments. I have also been energized by several ministerial appointments that these two prime ministers made to critical positions in the government.

Is this sufficient? Obviously not. As a country, we must set our sights on the long-term goals for development, and pursue them with discipline and single-mindedness. This can be the beginning of a wonderful journey towards instituting important reforms in our system.

How Can We Stop Corruption in India?

Every day we see news items like 'CID to probe top IPS officer', 'Notice served on Andhra MLA for fraud', 'IT Commissioner lands in CBI net' and 'MP gets jail term for tax evasion'. These are only a few of the umpteen headlines I have taken from English newspapers of India in the recent past. Corruption in India has become so pervasive that it has seeped into the most revered institutions. No wonder then that Justice Barucha was compelled to remark in 2001, 'About 20 per cent of the judges in the courts are corrupt; corruption among public servants has reached monstrous dimensions in India. Its tentacles have started grappling even the institutions created for the protection of the public.' Even a powerful prime minister like Rajiv Gandhi admitted defeat and bemoaned that: 'Out of every 100 crore allocated to an anti-poverty project, I know that only about Rs 15 crore reach the people. The remainder is gobbled up by middlemen, power brokers, contractors, and the corrupt.' President K.R. Narayanan despaired in 2001 that even convicted criminals were getting elected to legislatures. As much as Rs 37,000 crore or about 1.5 to 2 per cent of the GDP surfaced as part of the Voluntary Disclosure scheme in 1997 alone. It should surprise no one that Transparency International has ranked India among the top fifty-five corrupt countries in the world.

Is corruption the sole prerogative of the politicians and the

Published in *Business Today*, 2 January 2006

bureaucracy? I am afraid not. In fact, the biggest corruption cases have been outside the government. The Harshad Mehta scam of around Rs 10,000 crore and Ketan Parikh's scam of Rs 5,000 crore put other scandals to shame. It is estimated that non-banking financial companies have swindled over 30 million small investors. The other day, it was reported that a sizeable number of software professionals in a well-known multinational had fudged their bills. This morning, I received an e-mail from an erstwhile, dismissed colleague of mine arguing why she was not all that wrong in swiping an attendance card on behalf of another colleague! The cricket match-fixing scandal is still fresh in our memories. Several years ago, I sat through a long sermon from an NRI in Chicago on how Indians are corrupt; I had no hesitation in abruptly walking out from that meeting when he whispered a question in my ear regarding whether he could sell his dollars in black. The list goes on. It is very clear that corruption is now an accepted phenomenon in the psyche of Indians from all walks of life.

Corruption is not just a moral issue but also a powerful inhibitor to economic progress in a poor country like India. Most economists observe that corruption thrives when politicians and bureaucrats espouse the choice of unnecessary and unviable public projects, inflated costs, and selection of incompetent contractors. Those politicians who proclaim their commitment to improve the lot of the poor would do well to remember that it is really the poor that suffer most in a corrupt country.

Is there a solution to this seemingly unsolvable problem? Is there any hope at all? Will we ever see a corruption-free society? Can we at least work towards creating a corruption-free society for our children and grandchildren? I am an optimist and I believe that every problem can be solved. It requires leadership that is inspirational, selfless and courageous. We do have a few such people in India among our politicians, bureaucrats and corporate leaders. They have to come together to fight this scourge. Let me detail a few steps needed to fight corruption.

Fairness, transparency and accountability displayed by leaders are what instil confidence in a government, a community and a society. Unfortunately, in our society, the government rarely practises these attributes when it comes to the elite. Only when we practise these attributes in fighting corruption among the elite and the powerful, will we succeed in rooting it out. In the following paragraphs, I will detail how we can enhance fairness, transparency and accountability among the elite.

Let me first talk about fairness in ensuring that everybody in the land, no matter who he/she is, gets punished if guilty of corruption. It is important to create a climate of opinion that honesty matters and that the corrupt will be punished swiftly, and ostracized. This requires the active endorsement of honesty by not just politicians but also bureaucrats and corporate leaders and, in fact, every leader from every sphere. These leaders must be ready to sacrifice their positions rather than work with tainted colleagues. Whenever there is an accusation against a person, he or she must not be allowed to hold any office until proven innocent. Swift and harsh punishment must be meted out to the guilty. To me, this is the most important instrument we have for curbing corruption. Once we practise this for a generation among the elite, the next generation will automatically subscribe to this philosophy. This, in fact, was the norm in the early fifties. But today, we see many accused serving in the Central and state cabinets. There are many reasons for this. One of them is the ambivalent message that our leaders have sent on the issue of corruption. The current thinking among various politicians in the country is that corruption is a global phenomenon. This has created a notion that corruption will be tolerated. Further, we have been very lax in pursuing and punishing cases of corruption involving powerful politicians, bureaucrats and rich people. Such inaction in our system during the current generation has emboldened the rich and the powerful to embrace corruption with impunity.

Let me give you an example of how important it is for our leaders to send the right signal to the community. One evening in the mid-eighties, I met a friend of mine at Ashok Yatri Nivas in Delhi for dinner. He was known to be a good, honest and upright officer in one of the Central ministries. That day, he was very sad and it was clear he was facing a moral dilemma. Over dinner, he confessed that he had taken a bribe for the first time in his life and was very confused. I asked him what the confusion was about, since it was clear that taking a bribe was wrong. His answer stunned me. One part of his mind justified his action since he had seen his minister taking a bribe. The other part was tormenting him that he had done something terribly wrong. I have no doubt at all that he represented a large number of honest officers drawn into the dragnet of corruption, thanks to the examples set by their bosses. A leader must never put himself/herself in a situation which creates such moral dilemmas in the minds of the people.

Let me now give you a positive example of how corruption was fought in Singapore. This incident, according to my Singaporean friends, took place in the middle eighties. Quick investigations on the corruption charges levied against one of the ministers showed that there was a prima facie case against him. The concerned minister met the prime minister to find out whether he would be protected. The prime minister was very clear that the minister's career was indeed over, that he would be punished, and that he would never again be able to contest elections. The minister went home and put a bullet through his head. That sent a strong message to all Singaporean politicians that corruption would never be condoned.

Let me now get to transparency. The best return on investment in reducing corruption would come from setting right our election funding system. We have to adopt the German system of funding so that the politicians have less incentives to be corrupt. The funding available to each candidate must be made known to the public. We must set up a whistleblower policy so that any violation in fund inflow can be quickly investigated and appropriate action taken. The office of the Chief Election Commissioner must be strengthened. I do believe that the action of the Narasimha Rao government in diluting the power of the Chief Election Commissioner was a step backward in fighting election fraud.

Collecting data on the criminal and corruption record of each candidate and publishing them widely is extremely important in curbing corruption. The recent work of Dr Trilochan Sastry and his associates in this area prior to the last Central and state elections is a step that must be encouraged with full support and adopted universally across the entire country. This courageous act of an MIT-educated professor has yielded significant results in exposing the shenanigans of powerful lobbies.

Ideally, corruption in government service delivery is eliminated when the state interface is removed from any activity. For example, when the government removed licensing of computer imports, most of the corruption that was imposed on small entrepreneurs dealing with the Department of Electronics was removed in one shot. However, the government has a tendency to create more and more schemes which require businesses to seek government approval. In fact, it may be best if some of the services were moved from the government to organizations like the Unit Trust of India (UTI). For example, the recent decision of the government to transfer the process of allotting PAN numbers to the UTI has removed delays and chances of corruption.

Corruption opportunities are high when both the decision-making and the implementation of the decision rest with the same individual and when transparency is low. Hence, if we want to reduce corruption, it is best to implement e-governance. E-governance helps us to separate the decision-making around services and their delivery in an inexpensive manner. Second, we have to bring transparency into the decision-making process. If we use a workflow piece for every major decision-making involved in the government, we will know exactly where the delays are taking place. Thus, pressure can be brought on the government to deliver the required service.

Let me now talk about accountability. Swift and harsh punishment meted out to the guilty is what serves as a deterrent in developed countries. In India, Lok Ayuktas have failed since they are under the control of state governments and the quality of staff is rather poor except in rare cases. We have to create a separate judiciary with a jury system to dispose of corruption cases quickly. A jury system will bring better visibility to such acts of crime and, thus, perhaps, serve as a deterrent. Such a step would also reduce the load on the judiciary. We must not allow any further appeal once a jury has decided. Corruption courts must be chaired by eminent men and women who do not owe allegiance to politicians and bureaucrats. They must be outside the purview of state legislatures and be accountable only to the Parliament. The punishment must be very harsh in order to serve as a deterrent. In fact, the delay in punishing the guilty and the light punishment meted out to them are what have emboldened crooks to indulge in corruption time and again.

Unfortunately, the Central Bureau of Investigation (CBI) has not done a good job in tracking down and punishing the guilty. If anything, it has only deterred honest people from acting efficiently. Its success rate has been very low. The model of the CBI has to be changed drastically to reassure honest citizens that they will not be harassed unnecessarily. One way to do this would be to put the CBI under the supervision of a committee of eminent citizens with executive powers to enhance its credibility. This committee must ensure that the CBI has good and reliable data before it can file a case.

Corporate leaders also have to walk the talk when it comes to honesty. Then, they will have the moral authority to take swift action when they see a transgression of values. Infosys demonstrated this a few years ago when a senior member violated the value system of the company. It took us just a few hours of discussion to come to a conclusion and ask the person to resign.

At the end of the day, leadership is what determines the success of a corporation, community or country. If our leaders from all sections of society come together to fight this scourge, I am sure corruption too will disappear like dew on a sunny morning.

In Praise of Secularism

Secularism, according to Mahatma Gandhi, is 'equal respect, not equal disrespect, for all religions'. My own definition is that it is a system where transactions are conducted between individuals as well as between individuals and institutions without being prejudiced by either party's religious beliefs, and where equal opportunity is available for every person irrespective of his or her religious or caste affiliations.

I will dwell on some of the salient reasons on why we need to be secular. It is the duty of the sovereign to protect the life and liberty of its citizens since every citizen has subordinated his/her privileges to the sovereign. This is the fundamental duty of the state and cannot be argued away. Secularism ensures the right of every individual to seek solace and peace of mind, and to derive moral sustenance, hope and courage from any source of his/her choice. As every religion teaches us, God transcends all of us, and He does not have the imperfections of humans. Thus, arguing that my God is better than somebody else's is repudiating the greatness of my own God.

A democracy works best in an environment of pluralism, where there is respect for the opinion of others and where there is freedom to practise one's own beliefs. For democracy to prosper, we have to keep an open mind to learn what is worthwhile from others and create a mindset that highlights the commonness of our beliefs rather

Darbari Seth Memorial Lecture, New Delhi, 21 August 2002

than differences. A democracy based on such principles will be vibrant, and enthuse, energize and encourage citizens to integrate rather than create fissions.

To be part of a civilized society, each generation has to work hard and make personal sacrifices to ensure a better and happier society for the next generation. We cannot encourage any source of hatred if we want a better society for our children and if we want our children to become better citizens than we are. This will not happen unless we show them the path by fostering a social atmosphere devoid of hatred.

India is one family—a community that believes in 'vasudaiva kutumbam' (the world is one family). In such a family, the majority community is like the elder brother and should behave like one. This was well expressed by Mahatma Gandhi when he said, 'Forgiveness is the attribute of the strong.' Even if the younger brother acts childishly once in a while, the elder brother should not punish him. We all know that this is what every mother tells her children every day. Why not practise it?

It will be foolhardy not to enthuse our minority populations towards participating in India's well-being, given the fact that they form about 15 to 20 per cent of our population. There are thousands of examples of high achievers from each minority Indian community. Dr Abdul Kalam, George Fernandes, Ratan Tata, M.A.K. Pataudi and Dilip Kumar are but a few of them. In fact, we are all minorities in India given that our country is so vast and diverse. For example, I am a Kannada-speaking man—a minority; a Brahmin—a minority; educated—a minority; well-to-do—a minority; and English-speaking—a minority. Hence, we should collectively focus on commonality rather than dig deeper into divisive factors based on caste, race, class or economic status.

We are one of the poorest nations in the world. Most of our erstwhile third-world brethren have left us far behind. The need of the day is to create a laser-focus on economic development. For such progress, we need an environment of peace, unity, enthusiasm and hope. Any action that brings divisions across communities will not help this cause.

Once we start the divisive mindset, there will be no end—North Indians will discriminate against South Indians; Tamilians against Telugus; the Right against the Left; the educated against the uneducated; the rich against the poor; the urban against the rural, and so on. This is a one-way street with no U-turn, and it has no upside.

Let us ask ourselves the question—how secular are we? Thanks to visionaries such as Gandhi and Nehru, we have a strong foundation of secularism. Let me give a few examples of secularism practised in this country. One of my favourite examples is that of my son, Rohan, spending most of his time during his formative years at our neighbour Farhu's place, and the affection shown by them to him. President Abdul Kalam who has spearheaded our missile programme is another proof of the secular fabric of India. My confidence in India's secularism was enhanced when I saw, the other day, several Hindu musicians, who were much older, touch the feet of Ustad Zakir Hussain at Bangalore, demonstrating their belief that talent and achievement are more important than age or religion. Omar Abdullah, Dilip Kumar and Shah Rukh Khan, and music maestros like Ustad Ali Akbar Khan and Ustad Amjad Ali Khan are good examples of people from minority religious backgrounds who have gained acceptance nationwide. It is only recently that we have seen a few violations of our commitment to secularism.

We should take what steps we can to further the secular fabric of India. I will talk about a few important ones. Leaders should act as change agents of progress by raising the aspirations and confidence of all the people—Hindus, Muslims, Christians, Sikhs and every other religion flourishing in our country. They have to bring about a big-ticket change in the secular orientation of the masses. They should be 'uniters' and not dividers. This is the responsibility of the leaders of all communities, not just the majority community. The best way to do this is by walking the talk to demonstrate their total commitment to secularism. 'We must become the change we want to see in the world,' said Mahatma Gandhi. Our leaders have to demonstrate their belief in secularism in every action of theirs.

We should stop thinking in terms of leaders of a community and think only of leaders of the nation. We have to create a system where people elect leaders for their performance rather than their caste or religion. We should honour and publicize role models of secularism from every religion.

Successful leadership today is about dealing with the contemporary and the future issues of development. It is not about fighting for relics, icons and ideas of the past. A nation is judged by its contemporary status and not by its past. A confident leader looks at what he/she can do in the future to better the lives of people rather than digging up the past.

We have to work vigorously towards economic progress so that the youth have hope for the future. Let us remember Aristotle's words that hope is a waking dream. Most followers of divisive tendencies are youths who have lost hope in the future. Our leaders have to send the message of hope, tolerance, love and affection to the youth of the country through their actions.

We should not get worked up about some elements of our minority communities occasionally identifying with majority communities of other nations. We must understand that every minority basks in the glory of a majority with whom they share a cultural, religious or national heritage. This is as true of French Jews basking in the Israeli victory of 1973 as with Indians in England cheering the Indian cricket team in 1971. This is also true for a few Muslims in India cheering the victory of the Pakistan cricket team playing against India. This is natural and not something to be unduly worried about.

There are many people who believe that the country must have a uniform civil code. My own view is that this is not necessary as long as the country's economic progress is not hampered. The leaders of a given community whose personal code is not progressive or modern should be the ones to take up this issue if they want their community to prosper. Let the onus be on them.

Today, we need a climate of unity, enthusiasm and hope. This is no time for hatred. Let us unite as Indians and fight communalism. This is the only way to create a great nation that we can be proud of.

Time for Chak De, India!

The other day, my wife and I were perhaps among the very few post-fifty people in the mostly-twentyish crowd watching the film *Chak De! India* in Bangalore. You had to be there to believe the shouts of joy that accompanied every goal India scored in the imaginary tournament in the movie. The mood at the end was as if India had actually won the women's world cup in hockey. I can appreciate this mood since I too felt a similar joy and pride when hundreds of cameras clicked pictures of me holding our national flag, when India and I were declared the winners of the Ernst and Young World Entrepreneur Award from among the forty-odd competing nations at Monaco in 2003. As I exited the theatre after watching *Chak De! India* that day, several youngsters asked me for my reaction to the movie. My answer was simple. I said I wanted to see the movie become a reality not just in hockey but in every sphere.

The recipe for such a success was most beautifully conveyed by Shah Rukh Khan and those wonderful women hockey players in the movie. Let me recount the recipe here.

- We have to identify ourselves as Indians first and rise above our affiliations with our states, religions and castes.
- We must accept meritocracy and enthusiastically play the role we are best suited to.

Published in the *Times of India*, 8 September 2007

- We must embrace discipline while following the steps required for success.
- We have to put the interest of our nation ahead of our personal interests, subordinating our egos and biases.
- Finally, we have to put in tremendous hard work and make short-term sacrifices for long-term glory.

I have immense faith and optimism in the youth of this country. But will we get our leaders to set examples for hundreds of millions of Indian youth? I wish more and more of our leaders see *Chak De! India* and learn these precious lessons.

My Empowered India

Empowerment at Infosys is about providing opportunities to individuals to achieve their aspirations while ensuring that community objectives are met. To me, an empowered India is a country that provides opportunities for every child to achieve its potential through education, health care, nutrition, shelter and employment. At the same time, we must ensure that these children advance the interests of the country.

Given that, today, we rank extremely low on the Human Development Index, such empowerment seems a distant dream. However, I am confident we can achieve this dream if we accomplish a few things. What are they?

To achieve this dream of empowerment, we must take tough, unpopular and unpleasant decisions. The tragedy of India is that we shy away from bold and tough decisions because we do not want to displease anybody. To push these decisions through, we need strong political leaders. We need leaders who have the courage of conviction, the courage to dream big, to take difficult decisions, and to make sacrifices.

Our leaders have to be people who can straddle several worlds—the urban and the rural, the modern and the traditional, the rich and the poor, the educated and the illiterate. They have to appreciate the aspirations of all these worlds. They should not believe that

Published in the *Indian Express*, 5 September 2005

development is a zero-sum game where gains to one world means losses to another. I often hear my politician friends talk about how the IT sector has created a great divide between the haves and the have-nots, and how that should be checked. Sadly, they believe that the solution is to restrict the growth of the IT industry instead of encouraging the creation of a larger number of such jobs.

Our leaders have to believe that the only way of our solving the problem of poverty is to create more jobs and shift a large number of people from agriculture to manufacturing and services. They must be open-minded, and willing to learn from the experiences of leaders across the world. They must aspire to benchmark India globally. They must be action-oriented. We have become too much of a rhetoric-satisfied society. Success is all about execution.

Leaders must espouse meritocracy at least within their own caste or community, since caste has entered the DNA of our society. They must become role models for honesty, modernism, quick action and openness. How do we achieve this? The only solution is for the top leaders of every political party to demonstrate leadership by example. Leaders across political parties must come together and resolve to promote these values for the good of the future generations.

This is tough and seems virtually impossible. However I, for one, believe in the adage 'a plausible impossibility is better than a convincing possibility'. There is no other way to do this. In the beginning, we may see a few good leaders being cast away quickly. But, once we see this behaviour from a generation of successive leaders, it will become the norm. For example, at one time, it appeared impossible to stem the mass defection of Aayarams and Gayarams from one party to another. The practice came to an end because all our political leaders came together and stopped it.

We must have a bureaucracy that is competent, fearless and action-oriented. The major skills for economic development are simulation, planning, estimation, business plan preparation, project management and execution excellence. Our bureaucrats may be very good people but they are very poor in these skills if the performance of government-funded projects is any indication. They have to be trained in these skills.

We must create an environment within the bureaucracy where high-performers have incentives to perform without fear. It is best if we abolish the current tenure system and move to a five-year contract system and a promotion system based on performance. Every good deed from a bureaucrat must be appreciated and rewarded. On the other hand, institutions like the CBI which have been used more as instruments of terror than for catching the guilty must be wound up. Our philosophy of 'suspicion before proof' has to change to 'proof before verdict'. If we persist with these changes for a few years, we will see some wonderful bureaucrats emerge.

Finally, we in the corporate world have to change as well. We have to become men of steel, and stop genuflecting before politicians when they ask us to. I see umpteen cases of such behaviour even today. We have to learn to stop asking for sops from the government. For instance, I cannot understand how CEOs of companies that make thousands of crores of profit ask for tax exemption just because they are in the export business. We must accept that we are in the export business because it is a lucrative business. When we ask for favours from the government in order to create asymmetry in the market vis-à-vis our competitors, we get drawn into the system of corruption.

We must work assiduously towards reducing the social and economic divide in our society, and gain the goodwill of the people. We have to learn to put the interest of the corporation ahead of personal interest.

In the end, we, the fortunate elite of this society, have to take responsibility. No matter what our vocation is—whether we are politicians, bureaucrats, corporate leaders or academicians—we have a responsibility to show courage and lead by example in order to make this a better society for future generations. I know of no simpler mechanism to achieve change than this.

PART III

IMPORTANT NATIONAL ISSUES

Lessons from the Economic Reforms of 1991

History is useful because it is a valuable rear window to look into the past, learn, and move confidently towards the future. The economic reforms of 1991 marked a watershed in the history of post-Independence India. I am a great admirer of the economic reforms that P.V. Narasimha Rao, the then prime minister, Dr Manmohan Singh, the then finance minister, P. Chidambaram and Montek Singh Ahluwalia ushered in in 1991. In less than a week, India was transformed from a command and control economy to an almost free economy. My company Infosys has been hailed by many as a sterling example of the benefits of these economic reforms.

There have been several articles written and speeches given by Indian politicians, bureaucrats, journalists and academicians about the 1991 economic reforms. However, these articles and speeches suffer from a lacuna. That is, nobody who was deeply affected by the reforms has spoken about them. I personally experienced and suffered from the highly-controlled economy that stifled India's growth till 1991. I will focus here on how India's reforms helped businesses, fostered entrepreneurship and resulted in job creation. I will also talk about a few generic lessons to be learnt from these reforms, and how they can be used to bring about inclusive growth and benefits to the larger masses of India.

First, the liberalization programme of 1991 was a defining moment

Malcolm Wiener Lecture, Harvard University, 13 February 2008 in independent India's history. In fact, for most Indians, the reforms of 1991 rank with the fall of the Berlin Wall and the end of apartheid in South Africa as one of the most improbable but impactful events of our lives. While the year 1947 brought India political freedom, the year 1991 sowed the seeds of economic freedom. I am glad to have been part of that era. I was happy to see India wake up for the first time in my life, show confidence and swing into action, thanks to these reforms. Second, the timely and bold leadership demonstrated by Narasimha Rao, the then prime minister, should serve as a good example for our current and future leadership to take quick and firm decisions on several other important reforms that have been pending for a long time. Third, we have a plethora of reform issues lying unresolved at the state level. Unless reforms are successful at the state level, we cannot achieve an inclusive growth. Fourth, there are several developing countries which are still bogged down by doubt and debate about economic reforms. The example of India's economic reforms should help them resolve some of their dilemmas. Finally, and most importantly, I am convinced that the best way to ensure lasting peace in the world is to reduce the gap between the haves and the have-nots. Wherever I have gone—USA, Russia, Vietnam, Peru or South Africa—the dreams of young men and women are the same: good jobs, happy and joyful days, and a better future for themselves and for their children. It is only when faith and hope are lost that people resort to violence. Hence, our challenge is to create a world where hope, faith and confidence in the future are strong. To do so, poor nations have to accept that responsive governments, entrepreneurship and global trade are the best instruments for creating jobs and improving living standards. An environment conducive to entrepreneurship is possible only if governments become catalysts to businesses, and allow businesses full freedom to become market-oriented while focussing on efficient ways to deliver basic services like education, health care, nutrition and shelter to the poor. This is what liberalization and economic reforms are all about.

While Prime Minister Manmohan Singh often invokes Victor Hugo's famous words that no force can stop an idea whose time has come, he has also said it is so much better to make, today, the time for all great ideas rather than waiting for them. After all, let us remember Francis Bacon's words that 'a wise man will make more opportunities than he finds'! The time for India to become a much stronger economy has come. Our economy is growing at 9.2 to 9.3 per cent a year. Our exports are growing at 20 to 25 per cent a year. Our hard currency reserves are at an all-time high. Our stock markets are on fire. Our FDI in 2007 was estimated to be $25 billion, five times what it was three years ago. We are adding 9 million new phone lines a month. There is a sense of new-found confidence everywhere. The number of billionaires in India is the highest in Asia. Every week, in my city, Bangalore, one finds fifty to a hundred new, young hi-tech entrepreneurs raring to go. There is no better time to forge ahead, improve our prosperity, make it inclusive, and make real the dream of the father of our nation to wipe the tears from the eyes of the poorest of the poor.

Most people in India believe that slow progress is inevitable in a democracy and that we have to accept such a slow progress as the price for our democracy. As Bimal Jalan, former Governor of the Reserve Bank of India, has noted in his book *India's Politics*, the form of government in a country is only one of the factors that influence economic progress. After all, most developed economies are democracies. This belief that progress in a democracy will be slow is simply an excuse to justify inertia, apathy, incompetence, indifference and, in some cases, vested interests. I believe in Jawaharlal Nehru's words, 'Life is like a game of cards. The hand that is dealt you is determinism. The way you play it is free will.' It is this free will that democracy has bestowed on us to achieve extraordinary things. After all, which sane political party opposes job creation, enhanced tax collections, and use of such funds to improve education, health care, nutrition and shelter for the vast majority of poor people in the country? The reforms of 1991 disproved the long-held belief that any major policy change in democratic India requires long deliberations and cannot be implemented in a hurry. They also disproved various other myths that most bureaucrats had held for a long time. For example, most of my civil servant friends believed that the classical theories of economics did not hold good for a large developing country like India. They believed that slackening the control on foreign exchange outflows would lead to capital flight. They also believed that economic policy solutions that worked well for smaller East Asian countries would not work in India. The economic progress made by India since 1991 proved them wrong.

Here, I will describe just three major policy changes brought in by the 1991 economic reforms. These changes made, perhaps, the biggest impact on businesses in India. The examples I will use to describe the hurdles these policy changes removed vividly describe our former command and control economy at its most stifling, outdated, negative, fatalistic and suspicious mindset. These policy changes were not easy to push through. They were anathema to most Indian politicians who were brought up with the belief that poverty was virtue, businessmen were crooks, making profit was a sin, and government was the solution to every problem. These policy changes also took away most of the power and opportunity for rent-seeking from the bureaucracy. These examples describe to you how business-unfriendly India was prior to the 1991 reforms. Forget about foreigners, even young Indians, in their twenties, do not believe me when I tell them the horror stories of bureaucratic red tape we went through till 1991.

Let me give you some background about the work we do at Infosys to help you appreciate my instances better. We founded Infosys in 1981 to provide bespoke software development capability to customers in developed nations. To do so, our business required import of state-of-the-art hardware and software platforms from abroad, easy and hassle-free travel abroad to our customer sites by our staff, opening of overseas sales offices, and availability of a data communications infrastructure. Even though this industry was likely to provide India's large pool of technical talent good jobs with high disposable incomes, convincing the government that this was a godsend was easier said than done. Prior to 1991, one needed a licence to import computers. The process of obtaining a licence to import a computer was lengthy, arbitrary, expensive and sometimes corruption-prone. Generally, it took about three years and fifty visits to Delhi to obtain one. Assuming that the cost of each trip was about $1,000, it meant that the importer had already paid a duty of at least 50 per cent of the price of an imported computer (roughly $100,000) even before the computer had been ordered! This was not all. Since it took three years to obtain the licence, at least five to ten new models of every component of the system we were to import were likely to be released in the US market during the same period. But, changing the model number of even one component in the licence usually took at least nine to ten months! Thus, thanks to our bureaucracy, computer users in India remained at least two generations behind in any technology.

The second major stifling factor was the lack of current account convertibility, that is, the non-availability of hard currency to Indian firms for its staff to travel abroad, for opening offices overseas, and for hiring consultants from abroad in areas like quality and branding. Let me illustrate how bad the situation was. If I wished to travel abroad even for a day, I had to make an application to the Reserve Bank of India (RBI) and wait for ten to twelve days. It was not always certain that I would get a positive response. I also had to submit a report on my trip abroad after I came back. A friend of mine was to travel to meet a few business prospects—a couple of them in Paris and one in Frankfurt. He obtained approval from the RBI for two days' stay in Paris and a one-day stay in Frankfurt. When he reached Paris, his second prospect asked him to meet him in Frankfurt since he had to leave for an urgent meeting there. The result was that my friend spent two days in Frankfurt and one day in Paris while the approval was for the reverse. When he returned to India and submitted his tour report to the RBI, he was issued a 'show cause' notice as to why he should not be prosecuted for violating foreign exchange regulations! It is unimaginable that we have moved from that era to the present one, when it has become extremely easy for Indian companies to do business overseas. We have the former RBI Governors Dr Bimal Jalan and Dr Y. Venugopal Reddy, two of our best free market champions, to thank for this.

The third major stifling factor was the lack of market-based pricing for Initial Public Offers (IPOs) by companies. A major incentive for entrepreneurs the world over is to take their company public to create liquidity for themselves and for venture capitalists. In fact, one of the major reasons for the success of the USA in the hi-tech area has been the IPO mechanism. In India, prior to 1991, there was a government officer in Delhi called the Controller of Capital Issues (CCI) who decided on the IPO price for Indian companies going public. This officer had very little idea of capital markets since he/she sat in Delhi while the capital markets were in Bombay, and he/she rarely travelled to Bombay or bothered to understand the dynamics of these markets. He/she would look at just the past performance of a company and allow a very low premium, if any, for the IPO pricing. Such a policy of government-determined IPO pricing was a disincentive for entrepreneurs who had to give up a large part of their equity to raise small sums in the capital market. After all, capital markets are all about future potential rather than just about past performance.

All of this changed in a jiffy when the four reformers led by Narasimha Rao waved their magic wands. Just in a matter of weeks we were in a new orbit unconstrained by these three major debilitating forces. The government removed licensing in most sectors of the economy. Since 1991, I have not gone to Delhi to obtain a single licence from the government. The reforms provided full current account convertibility. In fact, today there is absolutely no restriction on any current account transaction. Even in the area of capital account convertibility, we hardly have any restrictions for corporations. Indian companies have been acquiring companies abroad like never before in the economic history of India.

The government, realizing the futility of mandating IPO prices, abolished the office of the CCI and allowed Indian companies to set the IPO price in consultation with their investment bankers. This has resulted in market-oriented pricing policies and has generated a lot of enthusiasm among entrepreneurs.

These three major reforms and a host of others that followed have influenced Indian businesses in many ways. First, the reforms enabled our business leaders to spend their time in focussing on the market, innovation and employees rather than spending their time lobbying in the corridors of Delhi. Second, they removed uncertainty in business decisions forced by bureaucratic delays and whims. In other words, post reforms, businesses are much more in control of their own destiny than before. There is no climate of helplessness in the board rooms. The market is the primary determinant of the success of companies. Third, the reforms reduced the tyranny of rent-seeking and corruption to a large extent. Fourth, these policy changes made it easy for the entry of world-class multi-national companies (MNCs) into India. Since Infosys focussed those days on global markets, the entry of MNCs did not have any impact on our customer acquisitions. However, the competition for employees heated up. So, we had to improve our focus on attracting and retaining top quality talent. Frankly, this focus on employee attraction and retention is a seminal gift of the reforms to my company.

Let me give some data to demonstrate the benefits of the economic reforms on Infosys business. Between 1982 and 1992, Infosys revenues grew from a paltry $130,000 to $1.5 million, a factor of just 12 on a small base over a period of ten years. However, after the reforms, our revenues have grown from $1.5 million in 1992 to a likely figure of $4.1 billion in 2008, which is a factor of 2,700 over a period of sixteen years! Today, we are listed on NASDAQ. We operate in seventy countries and have over 88,000 employees comprising over ninety nationalities. We have created over 2,000 dollar millionaires and about 20,000 rupee millionaires through our employee stock option plans. We have beaten every MNC in India to be voted the best employer, the best managed company, the best in corporate governance, and the best in investor focus. We pride ourselves as a shining example of all the good things that came out of the economic reforms of 1991.

The IT industry grew from a mere $100 million of revenue in 1992 to more than $40 billion last year. The country had foreign exchange reserves barely sufficient for fifteen days of essential imports prior to the reforms. The easing of controls has swelled that kitty to more than $280 billion today. Contrary to the popular belief that any slackening of foreign exchange controls would deplete our reserves due to illegal capital flight, today we see more and more Indian companies bringing in larger and larger hard currency funds into the country. No wonder the rupee has appreciated heavily. Thanks to global investor interest in Indian companies, our businesses have raised their level of corporate governance. Thanks to the competition introduced by the entry of MNCs, Indian businesses have stepped up to the plate and demonstrated that they are second to none in customer, employee and investor focus.

What are the lessons from the reforms for us, the Indian businesses? There are many. The reforms showed that it is possible to run businesses legally and ethically in India; to compete with the best MNCs and succeed; to benchmark with the best global practices, improve on them and create next practices; and that following the best practices of corporate governance will attract the best global investors and enhance market capitalization.

What are the major lessons to be learnt from the 1991 reforms by our politicians and bureaucrats? First, the reforms showed that courage is the first attribute of a great leader. They showed that leaders who believe in the adage 'a plausible impossibility is better than a convincing possibility', can indeed achieve extraordinary results. Second, they demonstrated that even in an argumentative democracy like India, quick and decisive leadership is likely to get accepted better than a slow and hesitant one. Third, the reforms proved that most of our fears and assumptions that led to the command and control economy were wrong. Finally, they reaffirmed that sound economic policies practised by developed nations do work even for a developing country like India.

While the initial set of reforms has helped the country improve the lives of middle class and upper middle class Indians, they have not impacted the poor significantly. We have the largest mass of illiterates in the world. Our agricultural growth rate has come down from 3.2 per cent prior to 1991 to about 1.9 per cent today. Thus, our villagers have hardly seen any benefit from the reforms and globalization. The disparity is increasing all the time. While the number of billionaires in India is growing rapidly, the poor are getting poorer. The buzzword today is inclusive growth. Inclusive growth is about extending the benefits of reforms to the vast majority of Indians who are poor. Prime Minister Manmohan Singh is a firm believer in such growth.

I believe the lessons from the 1991 reforms can be used to bring inclusive growth in our society if we understand what the poor want. It is instructive to ponder on the difference in lifestyles of the middle class and the elite in India on the one hand, and the poor in India on the other. The starkest difference is that the middle class and the elite have very little interface with the government. They mostly use services and facilities—schools, colleges, hospitals, banks and shops—in the private sector while the poor depend on the government for these services.

Since the rich and the powerful citizens in India do not use any of the government services except where there is no alternative, these services have remained inefficient and unaccountable. Inclusive growth requires that we do one of two things—keep government services away even from the poor, or bring efficiency, transparency and accountability to government services in India. I believe that neither is an easy task, given the various socio-political decisions we have taken over the last sixty years. Hence, we have to devise a hybrid mechanism of privatizing some of these services while improving efficiency, transparency and accountability in those services which cannot be privatized. Nothing short of this will achieve much inclusivity.

The second principle we have to keep in mind in order to achieve inclusivity is to target any subsidies directly to the poor, eliminating the middlemen. Generally, across-the-board subsidies tend to favour primarily the rich who create powerful lobbies to keep them going. For example, tax exemptions on agricultural income and fertilizer subsidies have primarily benefited large farmers who do not need such subsidies.

I am an admirer of Milton Friedman's voucher system. However, if such a system is difficult to implement in India, we may want to provide a direct cash subsidy through bank accounts to the women of families below a certain annual income. Such a directed subsidy will help families to spend the money on what they need the most. Parallelly, we must create a paradigm where the private sector can provide basic services to the poor profitably. This way, the poor will get the much-needed subsidy, they can decide how best to spend it, and they will get the best value for money.

The next set of reforms will have to focus on introducing a flexible labour policy, enhancing agricultural productivity, improving physical infrastructure, and upgrading the quality of basic and higher education, health care, nutrition and housing. Much has been written about these. I will not go into the details here.

The progress of any society is as good as the mindset of its people. Being a strong believer in Max Weber, I am convinced that the important prerequisites for economic growth are a good work ethic, honesty, humility, objectivity, high-quality leadership and societal commitment to people. I know this may be difficult, but I am a believer in John F. Kennedy's words, 'Our problems are man-made. Therefore, they may be solved by man. No problem of human destiny is beyond human beings.'

Population and Economic Development in India

India's low-cost, skilled labour force has been an important driver in its economic growth. India today has the second largest population in the world. In 1960, India's population was 548 million, with an annual growth rate of 2.2 per cent. Population growth rate peaked at 2.22 per cent in the 1970s. The growth rate began to fall in the 1980s with the introduction of family planning policies and slowed to 1.8 per cent in the 1990s. It has slowed down further to 1.5 per cent since 2000.

However, India's population is still growing at twice the rate of China's annually. India contributes to 21 per cent of the world's annual population growth, and its population stands at over one billion today.

Jawaharlal Nehru believed that India's large population was an important asset, and 'the key to the economic future of our nation'. Development models link human assets to economic growth. The macroeconomic development model pioneered by A.J. Coale and E.M. Hoover indicates that the rate of economic growth in a developing country is primarily determined by two factors: the growth in the labour force and the amount of capital available per labourer.

Today, 36 per cent of India's one billion people are below the age of fifteen. This means that, by 2020, 325 million people in India will reach working age. India will have the largest working population in

A.D. Shroff Memorial Lecture, Mumbai, 8 April 2004

the world. This expected rise in India's working population comes at a time when the developed world is faced with a large ageing population. Europe's ratio of working population to retirees, for example, is set to fall to just 0.9, compared to a ratio of 6.9 in India. It is estimated that, by 2020, the USA will be short of 17 million people of working age, China by 10 million, Japan by 9 million and Russia by 6 million. In this scenario, India will have a surplus of 47 million working-age people.

Such a demographic profile for India, at a time during which the high growth rate of the working population can be a fuel for faster economic growth, is a 'demographic window of opportunity' for the country. It is estimated that one-third of the economic growth in East Asia between the 1950s and 1990s came from a similar demographic window in these countries. A report by Goldman Sachs predicts that, of the four big emerging economies—Brazil, Russia, India and China—India alone, equipped with the advantage of a large, vibrant workforce, will grow at more than 5 per cent a year until 2050.

However, economic growth and prosperity require not just growing populations, but also what economists call 'good human capital': a population equipped with the skills and resources to participate in the economy. Good human capital contributes to high levels of labour productivity and entrepreneurship which, in turn, drive growth in the economy. The key to creating good human capital is human development supported by the right policy environment. Critical policy areas include education, public health, family planning and economic policies such as labour market flexibility. However, key indicators show how India has fallen behind in its efforts in human development. We rank 127th among 177 countries on the Human Development Index. Adult illiteracy in India is 39 per cent compared to 9 per cent in China. In absolute terms, over 300 million people in India are illiterate. India, according to Amartya Sen, 'is in danger of becoming one of the most illiterate parts of the world'. Twenty-five million children in India are out of school, accounting for a quarter of the world's 104 million out of school children. Malnourishment strikes 64 per cent of children in India.

China pulls 1 per cent of its population out of agriculture every year and puts them into construction and manufacturing. Such large-scale job creation has failed to happen in India due to labour market inflexibility and curbs on investment. The poverty rate in India stands at 26 per cent, compared to 11 per cent in China. The absolute number of poor in India is still over 260 million people—193 million in rural and 67 million in urban India. With limited progress in human development, India's large population can become a liability rather than an advantage. India's present rate of population growth translates into 16 million more Indians every year, rising to almost 18 million a year by 2016. India's population is expected to overtake China's by 2035 when both countries will have populations of around 1.5 billion.

A failure to stabilize India's population will have significant implications for the future of India's economy. A comparison of India and China's GDP growth versus purchasing power indicates the impact of population growth on per-capita income. Measured by purchasing power per person, China and India were at the same level at the end of the 1980s. In the 1990s, both economies saw spurts of growth. As the *Economist* notes, India's real GDP grew by 5.8 per cent a year from 1991 to 2003. China's GDP grew 9.7 per cent between 1991 and 2003. However, the GDP per person diverged faster than economic growth. China's GDP per person grew by an average of 8.5 per cent between 1990 and 2003, while India's grew by 4 per cent. As a result, adjusted for GDP per person, China has grown to be 70 per cent richer than India between 1990 and 2003. China's national income per head in 2003 was $1,100, compared to $530 in India, a considerable gap achieved in one decade. At the current rate of population growth, India must average an annual 9 per cent GDP growth rate till 2016 to achieve Indonesia's 2004 per capita income level of $980.

Today, high population densities have also led to overloaded systems and infrastructure in urban areas. More than 25 per cent of India's urban population today lives without sanitation, and 24 per cent lives without access to tap water. The population of India's major cities is expected to increase by an average of 25 per cent by 2015. Mumbai, one of the world's most densely populated cities, is expected to grow from 18 million people today to 26 million by 2015.

India's population will be 72 per cent urbanized by 2030. It is estimated that India will require the construction of 3.6 million housing units in urban areas every year to address housing needs due to the additional population. The annual growth in India's population alone is estimated to require the opening of 66,000 new primary schools and 3,000 new health centres every year. To provide for the food requirements of the additional population, India will have to consistently increase food production by 3 per cent every year.

Population growth today will have a key impact on India's future demographics. In 2003, less than 8 per cent of India's population was over the age of sixty. However, by 2050, over 26 per cent of the population will reach retirement age. India's ratio of working population to dependents will fall to 0.9. Consequently, the burden of the ageing population on India's economy will increase significantly.

The impact of the population increase on India's resources has been severe. According to the World Bank, resource degradation costs the Indian economy 4.5 per cent of GDP annually. Common property such as grasslands has declined by 25 per cent, through encroachments and over-cultivation. The water table in India is falling by an average of 6 feet every year. It is predicted that India will cross into water scarcity by 2025. An estimated half of India's 329 million hectares of soil is degraded. India will lose all its productive land to desertification within 200 years if the present annual loss of land continues. The implications of future consumption on India's resources are significant. Today, the per-capita consumption level in India is one-twentieth that of Europe. However, with economic growth, approximately 30 million people are entering India's middle class every year. India's household consumption spend is expected to double to $510 billion by 2008.

India is undergoing what the economist Stuart Hart calls the transition from a 'survival economy' to a 'consumption economy'. The demand of India's population on its resources will, as a result, increase significantly. China's consumption demands, for example, have soared with economic growth. China saw 11,000 new cars enter its roads every day in 2003. In 2004, China accounted for 20 per cent of the world consumption of aluminum, 35 per cent of the global demand for steel and coal, and 45 per cent of the worldwide purchases of cement. In fact, Chinese demand was primarily responsible for the 50 per cent rise in the *Economist*'s commodity-price index over the past three years.

The future energy demands of Indian and Chinese populations will put significant constraints on world resources. China's present demand of 1 million barrels of oil a day is estimated to have been a key factor contributing to the rise in oil prices in 2004. Goldman Sachs estimates that India's contribution to global oil demand growth will overtake China's within fifteen years. The related environmental stress will be unprecedented. According to the International Energy Agency, China and India will produce about one-fourth of the world's total emissions of carbon dioxide by 2010.

The environmental impact of economic growth in China is already significant. The World Bank estimates that environmental and resource degradation costs China 12 per cent of its GDP annually. Seventy million 'environmental refugees'—people driven from rural land due to soil degradation and drought—are floating labour in China's cities. In 2003, water scarcity cost China $28 billion in lost industrial output; acid rain cost the economy $13 billion; and desertification cost China $6 billion.

The rapid growth in emerging economies cannot be sustained in the face of mounting environmental deterioration and resource depletion. The consumption model of the European and US economies would have an irreversible impact on resources and environment in India and China. Consequently, the challenge for India today is double-pronged: to stabilize population growth; and combine economic growth with a 'sustainable economy'.

To stabilize India's population at 1.7 billion people by 2045, India has to achieve the replacement level of growth—a fertility rate of 2.1 versus the present 3.3—by 2010. I believe this can be done. 'The plague of overpopulation is soluble by means we have discovered, and with resources we already possess,' said Martin Luther King Jr. Efforts to bring down India's population growth rate must implement a combination of short and long-term goals—drastically reducing the birth rate in the short term, and implementing long-term policies to bring down fertility rates. India's family planning policy has only been partially successful so far in controlling birth rates.

There has been a failure at the state level in implementing family planning programmes. The unmet need of contraception, for example, is nearly 20 per cent in the state of Uttar Pradesh. There has been little analysis of the effectiveness of India's family planning programmes. Haryana, for instance, has implemented incentive-based population programmes but the state continues to have fertility rates higher than the national average. Local government bodies and NGOs must be consulted for better implementation and to create more effective programmes. Localization of family planning programmes will also help address specific needs of the local population, and create greater accountability.

The government must focus on creating a network of information management programmes to educate families on various contraceptive methods. Involvement and education of women in family planning is critical to increasing the use of contraception in families. Short-term, state-level performance targets are required to assess real progress. Family planning policy must also focus on long-term goals. In the long term, a focus on human development—improvement in literacy rates, and women's and children's health—would bring down fertility rates and population growth. It is India's poorest and most illiterate states—the states of Uttar Pradesh, Bihar, Rajasthan and Madhya Pradesh—that have the highest average fertility rate of 4.3.

A decrease in population growth, however, has happened in the southern states of Kerala, Tamil Nadu, Karnataka and Andhra Pradesh. Today, these states have fertility rates equal to or slightly higher than the replacement level of 2.1. State governments here focussed on human development, opened up local economies, and improved social services faster than in the north.

Rising female literacy in these states contributed to the success of family planning. The economist Ben Wattenberg has shown that, worldwide, the correlation between falling female illiteracy and falling female fertility is nearly exact. A focus on women's and children's health also contribute to population control. A decline in maternal and infant mortality rates lead to a fall in fertility rates. Today, in

Kerala, the maternal mortality rate is 30 per 1000, while in Madhya Pradesh it is 200. Clearly, human development goes hand in hand with lower population growth. To maximize human capital, we must empower people by creating access to key resources. 'The strongest principle of growth lies in human choice,' said George Eliot. People should be given the skills and resources to make employment choices. This means creating access to health and education resources, improved access to infrastructure, and job creation.

India cannot afford to ignore the implications of unsustainable economic and population growth. Today, we need strong, effective leaders who will create urgency for change. The first step towards change is awareness. Leaders must encourage public dialogue on the implications of India's population growth; the successes and failures of our population policy; and the need for sustainability. Leaders and policymakers must encourage research towards solutions to stabilize the population, and achieve sustainability. India's focus on sustainability must change from piecemeal projects aimed at controlling pollution, to long-term solutions with a broad focus on pollution prevention, conservation of resources and innovation for clean technology.

The population experts Paul Elhrich and Barry Commoner observed that the environmental and resource burden of a population is a function of three factors: consumption, population size and technology. Consequently, when population size and consumption levels are high, the key to reducing the resource burden and creating sustainability is innovations in technology. India has the opportunity to leapfrog old, inefficient technology and focus on new, sustainable solutions—more efficient transportation and sanitation systems, clean-fuel vehicles, better product and process technologies in manufacturing, and bioengineering of crops rather than the use of fertilizers.

The government must focus on conservation-friendly policies. For example, subsidies on conventional fuel make it difficult for renewable energy sources to compete and should be removed at least for rich and middle-class people. Flat-rate electricity pricing which results in over-pumping of groundwater should also be removed. The government can play a key role as a regulator in making Indian industry environmentally responsible.

As a country, we have significant social and economic challenges ahead of us. We face unique problems, which will require new, innovative solutions. We are a nation of great talent. I believe that we have the capability to face these challenges and the opportunity to transform our nation in the process.

A Framework for Urban Planning in Modern India

In 1971, Parameshwar Narain Haksar, one of the key policy planners of post-Independence India, planned Indira Gandhi's political campaign using the powerful slogan of *'Garibi Hatao'*, a direct call to war against poverty on behalf of 300 million poor Indians. The only way we can truly implement *'Garibi Hatao'* is by improving our urban areas, since cities have to bear the main brunt of any economic growth.

The vision outlined by the Indian government in 1956 of a poverty-free India, with full employment in twenty-five years (by 1981), still eludes us. Today, over 260 million people in India remain below the poverty line. More than 390 million people in the country are illiterate—the largest pool of illiterates in the world. Unemployment in India is estimated to be over 10 per cent. Experts opine that India has to create jobs at the rate of 10 million a year over the next five years to merely sustain the present unemployment rate. Yet, we have been creating less than 1 million new jobs a year. Our economic growth has not been dynamic enough to ensure sustained job creation and to facilitate broad-based, equitable development. I believe the key to unlocking India's vast economic potential, and creating rapid, sustainable economic growth lies in our cities. That is

P.N. Haksar Memorial Lecture, New Delhi, 18 February 2006

why urbanization and urban planning for modern India are of paramount importance.

Today, we are witnessing rapid urbanization in both developing and developed economies around the world. Globally, each year, around 70 million people are migrating to cities. The rate of urbanization is especially significant in fast-growing, developing economies like India and China. It is interesting to note that, in 1950, the United States had 50 per cent more urban dwellers than either China or India. By 2000, China had twice as many urban residents as the USA while India had 25 per cent more.

Since the reforms of 1991, the Indian economy has grown at an annual rate of 6 per cent, and is undergoing a rapid transition from a rural to a semi-urban economy. Over 30 per cent of India's current population is urban. By 2001, over 300 million Indians lived in nearly 3,700 towns and cities across the country. The number of Indian cities with a population over 1 million increased from twenty-three to thirty-five between 1991 and 2003. Indian towns and cities have registered an annual population growth rate averaging 4–5 per cent, driven by a combination of rural–urban migration and internal growth. Thus, the urban population in India doubles every fourteen to eighteen years.

The economists Stanley D. Brunn and Jack Francis Williams explain urbanization as 'a natural consequence of economic growth'. A country's cities, they note, are at the frontline of its economic development. Urban centres provide increasing returns on land, labour and capital through agglomeration and economies of scale. Cities thus become poles of attraction for capital and labour as businesses and individuals locate in urban areas to take advantage of higher efficiency and productivity. Thus, savings, investment and wealth become concentrated in cities. Clearly, cities are the 'theatres of accumulation' for the country's economic activities. The UN estimates that the per capita output of cities in an economy is, on average, 10 per cent higher than the overall per capita GNP. In countries like India, it is even higher.

The contribution of India's urban economy to overall economic growth is significant. The urban contribution to GDP has increased from 30 per cent in 1960 to 70 per cent in 2003. As the economist David McKee points out, urban areas clearly house the strengths of national economies, and consequently, 'the efficiency of national economies is impeded by anything that impairs the efficiency of the city'. An effective urban planning framework is essential, therefore, to ensure sustained economic growth, and to manage the pace of urbanization through the effective supply of land, shelter and employment opportunities.

Unfortunately, urban planning in India has not been given sufficient priority. The expansion of India's cities and towns has been unplanned and haphazard. Consequently, urban India faces critical inadequacies in coping with the rising demand for resources and services. The demand for clean water in cities exceeds the supply by an average of 30 per cent. Water degradation has led to increased health costs. Urban waste management systems are overstressed, with significant implications for public health. Over 40 per cent of the solid waste generated daily in urban areas goes uncollected. The housing shortage in India's towns and cities is estimated to be around 22 million. About 22 per cent of India's urban population lives in slums. Around 25 per cent of the urban population is below the poverty line. Traffic congestion in Indian cities has assumed critical dimensions. While India's vehicle population increased a hundred-fold from 0.3 million in 1960 to 30 million in 2004, the road network increased by just eight times in the same period—from 0.4 million km to 3.3 million km.

The problem has become worse since attempts by governments to divert industry, job creation and investment into rural regions have failed in the absence of even minimal infrastructure in rural areas. For instance, 40 per cent of rural areas lack all-weather access by road. About 28 per cent of India's villages lack a primary school. A whopping 54 per cent of villages are over 5 km away from the nearest health centre. Consequently, while India's urban economy grew at an average of 7.3 per cent over the last decade, the rural economy grew at an average of just 1.9 per cent. Hence, the contribution of rural workers to the GDP is less than 20 per cent that of workers in the urban economy. The average urban income is twice that of the rural income in India.

Clearly, we require radical, immediate reform in the planning and management of our cities. Effective urban planning, as defined by the World Bank, 'creates a competitive, well governed urban environment. It makes cities livable by ensuring a decent quality of life and equitable opportunity for all residents.'

To plan cities and towns which are livable and provide equitable opportunities, urban planners have to recognize the complexity of their brief. The need of the hour is a two-pronged approach to urban planning in India. First, planning should address existing, chronic shortages in urban infrastructure. It should provide accessible, low-cost infrastructure for urban residents like housing, schooling, hospitals, commercial activities, transport and support infrastructure. In addition, it should incorporate an effective framework for capacity building, and coordinate the expansion of infrastructure and services with urban growth.

Efficient land use and space planning is essential in building a livable urban environment. India's archaic land regulations and property tax systems have resulted in highly sub-optimal land use. For example, India's urban land ceiling act and floor space index (FSI) restrictions have created extremely low densities in land development. Additionally, rent-control and complex ownership regulations have prevented effective land-recycling and redevelopment. Consequently, today, FSIs average below 1.6 in urban India, compared to averages ranging from 5 to 15 in other Asian cities. Such low FSIs also result in higher wastage of energy for transportation and cause higher pollution levels. Such inefficient land use has created an artificial land shortage, and has led to significantly high costs for office space and housing in Indian cities. According to McKinsey, the average property cost relative to average urban income in India is the highest in Asia.

Unaffordable housing costs have contributed to the rapid growth of urban slums. India's urban slum population has been growing at 9–10 per cent a year. At the present rate of migration and housing development, 35 per cent of India's urban population will be forced to live in slums by 2030. As the economist Michael Leaf writes, our urban policies have created 'islands of homogeneity and wealth set in a sea of diversity and poverty'.

We must encourage high-rise and high-density cities for equitable, sustainable urban development. Urban FSI restrictions must be relaxed. FSI should be raised significantly in Central Business Districts (CBDs) to create affordable office space and make these areas accessible to small and mid-size businesses. We must also replace the 'policing' approach to land markets with an 'enabling' one. Land and housing markets must be deregulated. Property tax systems must be based on land value rather than rent to improve tax collections. A supra-judicial agency must be created to quickly resolve existing property disputes.

Planning must adequately address the shortage of low-cost housing in Indian cities. It is estimated that India requires the construction of 3.6 million housing units annually to merely address the annual growth in demand for urban housing. An example of a successful low-cost housing programme is Sweden's 'million programme', implemented by the Swedish government in partnership with private developers between 1964 and 1974. Within a ten-year period, the programme built a million low-cost dwellings for the poor. The houses were well-connected to the city through inexpensive tram systems, and provided with infrastructure like schools, hospitals and recreational facilities.

Private developers in cities may be given incentives like tax rebates to include low-income housing in their development plans. Reusing public land and abandoned lots for social housing will increase land available for such projects. This approach is not uncommon—abandoned buildings are upgraded and provided as housing to low-income families in New York and in Caracas.

A key drawback of India's urban policy is its land zoning regulations. These regulations mandate the division of cities into 'business' and 'residential' zones. However, these zoning laws were adopted from pre-1950 British urban planning models, and were intended to separate polluting industries from residential areas. Today, such regulations limit the opportunity for non-polluting commercial land use which can increase economic opportunity and enhance the quality of urban life. Modern planning models such as the smart-growth urban planning model suggest a 'mixed land use' system.

Such a system allows the planned construction of both commercial and residential buildings around employment opportunities. Such construction is also coordinated with the development of support infrastructure and the growth of schools and hospitals. Thus, housing, commercial activity, transport and support infrastructure are developed in an integrated, 'holistic' manner.

Today, the congestion of road transport in urban areas has become a critical issue. It is estimated that road congestion has cut road transport efficiency by 50 per cent in urban areas. There has been little progress in the development of mass urban transit systems in the country. Suburban rail transit systems exist in just four of the thirty-five Indian cities with populations in excess of 1 million. Dedicated city bus services operate in just seventeen cities.

Effective transport infrastructure forms the backbone of economic development in urban areas. As the economist Paul Krugman has pointed out, weak urban transport systems constrain economic growth as they 'limit urban agglomeration, and reduce labour mobility and economies of scale'. Unfortunately, there has been little focus on building efficient urban transport systems in India. Urban transit systems must typically address six key criteria well: connectivity and accessibility; efficiency; safety; urban aesthetics; financial viability; and affordability. Cities must implement an urban transportation system using multiple options. Road capacity must be enhanced. There has to be accelerated development of mass transit systems using metro rail, light-rail, mono-rail and bus services.

Existing shortages in road infrastructure should be addressed through the introduction of parallel service roads, and the construction of priority bus and taxi lanes. In addition, public transit systems must incorporate easy transfers between bus/air/rail terminals through a single-ticket system valid across the transport network. Such an integrated approach—similar to the Hong Kong and Tokyo transit systems—increases connectivity within transit networks, eases commuting and improves efficiencies for businesses.

Enforceable, well-defined standards in infrastructure planning and development are critical to enhancing the quality of life in our cities. Unfortunately, we do not see such enforceable design and execution standards in the construction of buildings, footpaths and roads, in support infrastructure, and in our water and sanitation systems.

Building standards should be realistic with broad enforceable guidelines and incentives for compliance beyond required norms. For instance, FSI entitlements in cities can be combined with 'bonus FSI' for buildings that implement design and construction quality standards above the required norms. This has been put in practice in New York City which allows greater FSI for buildings that 'enhance the public realm'.

Building standards should also mandate parking space requirements for commercial and residential units. The absence of such requirements results in overcrowding, road encroachments and parking on pavements. Regulations for the construction and maintenance of roads should include standards for user-friendly and accessible footpaths that effectively connect open spaces, parks and playgrounds. Road planning systems should include standards for related infrastructure like street lighting and signal systems for the road network. Conduits must be laid for cables, power lines and sewage systems. Such conduits also eliminate the repeated digging of roads and footpaths—a familiar sight in every Indian city.

To improve the functioning of urban infrastructure and services, these services can be contracted out to private operators. Creating a competitive environment in providing infrastructure and services to citizens will improve service delivery and efficiency, enable improved response to urban growth, and help lower costs. The management of public services like sanitation systems by private operators has been successfully implemented in Thailand and Malaysia. The participation of the government in these systems has been limited to a regulatory and monitoring role.

To address urban decay in cities, we must incorporate urban renewal activities within the planning framework. These can help promote new commercial and housing development in 'depressed' areas, and the creation of 'green areas' and open spaces in overcrowded districts. Cities can permit 'infrastructure endowments' in business districts where the government sells 'extra FSI' to developers above the existing, permitted value. The funds from such endowments can be demarcated for urban renewal activities.

Local governments should actively involve multiple stakeholders—industry, civil society organizations and citizen groups—in articulating a shared vision for urban planning. For example, Brazil's system of participatory budgeting in municipalities provides interaction between citizen councils and elected officials to decide priorities and expenditures in municipal budgets. A coordinated public–private approach to urban infrastructure can also improve the enforcement of design, execution and operational standards.

No urban planning exercise will be effective in the absence of effective governance systems. While urban governance is critical, it is, as the economist Barbara Boyle Torrey notes, often the resource in shortest supply. Urban governance in India has been weakened by complex administrative systems and highly fragmented responsibilities. Decision-making, financing and execution roles are split across state and city administrations.

In the present urban governance system, local bodies such as municipalities are responsible for providing services. However, they lack the mandate to generate financial resources to meet expenditures and take decisions on funding. Municipal areas in India generate 50 per cent of the total revenues for state and Central governments. Yet, municipalities receive less than 2 per cent of these funds directly. Funds are collected and allocated by the state. The state governments take decisions on important issues like user charges for municipal services and property taxes. Such systems severely reduce the ability of municipal corporations to deliver effective services.

The mayor of an Indian city is elected by city councillors, typically for a one-year term. The mayor lacks executive authority—his role is a ceremonial one and lacks real accountability on governance issues. The municipal councils do not effectively represent urban citizens. The citizen–representative ratio in India's urban areas averages over 4,000:1, compared to a ratio of 300:1 for rural governance bodies. To ensure effective governance, cities must have a mayor who is elected directly by the citizens for a period of five years. The mayor should be supported by an urban legislative body composed of councillors who have been directly elected from the city wards. Electoral wards should be properly demarcated and defined to reduce citizen–representative ratio averages to less than 1,000:1. This is essential to ensure that local governance concerns are adequately represented at the legislative level.

The legislative body, headed by the mayor, should have broad, effective authority and responsibility in all functions—financing, planning, execution and maintenance—for the city. The proposal of the Urban Renewal Mission to empower municipal bodies in tax collection and receiving funds is an excellent one and should be immediately implemented.

We must link the infrastructure investment and services provided to wards with the payments made by the ward citizens through tariffs and taxes. This 'social compact', as the World Bank notes, is key to restoring accountability in urban governance. We must financially empower wards through de-centralized tax collection, and give them the authority to levy and collect user charges for services. The management of services like electricity, water, sewage and roads should be handled in an integrated manner at the ward level.

The urban governance system should also handle urban planning and management for the wider metropolis. This can be achieved through a council of elected mayors of the cities who are responsible for addressing metropolitan concerns such as peri-urban sprawl, and for the planning and expansion of inter-city infrastructure. Additionally, an advisory city committee consisting of eminent citizens and urban planners should monitor the progress of urban projects and the overall spending of funds. They must be consulted before any large project is taken up. There must be periodic surveys to assess the satisfaction level among citizens.

It is critical that the city governments ensure the financial viability of urban services. In urban India, public services realize, on average, less than 12 to 15 per cent of expenditure through the recovery of costs. This is unsustainable. The pricing of services such as water, electricity and public transport must cover all effective costs incurred in providing these services. An efficient subsidy mechanism like the voucher system suggested by Milton Friedman can be used to provide directed subsidy for the low-income urban households.

It is estimated that the transaction cost of issuing a building permit or a business licence in India is at least 40 per cent of its total cost. Such inefficiencies in administration impose significant, unnecessary costs on urban development. This has to be improved.

There must be strong incentive systems to bring in efficiency and accountability in urban administration. Accountability in urban administration can be enhanced through the financing of urban projects by accessing capital markets, credit rating of municipalities and urban infrastructure entities, and competitive score-carding of city officers. In addition, IT tools such as MIS (management information systems) can be employed to improve efficiency and help better monitoring of public service delivery.

The urban transition of our economies must be viewed within a broader context of development. Urban strategies must be developed with an understanding of the contribution that cities and towns can make to the country's economic goals. The expansion of infrastructure and basic services into outlying areas is a necessary factor in synergizing economic growth outside existing urban centres. This can be seen in the present development of the Zhengdong district in China. The Zhengdong district is located in China's rural hinterland. To encourage urbanization, the district is being developed with state-of-the-art infrastructure for business, residential, high-tech, university and industrial buildings, and for support systems.

State governments must develop systematic regional plans to extend economic energy outside the existing urban centres. The growth of satellite townships must be encouraged through the establishment of effective arterial infrastructure networks, fast-paced transport corridors and efficient regional supply-chains.

Urban development must be part of a broader macroeconomic dialogue for economic growth. Weak national economic policies raise costs for businesses and households. They distort and limit private investment, the main source of urban wealth creation.

Today, we are in an age of rapid urbanization. The face of India's cities represents the future face of our country. Clearly, the way we manage the development of our towns and cities today will shape the success of our country for decades to come. It is best to remember the words of geographer David Harvey that 'cities are endowed with great character and with fascinating, ever-changing personalities'. It is the need of the hour to embrace intelligent, practical and effective policies for urban development and governance to transform our dynamic, fast-changing urban centres into truly sustainable engines of growth.

The Eight Visions that Changed the Face of India

India completed its sixtieth year as a free nation on 15 August 2007. According to Hindu tradition, the completion of sixty years is a landmark event in the life of any person. This event celebrates wisdom, maturity, accomplishment and the readiness to enter *vanaprastha ashrama* (a phase of life marked by renunciation of worldly responsibilities, and detachment from power, desire and wealth). However, sixty years is a short span in the life of a nation, and barely marks the first baby steps of a toddler. Hence, any assessment of India over this period has to be generous and optimistic.

We have made decent progress in several areas during the last sixty years. We have produced world-class scientists, engineers, journalists, soldiers, bureaucrats, politicians and doctors. We have built complex bridges and dams. We have sent satellites and rockets into space. We have increased the number of doctors ten-fold. We have increased average life expectancy from thirty-two to sixty-five years. We have built about 20 lakh km of new roads; we have multiplied our steel production by over fifty times and cement production by almost twenty times. We have increased our exports from a few million dollars at the time of Independence to more than $125 billion now.

There is an equally convincing set of data to show that we have a long way to go. A whopping 350 million Indians are illiterate; 260

Published in *The Hindu*, 15 August 2007

million people are still below the poverty line; 150 million people lack access to drinking water; 650 million people lack decent sanitation and 50 per cent of our children are below acceptable nutrition levels. Basic medicines are unavailable in 75 per cent of India's villages.

Be that as it may, I want to focus on a few major achievements that have taken place since Independence, transforming the lives of our people in a way we never imagined would happen.

The Green Revolution

Perhaps no other Indian initiative has enhanced the national confidence as much as the Green Revolution initiated by Dr M.S. Swaminathan. This revolution, which started in 1965, not only transformed India into a food-surplus economy from a food-deficit economy but also triggered the expansion of the rural, non-farm economy. The lives of at least 400 to 500 million Indians have been uplifted due to this initiative. From being a perennial importer of grains, India became a net exporter of food grains ten years ago.

The White Revolution

Coming from a generation which experienced an acute shortage of milk, it is unimaginable that, today, we have become the largest producer of milk in the world. The credit goes to the extraordinary vision of Dr Varghese Kurien, continued ably by Amrita Patel. In a nation where millions of children are malnourished, such abundance of milk has offered us the opportunity to fight malnutrition.

The economic reforms of 1991

The economic reforms of 1991, initiated by the late P.V. Narasimha Rao, Dr Manmohan Singh, P. Chidambaram and Dr Montek Singh Ahluwalia, opened up the minds of Indian corporate leaders to the power of global markets, helped them accept competition at home and abroad, and raised the confidence of consumers. Our hard currency reserves have gone up from a mere $1.5 billion in 1991 to over $220 billion today. The reforms encouraged entrepreneurship, and gave confidence to businessmen and entrepreneurs to dream big, create jobs, enhance exports, acquire companies abroad and follow the finest principles of corporate governance.

Independent media and brave journalists
The success of a democracy depends upon certain important values of governance—fairness, transparency and accountability. The freeing of the media, particularly television, has laid the foundation for improving these values in our governments. The courage, enthusiasm and the zeal to seek the truth demonstrated by scores of idealistic journalists and editors like N. Ram, Arun Shourie, Shekhar Gupta, Sucheta Dalal, Barkha Dutt and Rajdeep Sardesai, to mention just a few from the English press and TV, and a host of wonderful journalists and mediapersons from regional languages, are what makes us feel confident that the future of this country is safe.

The telecom revolution
No other technology has brought India—the urban and the rural—together as the 500-line EPABX designed and implemented by the Centre for Development of Telematics (CDoT) under the leadership of Sam Pitroda. This programme brought fresh confidence to the people as they could reach out to their loved ones, officials and doctors when they needed to. People no longer feel that they live in isolation.

Space technology and satellite television
Prof. Yash Pal's Satellite Instructional Television Experiment (SITE) blossomed into a full-scale television facility connecting millions of villages of India. The television medium has made our political masters realize that their actions and inactions will be seen and judged by every citizen—from the forgotten villages of Assam to the activist villages of Kerala. This technology has given voice to the opinions of a billion people—the rich and the poor, the educated and the uneducated, the powerful and the disenfranchised.

Atomic energy
Dr Homi Bhabha conceptualized the Indian nuclear programme and initiated nuclear science research in India. His programme has made the successful utilization of nuclear energy possible in defence, power generation, medicine and allied areas. Our peaceful use of nuclear energy has raised India's prestige as a mature and responsible player in this field.

The software revolution

N. Vittal's Software Technology Parks Programme, along with the economic reforms of 1991, laid the foundation for this industry's spectacular progress. India's IT exports grew from a mere $150 million in 1991-92 to $31.4 billion in 2006-07, and is projected to reach $60 billion by 2010. The IT industry is unique on several counts. It focussed on exports; benchmarked with the best global companies; followed the finest principles of corporate governance; created the largest number of jobs in the organized sector; and demonstrated that Indians too could succeed in the most competitive global markets.

Conclusion

What do these eight programmes have in common? They were all led by visionaries. These visionaries accepted global benchmarks and settled for nothing less despite tremendous odds. In each of these initiatives the national government was a genuine catalyst, supported by some extraordinary politicians and bureaucrats. These examples clearly show how the people and the government can work together to achieve what is at first thought impossible.

What do I expect from the India of 2067, after another sixty years? I want an India where every child will have access to decent education, health care, nutrition and shelter. I want an India where every child belonging to any race, religion and caste is confident that there is a bright future for him/her if he/she is honest and hardworking. I want an India which receives respect from every global forum because we will be high performers; we will be peace-loving; we will be gracious hosts; we will be fair; we will be pluralistic and respect every faith; and we will be trustworthy.

Software Enterprises:
The Temples of New India

It is not easy to talk about a colossus like Nehru. His influence has permeated every strand of developmental thought in the fifty years of India's independence. Undoubtedly, the generations to come will continue to benefit from his profound thought, philosophy and actions. The history of independent India is laced with the myriad initiatives that Nehru launched towards solving the problem of poverty. His pet theme was the creation of the temples of modern India—universities, dams and factories that comprised the foundation for the industrial infrastructure and associated pool of knowledge so essential for any modern nation-state. He knew that this was the only way of fulfilling Mahatma Gandhi's dream of wiping the tears of every poor man and woman in the country.

Let me recall a few words from his famous 'tryst with destiny' speech delivered on the eve of India's independence. He said, 'A moment comes but rarely in history, when we step out from the old to the new, when an age ends, and when the soul of a nation, long suppressed, finds utterance.' What a profound sentence! It held true that day and holds good even today when India is poised to become a significant player in the global hi-tech industry. To me, the hi-tech enterprises that have sprung up in great numbers in the country are

The twenty-third Jawaharlal Nehru Memorial Lecture, London, 4 December 2000

indeed the temples and shrines of the new India. I will talk about the importance of this phenomenon and also briefly touch upon what India needs to do to keep the momentum going.

While many tomes have been written on Nehru as a politician, statesman and administrator, very little is written about his belief that knowledge and scholarship would play a big role in the emancipation of the people of India. I would like to highlight three policy decisions that he took when he assumed the prime ministership of India. First, he created several institutes of higher learning including the Indian Institutes of Technology (IITs), the Indian Institutes of Management (IIMs), the Bhabha Atomic Research Centre (BARC) and the All-India Institute of Medical Sciences (AIIMS). Today, a majority of India's contribution to entrepreneurship in Silicon Valley, to leading academic institutions across the globe and to the pool of corporate talent in the USA comes from the IITs. The backbone of the engineering and managerial talent in India comes from this pool. The dream of making India a significant player in the global software industry would not have been possible without Nehru's vision.

Second, he insisted that there be no import duties on books, journals and any knowledge instruments, even in the context of an otherwise high-duty, protectionist mindset. Third, even in the fifties and the sixties, when foreign exchange was scarce, he ensured that every Indian who could afford to study abroad was given the required foreign exchange. I can imagine the intense opposition he would have faced from the jingoistic and less enlightened crowd, India having come out of a colonial regime only recently. These are truly the acts of a firm believer in the open flow of ideas from the best sources in the world. Nehru truly symbolized Andrew Jackson's words that 'one man with courage makes a majority'.

From time to time, we hear divergent opinions on the role of hi-tech enterprises in shaping the destiny of India. Given the pluralistic society that we live in, the vast disparity in education levels, and the long-term nature of the impact that hi-tech initiatives will have on the condition of the common people, it is natural that there are opposing views on this topic. Therefore, I would like to address the need for embracing technology in creating a better India.

The purpose of science is to unravel nature and that of technology is to make the life of human beings more productive and more comfortable. If a product has to succeed in the market, it has to do one of the following: reduce cost, improve productivity, save time or improve comfort. It is unarguable that IT products have met these requirements remarkably well. Who needs these more than the poor Indian with his/her low disposable income and the resultant difficulty in fulfilling basic human needs? Let me give you a few examples to illustrate the power of IT for the common man. Fishermen in Pondicherry use wave pattern data on the high seas broadcast by the US Navy to improve their yield by as much as 40 per cent. NASSCOM used IP-based videoconferencing to connect a taxi driver in Mumbai with his family in a remote village in Uttar Pradesh. Technology is a great leveller. It does not distinguish between the rich and the poor. For example, one of my younger colleagues who is a janitor at Infosys is extremely happy to use an ATM because it does not discriminate against him—unlike the clerk at the manned bank counter. Technology makes services cheaper. A balance inquiry at a manned counter costs Rs 40. The same transaction costs Rs 8 at an ATM while the Internet brings down the cost to just Rs 2. Who needs these more than the poor? The use of the e-governance paradigm for deployment of inexpensive, efficient, quick and corruption-free community and public services is another case in point. Information Technology can enhance transparency in decision-making and thus improve the confidence of our people in the government. The need of the day is for our leaders to become evangelists for the role of technology in improving the lives of poor people.

Now, let me come to why we should embrace global software opportunities wholeheartedly. Today, we live in a global village. No country can afford to isolate itself from the global market. Even countries that did so for a few decades realized this and went back to the global bazaar and have succeeded in enhancing the share of exports in their GDP. Software is a very lucrative area of export for India. We have to embrace an export orientation due to the following reasons:

i.   Every country leverages its competitive advantages to bring their products and services to the global market. This is an important avenue for creating jobs in India.

ii. I define self-sufficiency as being able to earn enough global currency from your competitive advantages to import the best products and services at the best prices from around the world. This definition is obviously at conflict with the traditional Indian mindset that emphasized vertical integration and import substitution. It is unfortunate that this mindset prevailed amongst our politicians and bureaucrats for well over forty years after Independence.

iii. You have to maintain a certain healthy proportion of exports and domestic consumption in order to ensure balanced and de-risked growth in the economy. The contribution of exports to the GDP of India is around 9 per cent which is low compared to countries like China (25 per cent) and Brazil (20 per cent). Given the unpredictability in prices of essential commodities like oil, the need to import technology, and the requirement that we have adequate foreign exchange reserves, it is essential that we enhance the contribution of exports to our GDP.

iv. An export orientation helps Indian enterprises benchmark their products and services on a global scale. If you succeed in the highly competitive global market, you are likely to provide high-quality products at the best prices even in the domestic market. For a long time, the Indian consumer has been forced to put up with shoddy quality. An orientation towards export will help us remedy this.

The first millennium saw India reach a high point in mathematics, astronomy, surgery and a few other similar areas, with people like Aryabhatta, Varahamihira, Brahmagupta and Susruta making seminal contributions. The second millennium was a disaster for India since the country was under foreign rule throughout this period, save the last half-century. Unfortunately, the early conquerors concentrated on arts and pleasure, and did not encourage the advancement of science and technology in the country. British rule started during an era when Indian curiosity, entrepreneurship and technology orientation was at an all-time low. Thus, India missed the benefits of industrialization. The Indian intellectual had to make do with pen and paper and show his or her contribution in matters of the mind like mathematics, algorithms and theoretical aspects of science. The emphasis, the world over, was on innovation in mass manufacturing till the advent of software technology. Fortunately for India, the last twenty years have seen tremendous opportunity in software development which is essentially about algorithms and conceptualization. Thus, the Indian intellectual has an arena where he or she can excel despite the tremendous handicap that India has had in the global marketplace.

India has several competitive advantages in the area of software:

   i.   a large pool of English-speaking, software-oriented talent
   ii. the project management skills of Indians in managing large software projects ensuring completion on time, within budgeted cost and with the requisite quality and productivity
   iii. the software-friendly policies that successive governments have instituted
   iv. the low cost of talent
   v.   the possibility of a longer work-day leveraging the time zone differences between India and the majority of the G-7 countries.

Indian software companies have concentrated on software services rather than on products. They specialize in designing, developing and maintaining software that is specific to a customer need. The strength of India, at this time, is in the production of customized software and not in mass marketing and brand creation. Products require physical proximity to the customer, an environment that reveres innovation, and considerable domain knowledge. At this point in time, we do not have these factor conditions in India. Thus, Indian companies have rightly concentrated on services.

It is fashionable amongst armchair pundits in India to criticize this approach and say that India should concentrate on products rather than services. Thanks to the strong influence of the Brahminical mindset among Indian intellectuals and the condescending attitude of the British civil servant towards the Boxwallah, the Indian intelligentsia has had a healthy contempt for business and for businessmen. Let me dwell a little on this issue of the Brahminical mindset. Ancient India encouraged the caste system purely based on the belief in specialization of successive generations of a family in a given vocation or trade or activity. That made eminent sense at that time. The result was that the Shudra tilled the soil; the Vaisya engaged in commerce; and the Kshatriya became the warrior. The Brahmin had the responsibility of connecting the rest with God and was also the champion of all intellectual pursuits. Since his primary responsibility was to think of the afterlife and to connect with higher powers, he had little or no interest in anything that had to do with the present or involved any physical activity. Learning for learning's sake was his motto. Using that learning to make any difference to society would be dangerous for two reasons—it would not be chic, and he might be held accountable!

This mindset is strong even today in India. For instance, when I interview young boys and girls, they insist on working in esoteric fields that have no relevance to solving the problems that beset contemporary India. Their first choice would typically be Artificial Intelligence (AI)! I have tried to elicit why they are interested in AI and their answer is usually that it is intellectually challenging and aspirational. They have no interest in real applications that have at least a semblance of relevance to India. You see the same attitude when our intellectuals comment on Indian companies not having a product focus. I tell them that product skills will surely be acquired and leveraged as Indian companies become more global and have better financial strength. The need of the day is to create a large number of high-income jobs for our young men and women. As long as we run businesses that solve problems of our society, create wealth legally and ethically, and provide challenging and lucrative jobs, it does not matter whether we are into rocket science or beekeeping.

There is also a belief that Indian companies do not do high value-add work. In my opinion, these criticisms are ill-founded. You will see an Indian software company behind most leading-edge IT applications in the world. Whether it is a next-generation securities trading system or a retailing system or a broadband wireless switch, you are likely to see an Indian company involved. The key questions to ask for Indian companies looking for such opportunities should be: Is there a market opportunity? Is this opportunity profitable? Do we have the capability to service the market? If not, what can we do to build up the capability? What role should the government and the academia play in this?

According to a study by McKinsey, the total market opportunity for software services in 1998 was $270 billion. Of this, $27 billion was the opportunity that could be outsourced to remote locations like India. Of this India had a share of $4 billion (15 per cent) in 1999-2000. This is likely to go up to $250 billion by 2008. The prime minister has set a target of $50 billion for software exports by 2008. Even this target is only 20 per cent of the worldwide opportunity for offshore services by 2008. As long as there are new innovations in IT, and as long as end-user corporations want to leverage the power of these innovations to create new competitive advantages in the marketplace, I see a significant role for Indian software companies. Market opportunity does not seem to be an issue at this stage.

For the first time in the history of India, we have received global acclaim. And this has been in just one field—software exports. While what we have achieved is creditable, we are still at the very early stages of our marathon. If we have to fulfil the target that has been set for us, there are certain urgent initiatives that the country—the political leadership, bureaucracy, academia and the corporate leadership—will have to take up. Let me talk about a few of these.

To bring the benefits of IT to the vast masses of the country, we need quick decision-making and focussed implementation of policies. These require a consensus amongst all hues of political thinking that IT will indeed help the lot of the common man. We cannot afford prolonged discussions on whether or not IT is good. In fact, our political leaders have to become evangelists for technology in general, and IT in particular. They have to lead by example by using IT themselves and by demonstrating how productive they have become by using IT.

As my friend Rahul Bajaj has said, the greatest management guru is competition. Unless Indian companies realize the importance of customer service, the use of IT will not become all-pervasive in the corporate world. This is especially true of government departments and the public sector. Heavy investment in IT is necessary for these institutions to deliver faster, better and cheaper services to their consumer by way of e-governance and e-commerce. We have to dismantle monopolies in vital sectors like telecommunications, insurance and airlines if we have to benefit from competition.

Today's competitive and dynamic business environment demands that quick decisions be made right in the boardrooms rather than after receiving approvals from New Delhi. In a country like India, the government plays a critical role in the destiny of a corporation. As Indian companies move towards increased globalization, they will have to push the envelope to embrace new rules of competition. Our government will have to play a significant role in creating such new rules. This requires quick and decentralized approvals from state capitals and proximate government offices rather than from New Delhi. The government has to become a catalyst rather than a controlling authority. My own experience is that the government has, by and large, become extremely responsive to the needs of the corporate world. It is just a question of fine-tuning in a few areas.

The software industry has shown a compound annual growth rate (CAGR) of over 40 per cent in the last five years. The domestic IT industry has shown a CAGR of over 25 per cent over the same period. The demand for IT exists today and is likely to continue to be strong over the next five to ten years. The need of the day is to improve the supply situation. The IT industry is absorbing a large number of fresh engineering and science graduates and also attracting a large number of professionals from companies in other engineering sectors including power, construction, automobile and steel. Further, several countries have launched initiatives to attract Indian software professionals. Thus, unless we take urgent steps to start new colleges to produce IT professionals as well as to enhance the intake at various existing institutions of learning, the industry will not be able to grow at the required pace to reach the $50 billion target by 2008.

The quality of education provided has to be improved significantly. This requires that we create competition by allowing private universities to come up and also inviting well-known educational institutions from abroad to establish a presence in India. Initiatives such as the Indian School of Business (ISB) and the Global Institute of Science and Technology (GIST) are good first steps in this direction. There is also a great need for increased interaction between Indian industry and academia to push the envelope in software applications and software engineering practices. This is particularly true if we want to become better at product development.

It is unrealistic to expect the IT and software industry to grow indefinitely unless we improve basic infrastructure like airports, roads, hotels, power and telecommunications. Generally, the development of a nation has to be organic and all-round. I do not see how we can reach a $50 billion target for software exports with our existing physical and technological infrastructure. If we want the Internet to be ubiquitous and benefit the common man, India's telephone density has to increase manifold from the current level of 3 per 1,000 people and also become far less expensive. India is perhaps the only country in the world that defies the basic laws of economics by imposing higher tariffs as the volume of telephone usage goes up! Further, in a developing country like India, the pricing of these services has to be looked at in relation to disposable income levels for various segments, rather than being linked to international prices.

In keeping with the significant progress made by the government in its liberalization efforts, it is necessary that there be transparency in awarding large contracts and in policy formulation. This is mandatory if we have to have the benefit of participation by world-class companies in our nation-building process and in making our IT industry strong enough to be globally competitive. In addition, e-governance will improve transparency, reduce corruption and improve consumer comfort.

India has done a good job in creating a suitable rule set for attracting venture capital to the country. The results are already perceptible. Indian rules on employee stock option plans are probably among the best in the world. However, in certain areas, we have to reduce the hassle of dealing with the complex rule sets of myriad state and Central government institutions, if we wish to fully reap the benefits from these progressive measures.

The Internet will be a key vehicle of growth for the Indian economy. Restrictions in India on voice-over-IP and on connectivity between the PSTN and private networks for voice and data should go. Tariffs for voice and satellite bandwidth should be reduced to globally competitive levels. Without this, it is unlikely that the vast majority of Indians will receive the benefits of the Internet. Also, given that world-class communication infrastructure is a key condition for software exports, such barriers may hamper the long-term growth prospects for this sector. Unless our hardware industry grows in a big way, we will not be able to leverage the power of IT for the common man. Hardware costs will consequently have to come down. This can happen only by increasing volumes, and requires a rationalized duty structure that supports value addition through manufacturing.

Attracting global customers and investors requires that we enhance their comfort levels by instituting global standards in corporate governance. Similarly, bureaucratic procedures in setting up trading offices by foreigners in India have to be minimized. We have to change our mindset from one of thinking it is a favour India is doing to the international investor, to one of making the international investor feel wanted. The government and the industry have to work together on this matter. The government has done a great job in reducing the import duty on software from a punishing 150 per cent once upon a time to zero per cent today. However, the duties on imported hardware will have to be reduced to facilitate large-scale computerization across the country. Vendors will have to talk to their principals and establish special pricing schemes for India keeping in view the vast market potential.

By and large, Indian hardware companies have had some focus in their operations. However, this can hardly be said of Indian software companies. In fact, the most common complaint of clients abroad is that most Indian software companies claim every area under the sun as their area of expertise! While there may be many reasons for this, including low volumes in specific areas, such unfocussed operations lead to erosion of credibility and low quality of service to clients. Rather, a stronger focus on specialization will help software companies obtain domain knowledge and thereby move up the value chain.

It is universally agreed that a key reason for the failure of IT projects in India is the inability of the end-users to appreciate the value that IT can bring to the table. An offshoot of this is the unwillingness of end-users to pay a fair price for software. Often, users do not show adequate interest in allocating quality time to project personnel from their IT vendors. This results in inordinate delays and cost overruns. Coupled with the fact that the opportunity cost of taking up an Indian project is very high for an Indian software company, this explains why most Indian software companies are loath to take up domestic projects.

High growth and high per-capita revenue productivity require attracting the best customers in the marketplace and the best employees from the local talent pool. This can be done by establishing strong brand equity on a global scale. India has not been able to create a single global brand so far. The software industry offers an opportunity to break this jinx. But this initiative requires visionary thinking, considerable spending and excellent execution.

Our desire to move up the value chain and to become innovators in IT requires that we leverage the capabilities of our academic institutions. Our brethren in academia also need to enhance their focus on problem-solving orientation rather than the traditional Indian mindset of research for research's sake.

As I think of the developments over the last ten years, I feel happy about the progress this country has made in competing in international markets, in accepting globalization, in reducing friction to business, in benchmarking with global best practices, and in accepting competition from outside. But, these are just the first few steps of the marathon. Jawaharlal Nehru laid the foundation for the knowledge industry in India. I am optimistic that the political leadership, the bureaucracy, the corporate leaders and the academia will move forward with even greater enthusiasm and fulfil the dream of our first prime minister.

PART IV

EDUCATION

What Would I Do if I Were the Principal of a Secondary School?

The principal of a secondary school has much to be proud of. He guides students through some of their most formative years and sends them up to nationally-recognized higher educational institutions. School principals are very important because they produce future politicians, scientists, engineers, doctors, lawyers, military generals, corporate leaders, administrators, judges and journalists. They are important instruments for the progress of the country.

The main purpose of education is to produce good and productive citizens. Aristotle said, 'A civilized society is one where good people become good citizens.' In a civilized society, each generation is expected to make the society better for the next generation. It is educated people who form such a civilized society. Hence, the school has a tremendous societal responsibility.

I thought I would muse about what I would do if I were the principal of a school.

I am very happy that the ICSE and ISC curricula have been constantly revised so that they have an intellectual rigour on par with the best. However, I would enhance the emphasis on problem-solving in each subject. I would attempt to make these problems address our real-life contexts much more. This is particularly applicable to subjects

A lecture delivered at the Conclave of Principals of Bishop Cotton Group of Schools, Bangalore, 5 January 2001

like Economics, Physics, Mathematics and Chemistry. I would use more models when demonstrating theory in class. This way, the students would gain the confidence to tackle actual problems in the world outside the school.

Today's students are very likely to become leaders in their chosen walks of life tomorrow. Unless they are taught to write well and speak correct English in a clear diction and without a pronounced accent, all the good things they learn in the classroom cannot be used by them to influence others. I would institute a compulsory course in English writing starting from the fifth grade.

I would make the classes interactive and encourage lots of questions from the students. That is how we can uncover the extraordinary curiosity among children to question, experiment and internalize important ideas. I would encourage children to practise independent thinking. The schools must foster openness to new ideas and new cultures among children. It would be for instance wonderful to have a course on the various religions so that our children learn the good things from each of our religions and become both secular and broad-minded.

I would reduce the class size so that better attention can be given to individual students. I would spend my time in class teaching concepts rather than dictating notes. I would use technology to have interactive sessions in teaching Science, Mathematics and Economics. Right from the fourth standard, I would introduce Algorithmic Thinking as a subject. Many schools now have courses on computer programming, but the PC-to-student ratio needs to be improved. The study of the Internet could be included as part of these courses, to give students the opportunity to experience this great new paradigm. Another idea would be to connect some schools in a given town for video-conferencing so that quality teaching resources, which are scarce, can be shared.

The standard of teachers is fast going downhill. Unless we can attract high-quality teachers, it is not possible to impart a good education to students. A way out may be to double or triple the salaries for worthy teachers. As long as the quality of teachers improves, parents will always be willing to pay higher fees. Fund-raising committees can also be created to collect money from alumni after they start working.

Children are keen observers. They want the principal and teachers to be the epitome of all that is good. Teachers are their heroes. If they do not see their teachers walk the talk, they will lose faith. So, the teachers must embrace good values, merit, honesty and hard work, and must be seen as being unbiased.

Many of these are the observations I have heard when I talk to parents about the schools that their children go to. It is only by bettering our education system that we can produce good future leaders.

A Framework for Reforms in Higher Education in India

My father was a teacher. He believed that a country is as good as the quality of the intellectuals it produces. I too subscribe to this view. Progress comes from thinking, articulating, discussing, debating and executing ideas in an environment of respect for pluralism. We should remember Benjamin Disraeli's words that a university should be a place of light, of liberty and of learning. The aim of a country's higher education system is sustainable development and improvement of the economy as a whole. It enables this through the creation, transmission and dissemination of knowledge that is vital for a country's economic and social development, thus providing a direction for future growth. Research has shown that, on average, countries that have higher levels of literacy and have invested steadily in raising the education levels of their labour force have sustained high levels of economic growth.

Science is about unravelling nature, and creating a foundation for technology to make life better for humankind. The higher the quality of university education is in a country, the more prosperous and competitive the people. As countries move up the ladder of development, the contributions of hi-tech manufacturing and high value-added services to the GDP become higher and higher. Consequently, today, the comparative advantage of a country is

---

The third K.C. Basu Memorial Lecture, Kolkata, 3 August 2006

increasingly determined by how well it uses knowledge and innovation. Success in leveraging knowledge and innovation is only possible with a sound infrastructure of higher education. The writer Clark Kerr has said, 'On a global scale, wealth and prosperity have become more dependent on the access to knowledge than the access to natural resources.' The role of education has, thus, become central to the development and competitiveness of an economy. The USA is the finest example of this thesis, since it has built a vibrant educational system which is the second largest in the world. Seventeen of the world's top twenty universities are American. Not only do US universities produce workers to drive economic growth, but they are also world-class incubators of innovation and knowledge creation. American universities currently employ 70 per cent of the world's Nobel Prize winners. They produce about 30 per cent of the entire world's output of articles in science and engineering, and 44 per cent of the most frequently-cited articles.

The American education system has helped seed the growth of key 'new technology' industries in the USA—the semiconductor, information technology, biotechnology and pharmaceutical industries—through the early discoveries of university researchers. In fact, the growth of Silicon Valley was initially driven by electronics and high technology companies around Stanford University which accessed the university's technology expertise and skills. The Massachusetts Institute of Technology (MIT) alone incubates around 200 companies every year. The result is the enhancement of prosperity and competitiveness of the US economy year after year.

Similarly, since the 1960s, the South-East and East Asian countries pursued a strategy of building a 'stock' of highly-trained human resources to attract knowledge-intensive investment and boost economic growth. The Republic of South Korea is a good example of such an economy. As early as 1980, the country had achieved a primary enrolment rate of 96 per cent, and a tertiary enrolment rate of 40 per cent, figures similar to the industrialized nations. The country's education policy has significantly contributed to South Korea's rapid export-led growth, the sustained economic development the country has experienced since the 1980s, and the rising prosperity of its people.

Even in India, the value of higher education was realized by our early leaders. India's first prime minister, Jawaharlal Nehru, recognized the importance of institutes of higher learning for the development of the country. It was this vision that led to the establishment of the IITs, the IIMs, AIIMS and the national laboratories, resulting in many high-impact initiatives including Vikram Sarabhai's space programme and Homi Bhabha's atomic programme. Nehru's and Indira Gandhi's belief in higher education was so strong that they forbade any restrictions on the release of foreign exchange for studies abroad and insisted, in the midst of the most punishing duty regime in the world, on a zero-duty regime for imported books and periodicals. They invited several well-known researchers to drive India's economic growth. M.S. Swaminathan's Green Revolution, Sam Pitroda's telecommunications revolution and Yash Pal's experiment in using satellite technology for instructional television are all good examples of success in the application of advanced knowledge for the betterment of the common man. Over the last two decades, India has made strong economic gains leveraging its educational infrastructure. India's vast pool of low-cost, educated workers has helped establish the country's burgeoning software, biotechnology and pharmaceutical industries.

The economist Jandhyala B.G. Tilak has assessed the contribution of higher education to GDP growth in India's post-reform period to be between 27 and 30 per cent. An educated workforce has played an important role in the growth of companies such as Tejas Networks, TCS, Infosys, Reliance, Bharti, TELCO, Ranbaxy and Biocon, just to name a few outstanding companies founded by innovative, educated entrepreneurs. Amartya Sen, Kaushik Basu, P. Balaram, C.N.R. Rao, Srinivas Kulkarni, C.K. Prahalad, Rajat Gupta and M.S. Banga are just a few names in the galaxy of great economists, scientists, management experts and corporate leaders that Nehru's and Indira Gandhi's vision has produced. The outstanding work of non-resident Indian entrepreneurs like Desh Deshpande, B.V. Chandrashekhar, Kanwal Rekhi and Vinod Khosla is yet another testimony to the success of India's higher educational institutions.

India has the third largest higher education system in the world—

after China and the USA—with 311 universities and 15,600 colleges as of 2004. The number of degrees awarded by Indian educational institutions has grown by 70 per cent between 1990 and 2004, and the number of engineering degrees awarded has grown by 90 per cent. Of the 10.5 million students attending India's universities, the majority of enrolment is at the undergraduate level with 88.9 per cent of students enrolled in undergraduate programmes and 9.4 per cent in postgraduate programmes. India produces 2.5 million graduates and 350,000 engineers every year. India's pool of university graduates alone is 1.5 times the size of China's and twice as large as that of the USA. India produces five to six times the number of engineers as the USA. But, despite being one of the largest producers of degrees in the world, the quality of education in India is still unsatisfactory. India has hardly produced any worthwhile inventions in recent years. Almost every technology we use is from abroad. The reason is the low quantity and quality of our doctoral programmes and our continued emphasis on rote learning. Today, India's pool of PhDs is less than one-tenth the size of the US pool. India's engineering and medical colleges, management schools and universities are facing a serious shortage of good quality academics with faculty shortages averaging over 20 per cent. Our annual output of PhDs in the Computer Science (CS) area is around twenty-five while the output of PhDs in CS in the USA exceeds 800 a year. China is estimated to produce more than 2,500 PhDs every year in the CS area.

Thus, despite its vast network of universities and colleges, India has failed to create a world-class higher education system. According to the academic ranking of world universities for 2005, India had just two universities in the top 500, while Japan had thirty-four, China eighteen, South Korea seven, and Brazil four. McKinsey estimates that only about 10 per cent of Indian students with degrees in the arts and humanities and 25 per cent of Indian engineering graduates are globally competitive. Twelve per cent of the country's 41 million unemployed have either graduate or post-graduate degrees, pointing to the serious failure of the country's higher education system. Clearly, outside a few islands of excellence, our higher education system has failed to produce quality institutions that can nurture the creative, intellectual leaders we require for sustainable growth.

The absence of research excellence has seriously impacted India's scientific and technological output. India ranks a lowly 119th among 149 countries in the citations index. A McKinsey study found that the typical IIT was granted three to six patents in a year as against sixty-four for Stanford Engineering faculty and 102 for MIT Engineering faculty. The number of citations per faculty over a five-year period was two to three for the typical IIT while it was fifty-two for Stanford Engineering faculty and forty-five for MIT Engineering faculty. India filed 363 patents in 2004, compared to 84,271 filed by the USA, 35,350 by Japan, and 5,938 by Taiwan. Since the contributions of M.S. Swaminathan, Vikram Sarabhai and Sam Pitroda in the 1970s and 1980s, the country has not seen any major scientific and technical adaptations. Not a single major invention has emerged from India over the past fifty years.

While there was tremendous emphasis by Jawaharlal Nehru and Indira Gandhi on building a sound higher educational infrastructure, successive prime ministers have not been equally enthusiastic about higher education. The drive to create world-class institutions of higher learning has almost disappeared. For example, while the country saw the establishment of five IITs during Nehru's time, we have seen only one new IIT in the last forty years, not counting the fact that Roorkee and BHU engineering colleges were designated IITs! Similarly, after nearly 100 successful years of the Indian Institute of Science (IISc), only now has an attempt to create a few more institutes of science started, thanks to the vision of Prof. C.N.R. Rao. We see the same story in medicine, agriculture and economics, just to mention a few fields.

India spends only 1.9 per cent of its GDP on higher education, the lowest among nations with a GDP higher than $500 billion. The IT task force report which suggested several solutions in the area of higher education to enhance our IT competitiveness has been gathering dust for the last eight years. The recommendations of the Kothari Commission's report suggesting that we raise spending on education to 6 per cent of our GDP has still not been acted upon even after thirty-eight years! It took more than a year for the Central government to release the grant of Rs 100 crore announced by the finance minister for the IISc during the 2005 budget speech. I can go on and on but the message is clear—excellence in higher education does not matter to the country's leaders.

Over the last thirty years, the stifling bureaucracy and excessive control over institutes of higher education have impeded their progress. Let me give you a few examples. A well-known professor of the history of science and technology from the USA wants to write the story of an Indian Institute of Technology but his request for a visa gets turned down, until some well-meaning people in the government intervene after a delay of eighteen months. One of the best private medical institutes in a southern state is denied permission to start post-graduate degree programmes for eighteen years while all sorts of dubious medical colleges in the same state are given permission to do the same. The director of an IIM attends a conference in China at the invitation of the president of a well-known university there. He invites the president in a reciprocal gesture to visit his IIM. The government refuses to clear the invitation. Five well-known non-resident Indians (NRIs) in the USA decide to use their stocks to create a corpus of Rs 5,000 crore in the late nineties to start four institutes of bio- and information technology. They approach the University of California, Berkeley, the finest public university in the world, for collaboration, and get their consent in two months. Then, they apply to the Government of India (GOI). Despite the request to the GOI by some of us to expedite the approval, to date, there has been no reply. In the meanwhile, the stocks which traded at around $300 in 1996 have reached rock bottom numbers and these NRIs are no longer in a position to support this initiative. The country has lost a golden opportunity. The condition of hostels in most IITs is totally at variance with our call to excellence in education at these places. A successful and generous alumnus uses his own money to build a decent hostel with all modern amenities at his alma mater, a well-known IIT. The then minister and his bureaucrats ask the director of the IIT endless questions on why this hostel construction was permitted!

No wonder, then, that India's pool of university-educated talent constitutes a mere 9 per cent of its population, compared to 15 per cent in China, 19 per cent in Thailand and 28 per cent in the Philippines. We can forget about comparing ourselves to developed countries.

It is important to consider the state of primary and secondary education in the country as well, since the secondary school system is the input channel for higher education. Without a vibrant primary and secondary education system, it is unlikely that we will have a sound university education system. By all counts, we have failed even in achieving our goals in basic education. Today, India is home to the largest number of illiterates in the world, with over 390 million illiterate people. Twenty-five million Indian children are out of school, accounting for 20 per cent of the world's children out of school. India spends just 2.1 per cent of its GDP on elementary education. The impact of our neglect of primary education can be assessed by the following example. A whopping 650 million people are estimated to be dependent on agriculture that produces just 25 per cent of the GDP, resulting in an alarmingly low per-capita income of less than Rs 12,000 a year, much lower than even the already low per-capita GDP of the country. These people can barely survive. The only hope is to move these people from agriculture into low-tech manufacturing. Alas, most of them are illiterate and unfit to be pulled out of agriculture. On the other hand, China which has reached an adult literacy of 93 per cent pulls 1 per cent of its population out of agriculture every year and puts them into construction and manufacturing.

Amartya Sen believes that access to basic education is a human right, and 'a vital part of people's capacity to lead lives they value'. In 1992, the Indian government announced a planned target of 'universalizing' elementary education in India. This goal was divided into three broad initiatives—universal access, universal retention and universal achievement—aimed at making education accessible to children, making sure that they continued their education, and finally, ensuring that they completed their goals. By the end of 2003, an estimated 90 per cent of India's rural population had primary schools within 1 km of their residence, and 84 per cent had upper primary schools within 3 km. Between 1991 and 2003, the gross enrolment ratio in primary education rose from 82 per cent to 95 per cent, and in upper primary education from 54 per cent to 61 per cent. These are good statistics. However, these education programmes have failed to build in accountability in implementation and outcomes. In fact, over 90 per cent of the government expenditure on elementary education goes towards the payment of teachers' salaries in state schools. The programmes have placed an overemphasis on increasing enrolment with little attention paid to retaining students or to learning outcomes. This lack of accountability has resulted in what one educationist has called 'universal sub-par education'. State schools often lack even basic infrastructure and facilities. On an average, 14 per cent of government primary schools across India are single-classroom or single-teacher schools. This number rises to as high as 40 per cent in states like Assam and Arunachal Pradesh. According to an assessment done at the national level, there is an estimated shortage of 998,000 classrooms as of September 2005.

The lack of focus on quality has severely impacted the teaching quality in schools. In 2003, World Bank researchers made random visits to 200 primary schools in India, and found no teaching activity in half of them. A survey by Harvard University's Michael Kremer found that one out of four teachers in India's government-owned elementary schools was absent at any given time. Teachers did not attend school at all for almost a third of the school year. The low quality of education across state schools has significantly affected learning outcomes—a recent national survey revealed that close to 35 per cent of the children in the 7–14 age group surveyed could not read a simple paragraph and almost 60 per cent of children could not read a simple story. Less than half of the children in the fourth grade could handle first-level mathematics. This apathy has also led to high drop-out and failure rates among students. The average drop-out rate in state schools is 53 per cent. In the state of West Bengal, it is estimated that of the 100 students who enrol in the first standard, only seventeen finish the tenth standard. At the national level, only 28 per cent of the children who enrol in primary school pass fifth grade. And of the children who drop out, 61 per cent come from the poorest 40 per cent of Indian households.

Weak educational standards in government schools have resulted in private schools mushrooming across the country. A recent study found that 16 per cent of rural children are now in private primary schools that charge an average of Rs 90 a month in fees, as opposed to free government education. Today, while private schools account for 10 per cent of India's primary schools, they account for 27 per cent of enrolment. Private schools also perform better than public schools. The economist Geeta Kingdon's survey showed that private schools are more efficiently run with lower unit cost per student compared to state schools. The children in such schools also scored 10 per cent higher on verbal and mathematics examinations than their peers in public schools.

Let me, now, return to the higher education system. Why is it that a system that attracted about 350 PhDs from abroad just to IIT, Kanpur in the mid-sixties, fails to attract even a handful to the same institution today? Why is it that a system that produced about fifty PhDs a year just in one department at IIT, Kanpur during the sixties, fails to produce even two a year today? Why is it that a system that attracted at least five to ten well-known professors from the best universities in the world to most of our top universities in the sixties, fails to attract even one today? Why is it that a system that produced thirty to forty world-class papers per year in just one subject from one institution, now fails to produce even two per year in the same institution?

These important questions have to be answered. We have to face the truth, no matter how bitter it is, if we want to leave behind a better higher education system for our children. That is what a civilized society is all about. We have to take tough measures which will benefit the whole society but which may be unpleasant for some of us.

If we want to improve the quality of our educational institutions, we must provide full autonomy to these institutions. What do I mean by autonomy? Autonomy for an educational institution is about the freedom to decide on selection criteria and the size of intake for students and for faculty; syllabi; fees and scholarships for students; compensation for faculty; interaction with the best scholars and leaders from all over the globe; plans for growth and plans for adapting to a changing environment. It is clear that, on all these aspects of autonomy, our institutions of higher learning score very low and have, in fact, been losing their freedom gradually. Let me give you a recent example of reducing freedom in our academic institutions. Only two weeks ago, it was reported that the Ministry of External Affairs was planning to issue a notice that all organizations, including those in the private sector, would be asked to get the ministry's approval before inviting a foreign delegation or accepting an invitation from overseas. Such restrictions on commercial and educational organizations will only hurt our competitiveness.

The first requirement is to raise the aspirations, confidence, energy and enthusiasm of our educational institutions. We must let competition drive progress through greater transparency and accountability for these institutions. We must clearly lay down a set of rules based on the best global practices in each of the areas that I have mentioned above. To do this, we should create a group for each area of learning, called a regulatory committee, comprising eminent men and women including well-known educationists from countries that are in the top five in global higher educational rankings. This group should meet twice a year to set the standard in each of the governance areas, and review the progress of our higher education system. These standards must be widely published in newspapers and on the Internet so that students and parents know what to expect from institutions of higher learning. Let the market create a ranking system based on the parameters that this regulatory group has set up. While the national dailies and weeklies should rank the top fifty institutions in each area in the country, the regional dailies should rank the top fifty in each state. The USA and many other countries have created a similar system.

All private institutions would be incentivized by the mechanism I have outlined above. Of course it is not possible for all government-funded universities to reach the same uniform level of excellence all at once. Let us classify our public universities into A, B and C categories based on their current level of performance. Let the regulatory committee set increasing standards for performance for each of these categories, and define increasing levels of autonomy and funding. Let the regulatory committee decide on a floor-level standard for these institutions that must be achieved before grants can be renewed or enhanced. It is important to create incentives for every university to perform better. It must also be remembered that even low-performing institutions must have a high level of autonomy in areas like selection and promotion of faculty, else they will not develop.

That brings me to another important aspect of excellence in universities—the quality of students. We must all accept that, as in most things in life, the quality of students follows a normal distribution. That is, there will be a small percentage of outstanding students, a majority of average students, and a small percentage of below-average students. While it is important to provide every child an opportunity to become the best, we must accept that not all of them will do so, since the outcome will follow a normal distribution. We have all seen a large number of cases where there is a significant difference in the performance of children from the same parents. Unfortunately, in India, we have a tendency to design our standards based on the worst performers, and demotivate outstanding students. The suggestion that Muslim students should not have to pass Mathematics and English at the secondary level is one such sad exercise that would further disable Muslim children. The current debate on reservation for low performers also belongs to the same category. While the solution suggested may provide opportunity in IITs and IIMs for 2,000 students from disadvantaged backgrounds, it does not solve the problem of helping 150 million disadvantaged children. The solution is to focus on primary education, and to spend more resources on enhancing the performance of low performers, not to dilute the performance standards in higher education. It is best to create a large number of preparatory institutions that will take such weak students from disadvantaged backgrounds and provide extra coaching, nutrition and financial support so that they become competition-worthy.

It is universally agreed that the quality of an educational institution is determined by the quality of students it attracts; the quality of faculty it attracts; and finally, the quality of research it produces. The quality of students an institution attracts is, generally, influenced by the quality of alumni, the quality of peers and the quality of the faculty. In fact, it is universally accepted that, in the absence of any significant financial incentives, it is the quality of peers that enthuses good students and faculty to join a university. All of the world's great universities have followed these cardinal rules.

Even among the students from the merit-based category, we must design special courses only for bright students so that they learn in an environment of intense competition among equally bright peers. In the USA, such courses are called Honors courses. Generally, the majority of students attend the normal version of the course while a small percentage of students attend the Honors version of the same. The Honors version is a faster-paced course that has more in-depth coverage of the subject, allowing you to cater to all students without bringing down the quality of the top students.

There is a tendency in India to descend to the lowest common denominator in everything we do. Several years ago, a committee of parliamentarians who visited an IIT even suggested that India introduce its own standard of research to accommodate less-accomplished students in the PhD programme!

We must remember that universities become great not just by good teaching but by undertaking leading-edge research. Research is about advancing the state of the art. It is about treading the untrodden path. It is about opening new vistas. It is about imagination. Research requires that the faculty work in an environment of debate, competition and aspiration among competent people. There is no place for mediocrity in research. In fact, Harvard always looks for the best talent on a global basis when a faculty position is to be filled even though there may be many internal candidates. Almost all US universities have a stringent peer review process, including internal and external experts, in deciding on the tenure for a given candidate. If we really want to enable economic development and improve the lives of poor people, we cannot dilute merit in faculty and student selection at least in the top ten universities in each subject. Otherwise, no matter how eloquent and passionate we are in espousing the cause of social justice, these will remain empty words. Let us be clear that we cannot enable social justice without an M.S. Swaminathan, a Sam Pitroda or a Vikram Sarabhai, and that such people will not emerge in an environment that shuns merit.

Unfortunately, even in our so-called best institutions, there is tremendous resistance to meritocracy in faculty selection, compensation and promotion from the faculty themselves. We must all recognize that, in a democracy, it is always the average performers who form the majority, and they set the rules. Let me give you an example. A few years ago, I suggested to the Computer Science faculty of a well-known institute in India that my wife and I wanted to create a corpus for giving an award of Rs 2 lakh for every paper published in an internationally known, refereed journal. I was surprised at the vehement opposition from the majority of the faculty who, I learnt later on, were all mediocre! Their objection was that the awards would go, time and again, to only a few of the faculty members. My suggestion that every faculty member should strive hard to produce good papers was met with a stony silence. The solution is to allow the best people to set the rules and implement these rules with fairness and transparency. As Mahatma Gandhi said, 'In a progressive society, measures must always be held superior to men who are after all imperfect instruments working for their fulfilment.'

Progress is all about positive but tough change. Such change requires good leaders. Leadership is about having the courage to dream big and creating a grand vision, about creating trust in people by leading from the front. It is about walking the talk in working hard and intelligently, and making sacrifices to achieve what appears impossible. Show me a great nation, a great institution or a great company, and I will show you a great leader behind it. Our challenge now is to get good people to lead our universities as vice-chancellors and support them with governance mechanisms that attract the best and the brightest people.

Unfortunately, today, both the Central and state governments have weakened the governance mechanisms in educational institutions by diluting the robust processes that we had set up in the fifties, and by filling leadership positions in our universities using caste and regional considerations. For example, till 2002, the selection of the directors of IIMs was decided by the board of governors with inputs from faculty and external experts. This has been changed now to remove any role for faculty or the board in the selection, contrary to the practice in all world-class universities abroad.

As I have said earlier, aspiration is the main fuel for progress. Raising aspirations requires that we benchmark with the best global standards. Indian universities should benchmark their performance with the best in the world in infrastructure, facilities, research and quality of curricula across various fields—engineering, medicine, pure sciences, literature, arts and law. To create a globally competitive mindset, we must proactively participate in global rankings and studies that benchmark India with other nations that are ahead of us in higher education. As a country, we have typically avoided participating in such rankings. An example of this is the benchmarking of nations in Science and Mathematics proficiency at the school level. When our level was found to be very low globally, we started avoiding such rankings. But participating in them is necessary to help us realize our problems and solve them.

Indian universities must cultivate an environment of openness, and set up interactions with the best universities in the world through collaborative research initiatives and exchange programmes for faculty and students. Thailand has enabled this through an Internet-based 'match-making' initiative called Project JUNO (Joint Universities Network Online) for Thai and US universities interested in developing linkage projects. The project enables Thai universities to explore potential opportunities for student or faculty exchanges, develop joint courses, and undertake collaborative research with interested US counterparts.

In India, I suggest an experiment where the top five institutions in each area invite five world-class faculty members to teach a course each year. Assuming we are looking at fifty areas, this is just a question of inviting about 1,250 faculty members at a cost of about $40,000 per semester per faculty member from abroad, and would cost about $50 million, or Rs 250 crore. Similarly, it should be possible to depute our students and faculty to the best universities to do research with well-known researchers. This will again not cost more than about $10,000 per student. If we send about 1,000 of the best students in various disciplines abroad every year, it will cost us just $10 million or Rs 50 crore.

We should allow foreign universities to come in freely, either through joint partnerships or independently. This will bring international competition to India, and enable student access to global universities at affordable rates. Today, it is estimated that about 100,000 students go abroad for higher studies and spend about $1 billion a year. Most of this expenditure can be saved if we have these world-class universities operating in India.

The practice of getting PhD theses evaluated by researchers from abroad—which was common in India during the 1960s and 1970s—should be re-introduced to benchmark our research work to global standards. Opportunities for undergraduate research—as in US universities—should also be made available to our students. Interest in research is kindled at an early stage by such opportunities and is likely to attract more students to academia than today.

The Department of Science and Technology (DST), the organization overseeing research in India, should be made independent and move towards a system of transparent, peer-reviewed research funding similar to that followed by the National Science Foundation (NSF) in the USA. Such a move will result in more effective research funding.

That brings me to the question of the finances of our institutions of higher learning. In a poor country like India, I believe that higher education, as well as primary and secondary education in urban areas, must be left to the private sector. The government must focus its attention and limited resources on building a mature platform for effective primary and secondary education in rural areas. Any subsidy in urban primary or secondary education must go only to poor children, and all subsidies should be provided directly to schools by the voucher mechanism devised by the well-known economist Milton Friedman. Every child worthy of admission to a college must receive either a scholarship from the college or a loan from a financing institution. The government must put in place a mechanism to force the student to repay the loan with interest, no matter whether he/she is in India or abroad. This will eliminate any need for the government to subsidize higher education or urban education. Such a paradigm will also allow higher educational institutions to charge suitable fees to provide competitive compensation to the faculty, and to create a modern infrastructure. There should be incentives for the faculty to perform better. I believe that a competitive environment in fees will eventually reduce the cost of education. When the higher education sector in Japan was opened to the private sector in the 1980s, the cost of education in private colleges was initially higher than that in public colleges. However, the private sector began to respond to the market and student choices by controlling the rise of tuition charges, and within a decade, the fee differential disappeared.

Now, let me turn to the subject of reducing the cost of admission for students. Today, students spend lots of time and money in taking multiple admission tests. I suggest a national aptitude test, similar to the American Scholastic Assessment Test (SAT) to streamline the system of admissions testing across the country. Colleges can then frame their own admission requirements through weightings using factors like national test scores, school records, academic and extra-curricular achievements, interviews, recommendations, leadership and competitive abilities. However, colleges must be transparent in their weighting systems, and publish the average admission test score of their students.

University affiliations must not limit colleges in their ability to follow their own admissions criteria. For example, the University of California (UC) is among the most prestigious universities in the USA, spanning some 150 disciplines. More UC academic programmes are rated among the top ten nationally than any other public or private university. All the ten UC university campuses have independence in both admissions and functioning.

To enable educational institutions to cater effectively to changing economic and industry needs, our educational policy should encourage greater collaboration between industry and universities in curricula and course design, as well as industry research. There are several examples of industry–academia collaboration in India. ICICI Bank has worked closely with deans and professors of several colleges to help develop course content and to provide visiting faculty to these colleges. Bharti Tele-Ventures has set up a telecommunications training school at IIT, Delhi. Infosys has established Campus Connect, an initiative to enhance the quality of teaching in technical colleges in India. Infosys also provides twenty-six PhD scholarships in the IITs, the IIMs, IISc and a few engineering colleges. The government should also encourage more collaboration between industry, research institutions and colleges through tax incentives and a deregulated environment for research.

Let us remember the words of the scientist J.J. Brunner, who said, 'As we enter the twenty-first century, the challenge faced by developing countries is to advance rapidly along the path of growth and, at the same time, to join the emerging knowledge-based economy, and the global information society.' Making our universities globally competitive will require courage in making the right changes, and perhaps, some money. I hope our leaders will summon the courage needed since every deep transformation requires courage—the courage of conviction, the courage to dream big, and the courage to face the wrath of vested interests. As far as money is concerned, I am not sure we need too much money. But, even if we need more monetary resources, we would do well to remember the words of Robert Bok, the former president of Harvard University who remarked, 'If you think education is expensive, try ignorance!'

It was Jawaharlal Nehru who said, 'For growth, our country needs a scientific temper . . . only science, education and the pursuit of knowledge can help solve our problems of poverty, of superstition, of vast resources running to waste, of a rich country inhabited by a starving people.' By enabling a renewed, re-energized education sector, we have the potential to transform our country into a true knowledge power, and realize a future of prosperity and growth.

The Unfinished Agenda

As I stand before you, my mind marvels at the vision of Ezra Cornell and Andrew White in creating 'an institution where any person can find instruction in any study'. I salute the sustained efforts of successive presidents and all of you in strengthening that vision. What an institution they have created! Four Nobel laureates, two Turing award winners and three Pulitzer Prize winners, just to name a few awards that your distinguished faculty has won. I am awestruck when I realize that this was the place where Hans Bethe spent his research career. Your alumni include such venerable names as Pearl S. Buck, Willis Carrier, Ruth Ginsburg and Sheldon Glashow and, of course, our own Jeffrey Lehman. You have been a leader in several areas including genomics, computer science, nanotechnology, agriculture and hotel management. Your research has spanned a wide canvas from the microscope to the telescope, from Asia to Latin America, and from Sanskrit to Swahili. You have indeed fulfilled the wish of Louis Agassiz of Harvard, who, at the time of inauguration of Andrew White, said, 'I hope I shall live to see the time when all the old colleges will draw fresh life from this young university.'

The world, in general, and Cornell, in particular, has made tremendous advances in science and technology. The United Nations Development Report says, 'Technology has created the potential to

A lecture delivered at the inauguration of Jeffrey Lehman as the president of Cornell University, 16 October 2003

realize in a decade, progress that required generations in the past.'
We have sent men to the moon, scaled Mount Everest and explored
Antarctica. We have conquered time and distance using digital and
satellite technology, enhanced longevity, conquered diseases and
improved health. We have increased the world GDP six-fold in the
last fifty years. We have used technology to create more economic
capital, albeit for a small part of the planet.

However, we have not made significant progress in enhancing
social capital in the world—trust, concern for the less fortunate,
honesty and fairness. The disparity between the rich and the poor has
increased. In fact, World Bank studies show that the gap between
rich and poor countries has doubled in the past forty years. The
average income in the richest twenty countries is more than thirty-
five times higher than that in the poorest twenty. It takes a worker
in a developing country producing Disney clothes and dolls 166 years
to earn as much as what Michael Eisner, the Disney president, earned
in a day. There are 1.2 billion people in this world who live in extreme
poverty on an income of less than $1 per day. About one billion
people lack access to safe drinking water. How unfortunate it is that
some still bemoan the fact that the 'four hundred richest in America'—
with a wealth exceeding the combined wealth of a billion people in
India, Bangladesh and Nepal—find it difficult to make both ends
meet since the price of a one-kilo tin of caviar has gone up by 28 per
cent to $1,048!

We have created a situation where a poor child is ashamed that
she cannot afford to buy lunch at school while hundreds of poverty
alleviators from multilateral institutions treat themselves to sumptuous
five-course meals next door. The ill-gotten deposits in Swiss banks
made by third-world despots vastly exceed the GDP of these countries.
There is a danger of protecting the interests of 6.5 million farmers in
the developed world while ignoring the interest of over a billion
farmers in the developing world. There is a continued concentration
of wealth in the hands of a few, not just in poor countries but also in
rich countries like the USA. We would do well to remember the
words of John F. Kennedy who said, 'If a society cannot help the
many who are poor, it cannot save the few who are rich.'

In a well-known corporation in the USA, while more than 3,000 employees lost their savings and were fired, the top managers made millions of dollars in bonuses and stock sales. According to a senior Securities Exchange Commission official, the senior executives of another corporation treated the company as their private bank, taking out hundreds of millions of dollars in loans and compensation without even informing the investors. In yet another case, a CEO used millions of dollars of company funds to throw a lavish party on his wife's fortieth birthday. It is not uncommon to see CEOs canvass enthusiastically for mergers and acquisitions with promises of a better bottom line. They achieve such bottom lines not by any corporate wizardry but by eliminating a large number of ordinary jobs. It is surprising that these CEOs and senior managers have to be paid retention bonuses to stay in the company after a merger that they argued for very passionately. At one company, the CEO's employment contract not only set out the model of the Mercedes the company would buy him but also promised a monthly first-class air-ticket for his mother along with a cash bonus of $10 million and other benefits. Not surprisingly, this company has already filed for bankruptcy. According to a study, the average salary of the CEOs of the Fortune 500 companies has gone up by 535 per cent in the last ten years. At the same time, the compensation of the average worker has gone up only by 32 per cent during the same period. No wonder then that Alan Greenspan was prompted to talk of this 'infectious greed' among CEOs. What is tragic is that most of the compensation is not even for true wealth created. Less than 3 per cent of the daily global flow of capital of more than $1.6 trillion is about trade. It is the same greed that you see in a casino. I am reminded of the words of the economist-thinker John Maynard Keynes who said, 'When the capital development of a country becomes the by-product of the activities of a casino, the job is likely to be ill-done.' It is not much of a consolation that such behaviour is not limited to one country but is a discernible pattern in almost every country today.

Corporate governance, which is about enhancing shareholder value on a sustainable basis while ensuring fairness to all stakeholders—customers, employees, investors, vendor-partners, the government of the land and society—is at an all-time low these days. Henry David Thoreau said, 'It is truly enough said that a corporation has no conscience. But a corporation of conscientious men is a corporation with a conscience.' However, the ability to put the interest of the company ahead of the individual is becoming rare. In a civilized society, every generation works hard to make life better for the next generation. Aspirations, value systems and confidence are being depleted. Franklin Roosevelt put this forcefully when he said, 'Small wonder that confidence languishes, for it thrives only on honesty, on honour, on the sacredness of obligations, on faithful protection and on unselfish performance; without them it cannot live.'

Why have we seen such a sharp decline in aspirations and values these days? I believe we have to bring old-fashioned leadership into vogue once again. What do I mean by this? Every nation, every company or every community that has brought about a big change has had a visionary leader leading this change. George Washington, Abraham Lincoln, Mahatma Gandhi, Winston Churchill, Martin Luther King Jr. and Nelson Mandela are a few names that come to mind immediately. In the corporate world, we have had the likes of Akio Morita of Sony and Jack Welch of General Electric.

What is common to all these people? They took a set of average people and turned them into an extraordinary force creating a better future for their country and their companies. The only resource they had was the power of the human mind. Aspiration was the main fuel to ignite these minds. They raised the aspirations of their people and encouraged them to dream the impossible, and then to work hard and smartly to convert that dream into reality. They inspired their followers to believe in themselves. Their principles are best described in the words of Ralph Waldo Emerson who said, 'What lies behind us and what lies before us are small matters compared to what lies within us.' Who would have thought that thousands of young men and women would sacrifice their lives to lead India to freedom? Who would have thought that a tired, African-American housemaid called Rosa Parks would have the courage to refuse to vacate her seat on the bus? These acts were the result of the high aspirations created by leaders like Mahatma Gandhi and Martin Luther King Jr. Aspirations build civilizations. The difference between a great country and an ordinary one is the quality of its leaders.

Today, we have to ask ourselves a fundamental question. Is the agenda of Cornell just bringing about great advances in engineering, science and liberal arts? Or do we stand for a nobler purpose? Can we make the world a better place? Do we fight for better justice in this world? Can we be catalysts in wiping the tears from the eyes of the poorest of the poor? Can we bring solace not just to the chosen few but to a forlorn child in the remote lands of Africa? Hunter Rawlings III said, 'Cornell's greatest contribution derives not from the significant knowledge that its scholars and researchers produce, but from the women and the men who carry its values with them into the world.' How can we implement his wish? Can the Cornell chime bring solace not just to the chosen few on this campus but to a forlorn child in the remote lands of Africa? It is time we stretched ourselves to address the issues beyond the boundaries of this noble country.

How can we address the myriad problems that cripple the development of mankind as a whole? I believe we can contribute significantly to solving these problems by creating Cornelians who have the courage to dream big, and the courage to stand for their convictions. They have to create trust and instil hope. For this, they have to abide by the value system of the community. A value system is a protocol for behaviour that enhances the confidence, commitment and enthusiasm of the people. It allows the community and the individual to progress on a sustainable basis. Compliance to a value system requires people who have high aspirations, self-esteem, confidence in the future and enthusiasm to take up apparently difficult tasks. We need people who will walk the talk in demonstrating their commitment to a value system. Remember Mahatma Gandhi's words, 'We must become the change we want to see in the world.'

Our agenda is still unfinished and will not be finished until we can help improve leadership across the globe. Robert Kennedy summed up the leadership challenge best when he said, 'Some men see things as they are and ask why; I dream of things that never were and say why not?' I want to see Cornell as a fertile place to produce such leaders in plenty. Knowing President Lehman and the extraordinary faculty, I have no doubt you will succeed in this noble task.

PART V

LEADERSHIP CHALLENGES

On Leadership: Lessons from the Infosys Journey

About Infosys

Infosys was founded in 1981 by seven software professionals with complementary skills, a similar value system and a modest capital of $250. The idea was to specialize in developing large, customized software applications for global customers. In the beginning, we were just seven, the founders. We started Infosys out of my bedroom, a 10x10 ft room. We were strong on hard work, commitment, energy, enthusiasm and confidence but short of money, since $250 did not really get you too far, even in 1981. I must acknowledge that there was tremendous commitment to take the company far. Now, in 2007, we will exceed $3 billion in global revenue. Infosys has been voted the most respected company, the best employer, the best managed company, and the best in corporate governance in India. It has won most of the awards in Asia and several on a global scale. The company got listed in India in 1993 and on NASDAQ in 1999, and its market capitalization is around $27 billion.

What is leadership?

Who is a leader? What are his or her attributes and responsibilities? Prosperity in a community, corporation, society or a nation comes from economic progress, stability, peace and harmony. Progress is

---

A lecture delivered at the Bloomberg Leadership Conference, New York, 26 February 2007

positive change. A leader is first and last a change agent. Progress is his agenda. His responsibility is to raise the aspirations of his people, to make them more confident, energetic, enthusiastic, hopeful, and determined to seek a glorious future for the community and for themselves.*

Leaders obviously have to walk the untrodden path, the road less travelled, and they have to take huge risks. Robert Kennedy summed up the leadership challenge best when, borrowing the words of George Bernard Shaw, he said, 'Some men see things as they are and ask why; I dream of things that never were and say why not?' To me, this is perhaps the best summation of the leadership challenge. The challenge is to see what most people do not see, to accept what most people wonder about and are scared of, and then say, 'I will take up this challenge because it is aspirational, honourable and the right thing to do.'

Vision
What is the first task of a leader in energizing his people? It is creating a grand vision—a purpose which is noble, lofty and aspirational. It is a dream that should excite and energize everybody in the community or corporation. The leader has to craft and articulate a vision in which everybody sees a better future for himself. The vision has to be powerful enough to make every tired mind and body that leaves the office in the evening come back early the next morning, saying: 'I am proud to belong to this company and I will work hard to make it a better company.'

When seven of us met in the small bedroom of my apartment in Bombay in May 1981, we had a four-hour-long discussion on what the dream for the company should be. We started off with the dream of becoming the software services company with the largest revenue. I rejected it. The next idea was to become the largest job creators in India. I said 'no' to that as well. Then, we moved on to whether we should strive to be the software services company with the highest market capitalization. When I rejected that too, there was considerable

---

*For the sake of brevity, I will use 'he' to denote both genders.

consternation among my colleagues. Finally, they got tired, and asked, 'What do you want to do?' I said, 'I want this to be the most respected software services company in the world.' And I continued, 'If you seek respect, you will not short-change your customers, you will be fair to your colleagues in the company, you will be transparent with your investors, you will treat your vendor partners with care and understanding, you will not violate the laws of the land in whichever country you operate, and you will live in harmony in whichever society you operate in. My conviction is that such a pursuit will bring revenues, jobs, profits and market capitalization.'

I was happy that all my colleagues accepted the idea. They perceived this vision as something larger than life, and something more inspirational to go after than mere profits, revenues and market capitalization. Thanks to this dream of seeking respect, revenues have come in, jobs have been created, profits have accumulated and market capitalization has been achieved. And this has all happened in an environment of energy, enthusiasm, happiness, joy, satisfaction, and confidence amongst all my colleagues—fifty thousand Infoscions today. Similarly you, as leaders in whatever area you operate in or whatever function you are in charge of, have to define a vision which transcends the mundane day-to-day challenges to get the best out of your people.

Communicating vision and values
Having defined a powerful and attractive vision, you have to communicate the power of that vision to a large number of people in your organization. It is very unlikely that you will be able to meet everybody you work with. Today, we are a company with fifty thousand people; we operate in thirty-eight countries; and we have people of forty-five nationalities. No matter how hard I try, it is not possible for me to interact one-on-one with every one of these people. Hence, we use several indirect and surrogate mechanisms to communicate our vision to a large group of people in the company— simple and powerful messages, multiple tiers of leaders, meeting in small groups and, most importantly, leadership by example.

Communication is most impactful and yields the best results

when you use simple, direct and powerful statements or quotes to convey your ideas. At Infosys, our vision is 'to be a globally respected software corporation that delivers best-of-breed, end-to-end business solutions leveraging technology and employing best-in-class professionals'. This is a good vision but would have failed unless we brought exhilaration, joy, enthusiasm and energy to the minds of our people to translate this vision to reality. Hence, we use the famous adage 'A plausible impossibility is better than a convincing possibility' to make every Infoscion remember that his mission is to satisfy our customers by making the plausibly-impossible happen. We want him to reach for the impossible in every situation because it is plausible, it is inspirational, and it is desirable, rather than reaching for the mundane and easily-attainable goals in satisfying the customer.

Similarly, we use a few other sayings to facilitate easy and direct communication of our values, duties, obligations, beliefs, dreams and aspirations. For example, our value system is communicated by the simple adage, 'The softest pillow is a clear conscience.' Our commitment to transparency is communicated by the adage, 'When in doubt, disclose.'

Trust is very important

Every aspirational objective requires tremendous courage, hard work, teamwork and sacrifice. How does a leader ensure that his people commit to such hard work and sacrifice in the short term with the hope that he will be better off in the long term? To get such commitment from his people, a leader has to become trustworthy. When you articulate your vision to your group or function, it is generally seen as pure rhetoric or, at best, a statement of lofty purpose, since there is no data to prove that you will indeed be successful. There is an element of huge risk since you will take your team on a road less travelled or sometimes even a road not travelled at all.

If you want your people to follow you like the faithful followed Moses, they have to have implicit trust and faith in you. How does a leader create trust? At Infosys, we have looked at various instruments to create trust. After considerable thinking and researching, we realized, pretty early in the founding of the organization, that the best instrument for creating trust is to demonstrate our commitment to our vision and our values through leadership-by-example or 'walking the talk'. After all, if thousands of people who work with you see you practising your precepts in pursuit of lofty goals of the corporation, they are likely to believe your words and trust you.

Courage is the first attribute of a great leader

I was once asked by the CEO of a Fortune-10 corporation what was the first attribute a leader must possess if his other attributes have to find utterance. It took me ten seconds to say it was courage. He asked me, 'Why do you think courage is the most important attribute of a leader?' I replied, 'If you want to walk the untrodden path, if you want to dream big, if you want the organization to take risks, if you want to have conviction, if you want to go against the conventional wisdom, if you want to take tough and unpopular decisions, if you want to communicate to your people that a plausible impossibility is better than a convincing possibility, then you must have courage.' I do not know of any great leader, whether in a corporation or a nation, who has not demonstrated courage.

Demonstrate your commitment to values

If we want our people to be enthusiastic about the future and make sacrifices, we have to create a climate where everybody is confident that nobody else in the team will short-change him. That, to me, is the value system. A value system is the protocol for behaviour of an individual in a group required to enhance the trust, confidence, energy, enthusiasm and hope of every other individual in the group. That is, if I am a member of your group, I must conduct myself in such a manner that every one of you would say, 'I am much more optimistic about this group today than yesterday.' That is where a value system becomes extremely important. Progress involves teamwork and sacrifice from every member of the corporation. Progress happens when every member is confident that everybody else is also putting in the required hard work and making the necessary sacrifices.

A value system cannot remain purely rhetorical. It has to be demonstrated in action from time to time by the leaders. Let me give you an example. In 1995, we had to wait for a few months for permission from the Government of India to start an office in Boston. So, we decided to invest the money earmarked for setting up the new office in the secondary market, hoping we would get some decent returns in the interim. It turned out that we did not have enough expertise to invest our free cash successfully in the secondary market, and we incurred some losses. At that time, according to the Indian GAAP (General Accepted Accounting Principle), it was not mandatory to provide low-level details of losses in non-core business activities. But since we had made a commitment to our shareholders that we would bring the bad news early and proactively to them, I said, 'I want to be known to our shareholders as an honest person first, and then as a smart person. So, let us give them full details of our losses.' We went to the shareholders and said, 'We have lost this much money by investing in the secondary market. This was a mistake. We have learnt our lesson. We will not repeat this mistake.' Many of my friends in the Indian corporate world were surprised by this. But the shareholders were happy about our transparency. We have many schemes in the company to honour compliance with our value system. For example, the person who demonstrates the best compliance with the Infosys value system during the year is recognized and honoured as the Value Champion of the Year.

Openness and fairness

I believe that openness and fairness is another powerful instrument leaders have to earn the trust of their people. In the Indian culture, the family is a very strong unit and brings the best of sacrifice, kindness, openness and fairness from all the members. So, I often tell my colleagues, 'When you deal with your colleagues, you have to operate as if you are in a family.' At all points of time, all doors are open at Infosys and any employee is welcome to walk into anyone's office to discuss issues. The best way of ensuring fairness in a transaction is to use data and facts to decide on the merits of the transaction. By doing so, you raise the confidence of your colleagues in the fairness and openness of the system. Even those who lose a transaction are likely to say, 'My boss tried hard to be fair to me.

Next time, if I have better data and facts on my side, I will win.' This way, people are confident to work smarter and harder even after they lose a transaction. Our commitment to openness and fairness is exemplified by the famous adage, 'In God we trust, everybody else brings data to the table.'

Create an inclusive environment

Another important lesson we have learnt in motivating people is the power of inclusion. A great motivator for human beings is self-esteem. Self-esteem gets enhanced when people participate in making decisions that affect them. In other words, you cannot create two classes of people—those who rule and those who are ruled. An inclusive system enhances the self-esteem, enthusiasm, energy, confidence and hope of everyone in the organization. Such a system helps people deal with their fellow colleagues with respect, dignity and affection. We use the adage 'Praise in public, criticize in private' to communicate the power of such courtesy to fellow employees. This is also a sure way of holding your people accountable for performance. As long as you praise people for their performance in public, you will earn the right to criticize them in private. We use the adage 'You can disagree with me as long as you are not disagreeable' to emphasize the importance of being courteous in dealing with colleagues.

A leader is nothing without people to lead

Leadership is not about you. It is about how you can bring aspirations, confidence, joy, hope, enthusiasm and energy to your people. To do this, you must behave in a manner that people flock to you to seek help, solace, guidance, confidence and joy. A good leader makes people feel an inch taller in his presence. He is generous. He is confident and decisive. He is firm but courteous. He shows his frailties since people want to see him as a normal human being rather than a superman. After all, he is their role model and people want to emulate him and reach his position. Show that you have emotions; that you laugh, cry, can be frustrated and even fail. Above all, be humble. Take your work seriously but not yourself. You are not indispensable. The world continued to prosper even after some of its finest leaders departed, and will do so even without the best of you.

The power of feedback

Feedback from known and sometimes even anonymous sources is the best instrument that a leader has to correct his mistakes and calibrate his performance. I know several powerful corporate and national leaders who failed miserably because they ignored feedback.

Enduring attributes of a successful corporation

What are the most important, time-invariant and context-invariant attributes for the success of a corporation? They are: openness to new ideas, meritocracy and justice, speed, imagination and excellence in execution. Openness to new ideas is very important to raise the confidence and self-esteem of people and get the best out of them in the organization. It is also a sure way of fostering innovation. An ideal organization is one which practises the hierarchy of ideas rather than the hierarchy of titles. Such an organization puts the best person in each position, creates an open environment and harvests the best ideas, ignoring the hierarchical rigidities of the organization. As long as you constantly ask the questions, 'Can we do things faster today than yesterday, last month, last quarter and last year?', 'Can we bring better ideas to the table today than yesterday, last month, last quarter and last year?', and 'Can we execute those ideas with a better level of excellence and quality today than yesterday, last month, last quarter and last year?', I believe you will create a learning organization and will succeed on a sustainable basis. I strongly believe that these attributes are extremely important for the enduring success of a corporation.

I also believe that every organization must look at two very important financial parameters for measuring success, in addition to many non-financial parameters: first, the per-capita revenue productivity, and second, the net-after-tax dollars earned per employee per year. The latter measure has a direct impact on your earnings per share, enhances the confidence of your employees, and allows you to pay your people better. At Infosys, these two measures are used as primary financial parameters to measure the success of every group.

The primary responsibilities of a CEO

The primary responsibilities of a CEO at Infosys are summed up by the acronym PSPD. The first P stands for 'predictability of revenues'. That is, how good your forecasting system is, and how well you can predict the company's revenues for the next month, quarter and year. S stands for 'sustainability'. It tells you how good your system is to actually achieve the sales forecast; how smart your sales people are in beating the pavement, making customer calls, persuading them and closing sales; how good your company is in delivering what was promised, on time, within budget, and with the requisite quality; how efficient you are in raising invoices on time; and, finally, how good you are in collecting the full invoice amount on time in a friendly manner from the customer. The second P stands for 'profitability'. I believe that every great corporation has to make money hand over fist. Unless you are profitable, there is no point in playing the game. Unless you have the best profitability in the industry, you are not the smartest. Of course, you have to achieve such profits legally, ethically and in a manner that makes every one of your colleagues happy and proud. Finally, the last letter, D, stands for 'de-risking'. De-risking is about the systems, processes, information and actions that ensure minimization of risk to the corporation in every dimension of its operation. At Infosys, we have created the Risk Mitigation Council to ensure that we do not depend too much on one customer, one country, one key employee, one technology, or one application area. This is how we endeavour to make the future of the organization safe.

Good corporate governance is the bottom-line

Let me end by reminding you of the importance of complying with the best principles of corporate governance in these troubled times when the credibility of our community is low. This is key to long-term success, and is a tenet that I believe is at the heart of Infosys's reputation.

A Leadership Mindset for a Resurgent India

We live in extraordinary times. Never before in the last three hundred years has India received the kind of attention that it does today. Whichever conference I attend around the world, India's growth is talked about and India is mentioned along with China. There are umpteen books written about India. People ask me about the secret sauce for India's success in software and BPO. Taxi drivers in places like New York, London and Sao Paulo ask me about how India has managed to attract the attention of the world. The figures substantiate these perceptions. We have become a trillion dollar economy. Our exports have doubled in the last three years. The rupee is becoming stronger by the day. In July 2007, we added 8.4 million new mobile telephone subscribers. Our FDI in 2008 will be around $25 billion, five times what it was two years ago. New airports are being built in major cities. In Delhi, you see work on the expansion of the metro rail wherever you go. An Indian, Mukesh Ambani, was the richest person in the world for a week, and remains among the top five in the world. The list is endless. This is the time for us to consolidate on this progress, work harder and smarter, and bring about inclusive growth. We have to invest the benefits of our economic growth into making life better for all Indians, not just the elite as it has happened so far. This is possible if we focus on improving infrastructure, improving agricultural productivity and moving people

Published in *Business Today*, 7 January 2008

away from agriculture to low-tech manufacturing in rural and semi-urban areas. All of these are possible if we break away from our traditional mindset, stop denying we have problems, become open to new ideas and possibilities, and create a culture of high performance.

In my opinion, openness to new ideas, the ability to learn from people who have performed better than us, openness to admitting problems and to accepting that there is room for improvement are important attributes of an effective leader. Here, I will talk about how such changes in mindset are taking place in the country from the top to the bottom. I will give some examples of how openness to new ideas is enhancing the image of the country. I will also describe a few examples of how rigidity and adherence to the old mindset at certain levels of the bureaucracy is blurring that image.

Accepting that we have problems is crucial to our progress. In my opinion, this progress is more important than the ones we see in our economy, in our physical infrastructure or in our stock markets. This openness stems from self-confidence. This openness is what will help us to accept challenges and solve our problems, rather than being in the state of denial that our leaders have become habituated to. For the first time in the last forty years, I see a few of our leaders confident enough to accept that we indeed have problems in basic areas of education, health care and nutrition, that other nations have performed better than us, and that we will solve our problems by working hard and intelligently. At the recently-concluded Asia Business Council (ABC) meeting in New Delhi, my foreign CEO friends from Asia, Europe and the USA were very impressed with the openness of Prime Minister Manmohan Singh, Rahul Gandhi, Montek Singh Ahluwalia and Kamal Nath. In every one of these meetings, our leaders were gracious, modest, confident, used data to argue their points, and did not use superlatives to describe India's progress. They admitted that we have problems of income disparity, that we lack basic infrastructure and that we have a big job to do in the areas of primary education, health care, nutrition and shelter. My interaction with our Central ministers indicates that this change is becoming pervasive and that you do not see the ghost of the argumentative Indian in our leaders as often as we saw earlier. This is the start of a great journey.

While I see this mindset of openness taking root at the Central level, I still see a challenge at the level of the states. However, there are several good examples of a progressive and open mindset among ministers at the state level as well. Vijayaraje Scindia, Uma Bharati and Buddhadeb Bhattacharya, who have been chief ministers of Rajasthan, Madhya Pradesh and West Bengal respectively, are good examples of such openness. D.B. Inamdar's name comes to my mind when I talk of open mindsets among ministers in Karnataka. Inamdar was the Information Technology minister several years ago when the board of governors of the Indian Institute of Information Technology, Bangalore (IIITB) was solving the difficult problem of finding a permanent home for IIITB. But for his proactive and open mindset towards solving problems quickly using new paradigms, I do not think we could have gained such a beautiful home for IIITB. Similarly, Minister H.D. Revanna's progressive policies and quick decision-making helped Electronic City get the much-needed sub-station to handle its power problems.

My friend Raghunath Mashelkar (former Director General, Council of Scientific and Industrial Research) often says we fight a constant battle between our mind which is the engine of problem-solving, and our mindset which is a set of beliefs and dogmas. He notes that the mindset prevents the mind from taking bold and innovative decisions based on openness to data and facts. He believes that only those of us who win the battle in favour of the mind will make progress. Today, I see a slow shift towards putting the mind over the mindset among our leaders.

While I see a fundamental shift towards openness among most of our senior bureaucrats, I do not see that shift percolating downwards. I will give you two examples to demonstrate this. The first is about my experience with Shiv Shankar Menon, our current Foreign Secretary. Mr Menon is one of the finest bureaucrats this country has produced. He is a fine gentleman, courteous, always willing to help, and constantly on the move to improve the efficiency of his department. A couple of years ago, the government had issued a sixty-four-page passport, but had quickly stopped that practice and continued with the usual thirty-six-page version. Last year, I requested Mr Menon to provide a 240-page passport to those of us travelling abroad frequently, so that we do not have to get new passports every few months. This would also increase the validity of our visas since many countries require us to obtain new visas whenever we change the passport, New Zealand being an example of this policy. I told him that the sixty-four-page passport was not very convenient since the frequency of travel abroad was high in our industry, and that we would be happy to pay all the expenses needed for a 240-page passport. Being an extraordinarily open-minded leader, he readily agreed and promised me that we would have such a passport. He obviously and rightly expected people in his department to handle this task. A few months later, I was informed that there would be a ceremony in Bangalore where the minister of state for External Affairs would give me the first new jumbo passport. I was thrilled. But when I received the new passport, I found that that it was the same old sixty-four-page passport. The officials present explained that it was not possible to produce a 240-page passport since the ministry press did not have a machine which could stitch 240 pages! It is surprising that, at a time when India plans to land a satellite on the moon, we cannot import, if not produce, a machine that can stitch 240 passport pages. The problem lies in the mindset of the people lower down in the Ministry of External Affairs. This example shows how an extraordinary leader's initiatives can be derailed by the outdated mindset of a few people working under the leader. This has to change.

I will give you one more example of our antiquated mindset. The CEO of a very famous Fortune 500 US company wanted to get an Indian visa to participate in the Asia Business Council (ABC) meeting in New Delhi. When his office contacted the Indian Consulate General's office in his area, his secretary was told that he would have to leave his passport with the Indian Consulate for thirty days to get a visa! The CEO informed the ABC secretariat that his frequent travels would not allow him to leave his passport for so long a time, and that he would therefore not be able to attend the ABC conference in Delhi. Ronen Sen, our ambassador in the USA, came to know about this through a cabinet minister in Delhi. He picked up the phone, called the CEO, apologized and requested his staff to expedite the process. His department immediately carried out the mandatory checks and issued a five-year multiple-entry visa, gratis, the same day. I heard endless praise for India from the CEO. Such fulsome praise made the country look good in front of ABC members whose companies have a total market capitalization of more than a trillion dollars. This is another powerful example of how some people within our government institutions have still not adapted to the changed circumstances and blur the good image of the country even though the top-level bureaucrats have made tremendous efforts to bring about a new mindset into the government. If we want more FDI, as the prime minister has indicated several times, we have to make it comfortable for international business leaders to visit India. We cannot take refuge under the reciprocity issue which is the argument used by some junior bureaucrats to justify outdated procedures.

While I am worried that the desire for openness has still not become pervasive across all levels in our government institutions, I have come across several examples of positive change. The pro-action of the Income Tax department at Bangalore in introducing IT systems for filing income tax returns by our employees electronically, the extraordinary work of the Software Technology Park in being a catalyst to the IT industry all over the country, the efficient officials of the customs department at Bangalore, and the 'under-promise, over-deliver' attitude of Maharashtra, Rajasthan and Orissa government officials are all good examples of such an open mindset that admits we can improve and takes steps to improve.

How does one instil in our people an openness to accept that one could be wrong and somebody else may have a better idea? At Infosys, we realized early enough that the best way to focus on the best solutions and to solve problems quickly is to start every new transaction on a zero base, without any bias from previous transactions, and to use data and facts to argue our case. Such an approach enhances the confidence of our youngsters in meritocracy, in our fairness and in our desire to be inclusive. That is why the famous adage, 'In God we trust, everybody else brings data to the table' is very popular at Infosys.

PART VI

CORPORATE AND PUBLIC
GOVERNANCE

Good Corporate Governance:
A Checklist or a Mindset?

I am going to focus on a topic close to my heart and crucial to the survival of businesses across the globe: good corporate governance. In recent times, this topic has received much attention throughout the world including the emerging markets. We in India have made considerable progress in this area over the last ten years.

I will focus primarily on the advances in corporate governance that have been made in the USA. The USA is the world's most dynamic capital market, and US financial institutions have been leaders in helping corporations across the world raise capital. It is fair to say, therefore, that governance initiatives in the US capital market serve as the harbinger of things to come in other capital markets. 'When the US capital market sneezes, capital markets in every other country catch a cold' is a well-accepted saying. Thus, any observations regarding the US market are bound to be valid for other markets as well.

I have used examples of the violation of corporate governance among US corporations since these are big-ticket items. My own belief is that the incidence of corporate fraud is about the same everywhere.

Corporate governance, to me, is about maximizing shareholder

Robert P. Maxon Lecture, George Washington University, Washington DC, 6 February 2006

value legally, ethically and on a sustainable basis while ensuring fairness to every stakeholder—the company's customers, employees, investors, vendor-partners, the government of the land and the community. Thus, corporate governance is a reflection of a company's culture, policies, how it deals with its stakeholders, and its commitment to values.

Good corporate governance serves several important objectives. It enhances corporate performance by creating an environment that motivates managers to maximize returns on investment, enhance operational efficiency and ensure long-term productivity growth. Consequently, such corporations attract the best talent on a global basis. It also ensures that corporations conform with the interests of investors and society by creating fairness, transparency and accountability in business activities among employees, management and the board.

Longevity is the best index of the success of a corporation, and good governance is a necessary condition for longevity and growth. Corporate growth requires investment. Good corporate governance increases public confidence in a corporation, and is likely to lower the cost of capital for investment. According to a McKinsey study, over 60 per cent of investors cite good governance practices in a corporation as a key factor in their investment decisions.

Today, global capital is not constrained by national boundaries, and flows where it finds a hospitable climate. There is tremendous competition among all nations—developed and developing—to attract global entrepreneurs to create high-quality, high-income jobs. These entrepreneurs require massive inflows of capital and they realize that an effective governance model is a big plus in attracting investment.

Let me now trace the history of efforts towards improving corporate governance. The trigger for the Great Depression of the 1930s in the USA, as the writer Joel Bakan notes, was corporate mismanagement and indifference towards workers. It even led, as Bakan points out, to a 1933 Supreme Court ruling which condemned corporations as 'Frankenstein's monsters, capable of doing evil'. The public perception resulted in the establishment of the SEC (Securities and Exchange Commission) in 1934, leading to regulatory reform defining corporate ownership and control. However, the legislation failed to clearly address responsibilities relating to 'acceptable behaviour' and levels of disclosure for corporations.

During the 1970s, a series of business scandals led to an unveiling of pervasive, unethical practices in US corporations. SEC investigations revealed widespread illegal contracting practices, insider trading, deceptive advertising, and savings-and-loan scandals. The lawyers Alton Harris and Andrea Kreamer note that over 500 publicly-held US firms, including 117 of the then Fortune 500 companies, were charged by the SEC or confessed to corporate misconduct.

The governance failures of the 1970s and 1980s set the minds of the public and the regulators on improving the governance of corporations. The best minds were deployed to create frameworks for enhancing the accountability of corporations to shareholders-at-large. The result was a surfeit of good governance codes issued across the globe by securities exchange commissions, stock exchanges and investor associations. Some of the most influential initiatives have come from the Treadway Commission and the SEC Blue Ribbon Committee in the USA, the Cadbury Committee in the UK, the Vienot Report in France, and the Peters Report in the Netherlands.

The common view of all these committees was that good governance required effective board functioning through informed, independent directors, empowered board sub-committees, and improved board transparency to management functioning. They also recommended enhanced disclosure levels in financial and risk reporting to shareholders.

Outside the USA, the UK Cadbury Committee report has served as a pioneer in advancing the levels of corporate governance across the globe. This committee, as the writer Paul Coombes points out, made significant recommendations on the structure, independence and responsibilities of boards. It also made recommendations towards effective internal financial controls, and the remuneration of directors and executives. This effort contributed to the increased effectiveness of corporate boards in the UK, and sparked similar initiatives in the British Commonwealth countries.

In the USA, recommendations for auditors were taken up by the

1999 SEC Blue Ribbon Committee. The recommendations aimed to improve the independence, operations and effectiveness of audit committees. These recommendations became law.

Coombes also notes that the most effective codes such as the Cadbury Code have operated on a 'comply or explain' basis. That is, corporations are not required to comply with any provision of the code. However, if the corporation decides against following any of the code's provisions, it must explain its reasons for not doing so.

It was expected that the efforts of the Cadbury Committee and SEC committees would usher in an era of disciplined corporate behaviour and good governance. Unfortunately, this confidence was short-lived. Prescriptions from the wise men and women of these committees failed to curb financial mismanagement and the rise of corporate fraud in the late 1990s and the early part of this millennium.

As a result, the 1990s was the era of the stock-option-fattened, superman-superwoman CEOs who could do no wrong in the eyes of their admiration-heavy boards, and who were seen as demigods. Lax oversight by boards made these CEOs more or less omnipotent. The boards became corporate allies of these CEOs primarily to serve their interests. In this environment, the regulations achieved little. As McLean and Elkind put it in *The Smartest Guys in the Room*, regulatory compliance 'equated telling the truth to making sure that no one could prove that you lied'. Accountants found ways to circumvent accounting rules, and investment bankers invented complex financial structures to make mandatory disclosures look rosier. Reward-hungry employees followed illegal orders without a murmur.

It is no wonder that this climate led to Enron's spectacular collapse in 2001 and the collapse of WorldCom, Qwest and Tyco in 2002. Significant accounting irregularities emerged—the overstating of profits by billions of dollars, and illegal, off-the-book partnerships and loans. These corporations exemplified entire organizational cultures dominated by greed, arrogance and utter disregard for the law to the immense cost of shareholders. It is estimated that the scandals at Enron, WorldCom, Qwest, Tyco and others resulted in a loss of more than $7 trillion in market capital, the largest in the history of capitalism.

The general belief is that such abuse of power was not confined to these corporations alone. According to Malcolm S. Salter, the lack of corporate governance 'was not a case of the odd duck or the five-legged cow, but one of widespread malfeasance'. The excessive pay for senior management has been just one illustration of a broad failure in governance. The ratio of US CEO compensation to the pay of the average production worker jumped to 431:1 in 2004. In 1990, that ratio was 107:1, and in 1982, it was 42:1. The aggregate compensation for top-five corporate executives in the USA was 10 per cent of aggregate corporate earnings in 1998–2002, up from 6 per cent of aggregate corporate earnings during 1993–97.

The high-profile scandals and rising investor dissatisfaction with governance practices led to demands to 'raise the baseline' of mandatory disclosure and compliance by corporations. 'No longer is corporate governance an arcane topic for high-minded legal debate. Today there is new, widespread concern regarding the standards of corporate behaviour,' is how the then SEC chairman Arthur Levitt reacted. These concerns have triggered a shift away from 'soft law' such as comply-or-explain requirements. The emphasis is now on 'hard law'—mandatory compliance requirements, with governance practices strictly supervised by the regulator.

In the USA, the Sarbanes–Oxley (SOX) Act and the revised New York Stock Exchange and NASDAQ listing rules have created more stringent standards for financial disclosure, committee and board nominations, and audit policies. Other countries have followed the USA in implementing stricter compliance. For example, a proposed legislation in the UK would give investors the right to sue directors for negligence and breach of duty. The European Commission expects that its new corporate governance directive, scheduled to take effect by 2009, will enhance transparency laws and empower shareholders. In Asia, revised corporate governance regulations in several countries such as Hong Kong, Singapore and India mandate a much stricter standard of compliance for corporations.

Let me now talk a little bit about the Sarbanes–Oxley Act (SOX). This act represents a shift towards government regulation of corporate standards relating to auditing, accounting, quality control, ethics and independence through the Public Company Accounting Oversight Board (PCAOB). In many ways, SOX represents meaningful progress in restoring management and board accountability, increasing shareholder responsiveness and ensuring sound governance. For example, SOX has mandated the adoption of a code of conduct and ethics for principal officers including the board of directors of the corporation. It requires well-defined processes for the protection of whistleblowers within the company.

SOX has also mandated new audit requirements and increased independence for audit committees. New performance measures have shifted focus towards long-term shareholder value creation. It has also renewed information transparency through organization-wide ownership of risk controls. A landmark development through SOX is Section 404 which requires the company's CEO and CFO to annually assess internal controls and sign written statements, acknowledging responsibility in maintaining controls over financial reporting. Any violations and false declarations can result in heavy penalties including imprisonment and fines of up to $20 million. As of December 2005, approximately 12 per cent of corporations worldwide had failed the SOX 404 test.

There are areas for improvement within SOX as well. It has to focus more on substance than form, and move from rule-based accounting to the setting of objectives-oriented accounting standards. It must address the inadequacy of the current business reporting framework. Both the management and investors need more 'qualitative' information like business opportunities, risks, strategies and plans. Such information permits a clear assessment of the quality, sustainability and variability of a corporation's cash flows and earnings. The SOX framework must clarify the role of the audit committee. It must also help enhance the base of accounting firms and develop a broad, competitive audit market.

The recent move by the SEC to mandate full disclosure for managerial compensation and perks is a welcome one. Without such disclosure, we have to agree with Nobel Laureate economist Joseph Stiglitz's observation that 'we have distorted knowledge of how company value is distributed among shareholders, employees and management'. As I described earlier, many CEOs have created significant asymmetries in compensation within their corporations through undisclosed perks and incentives. For example, one CEO was paid $800 million including perks over a thirteen-year period—a period during which his company profits had plunged, and shares provided lower returns than even Treasury bonds.

While SOX and other initiatives have created a good framework for better governance, I do believe that such focus on rules-based regulation can only succeed if we create a mindset for decency, honesty and respectability among corporate leaders. It is true that, by and large, most business leaders are committed to these values. However, our focus has to be towards creating disincentives for the small minority who disregard them.

A continued shift towards 'hard law' and greater regulation in corporate governance can result in what the *Wall Street Journal* calls 'governance at gunpoint'. Regulating every aspect of corporate behaviour is impossible without adversely impacting operational flexibility of a corporation, discouraging risk-taking, and penalizing the progress of even honest corporations.

Government regulation is, after all, a form of ethics that is externally mandated. It is instructive to remember the words of former US President Bill Clinton who said, 'We must consider how excessive business regulation and "box-ticking" will ensure business performance.' An unethical company can bypass even the most draconian regulation. It can incorporate every governance practice in form, and still possess none in substance. Consequently, good corporate governance cannot be legislated through a mere 'checklist' of rules and regulations. Let us remember that despite increasingly stringent legislation, excessive top management compensation—the most visible sign of management power—has continued unabated in the last few years. In 2004, corporations that comprise the S&P 500 index saw median chief-executive compensation increase by 30.2 per cent to $6 million, compared with a 15 per cent rise in 2003. Clearly, we must address the basic cause of corporate malfeasance—the lack of a strong environment for good governance within the corporation. My belief is that any system is as good as the people who use it.

Hence, the focus has to move towards creating an environment where respectability matters.

The first area of focus is bringing better balance of power between the management and the board. As we have seen, governance reform has, so far, failed to create an effective balance of power between shareholders, management and the board of directors. Board independence from management continues to be affected by directors who have limited accountability to shareholders, and are ill-equipped in exercising management oversight. It is estimated that, on average, one-third of the board members of American corporations lack the necessary industry knowledge and experience to contribute effectively to management oversight. My guess is that this percentage is even higher among most other countries. This lack of expertise has resulted in an asymmetry of power favouring management in most decision-making in corporate boards.

Hence, the first step is to select informed people with integrity and independence of mind for board positions. These people must be taken through a robust training and certification programme on board governance. The business-specific part of the programme may be held by the officers of the corporation while the board governance training can be held by specialist organizations.

Secondly, every year, there should be a peer evaluation for each member of the board. At Infosys, this exercise is handled by the chairman of the nominations committee. The parameters used for such an evaluation are in the realm of board governance. The chairman of the board sits with each board member, discusses his/her evaluation, and suggests remedies and course-corrections. The chairman's performance review is handled by the lead independent director.

Corporate governance suffers in companies where the allegiance of independent directors is to the officers of the company rather than to its shareholders. To make the shareholder–board relationship more effective, we need better shareholder surveillance. Shareholders must actively step up as owners, and engage directors on corporate issues. Independent directors in general, and chairmen of all committees in particular, must participate more actively in annual general meetings by owning up to their board decisions and answering shareholder queries.

The abuse of corporate power results from incentives within firms that encourage a culture of corruption. For example, former employees within a now-demised corporation described a 'yes man' culture in which only those employees who did everything to please their bosses prospered. As Tom Tierney, former managing partner of Bain Consultancy remarked, 'Corporate culture is what determines how people behave when they are not being watched.' Unethical companies have typified corporate cultures that voiced their commitment to one value system while their processes and incentives reflected an entirely different value system in practice. The responsibility to change this lies with the top management.

Clearly, good governance requires a mindset within the corporation which integrates the corporate code of ethics into the day-to-day activities of its managers and workers. As the sociologists Rossouw and van Vuuren note, companies must move from the 'reactive and compliance mode' of corporate ethics to the 'integrity mode', where the functions of the entire organization are completely aligned with its value system. To achieve this, we must address the system of incentives that exists within corporations.

Corporations must integrate their value systems into their recruitment programmes. They must mandate compliance with their values as a key requirement from each potential employee. They must ensure that every employee owns responsibility for accountability and ethics in every transaction. Corporations must also publicly recognize internal role models for ethical behaviour. They must reinforce exemplary ethical conduct among employees through reward and recognition programmes. Ethical standards and best practices must be applied fairly and uniformly across all levels of the organization. Any non-compliance must be swiftly dealt with and publicized. Additionally, there should be strong whistleblower mechanisms within the corporation for exposing unethical or illegal activities.

The need of the hour is for all voices in a corporation to unanimously extol the values of decency, honesty and transparency. In other words, every employee has to appreciate that the future of the corporation is safe only if he/she does the right thing in every transaction. At Infosys, every Infoscion is encouraged to act according to our belief that 'the softest pillow is a clear conscience'.

Corporations have to create systems, structures and incentives to promote transparency, since transparency brings accountability. At Infosys, every employee remembers and follows the adage, 'When in doubt, disclose.'

None of this can happen unless corporate leaders believe in the values of the company, and walk the talk. Corporate leaders are powerful role models. Every employee watches them carefully and imitates them. For example, many corporations talk about cutting costs as a way to improve profitability. Such cost consciousness has to come from the top. If we want our employees to spend carefully, we, the leaders, have to show the way. Unfortunately, this rarely happens. It is instructive to remember Peter Drucker's observation that 'corporate leaders wear a badge of increased distinction and responsibility'. They must, therefore, be held to a higher standard of behaviour. We need CEOs who are men and women of integrity—people who will walk the talk in demonstrating their commitment to a strong value system.

Great corporate leaders are expert simplifiers. They operate on simple business rules. Such rules are easy to understand, easy to follow, and easy to communicate. After all, you cannot cheat people with simple rules. Without exception, every corporation that violated basic governance principles did so by creating a web of complex and confusing rules.

We need broader market reforms to create incentives for good governance. As John Bogle, the former CEO of Vanguard Mutual Funds notes, 'Our markets have played a key role in creating incentives for the mismanagement of funds by corporations.' For example, speculative investment and an emphasis on short-term gains in capital markets have limited the focus on sustainable business growth. Industry reforms which emphasize the long-term performance of fund managers and institutional investors would encourage a focus on sustainable business growth. Additionally, we must focus our efforts towards streamlining corporate taxes. Multiple tax shelters disincentivize compliance.

These are the days of globalization. In a global environment, it is best if all nations can agree to quickly adopt the IAS (International Accounting Standards) as their accounting standard. This move will make it easy to compare the performance of corporations in an industry across countries. In the absence of such a uniform accounting standard, Infosys has demonstrated its investor-friendliness by becoming the first company on NASDAQ to produce its balance sheet and income statement according to the GAAPs (Generally Accepted Accounting Principles) of eight countries from where we have investors—India, USA, Canada, UK, France, Germany, Japan and Australia.

Corporations must ensure that incentives for senior management and board members are effectively aligned with responsible governance and long-term corporate health. The pay of principal officers must be directly linked to overall performance covering all functions of the corporation—operational health and efficiency, client and employee satisfaction, and shareholder value.

Warren Buffett believes that CEO pay remains the acid test if corporate America is serious about reforming itself. Senior management compensation must be based on the principles of fairness, transparency and accountability. Fairness of compensation with respect to the compensation of the lowest level employee is crucial to gaining the trust of employees. After all, no leader can be effective in a vacuum. He/she requires the dedication and commitment of each one of his/her employees for success. Transparency of compensation vis-à-vis shareholders and employees creates a climate of trust in top management. Shareholders will then know what their leaders are costing them. Additionally, accountability is best implemented by linking a significant part of senior management compensation to the long-term success of the company.

The current practice of the 'platinum handshake' in the form of huge severance pay norms for top management should be stopped. It should be changed to a uniform norm valid across all levels in the corporation. These days, it has become common for a CEO who argues strongly in favour of a certain merger or acquisition to expect a retention bonus after consummating the merger/acquisition. This practice simply does not make sense and has to stop.

There is a lot of concern among corporate leaders about the corporate control market and its implications for them. My personal belief is that excellence in corporate performance is the best defence against takeovers.

Corporate leaders have to create a climate of opinion that values respectability in addition to wealth. Seeking respect forces a CEO to do the right thing by every stakeholder. Such behaviour ensures better employee retention, better sales and profits, better market capitalization, and better compensation for the CEO and others.

Business leaders must openly condemn peers who do not follow a proper code of conduct, however influential they are. The economist Robin Matthews has noted that once we create a mindset where the role of honesty in our social contracts becomes significant, the very threat of 'losing honour' within society becomes a preventive measure for greed.

We must institute international awards for good corporate behaviour, and promote a global corporate governance ranking system for Fortune 500 corporations. CEOs must be ranked globally on respectability. Respect has to become as important as wealth. There must be awards for such respected leaders on platforms like Davos. We have to create mechanisms to evaluate the contribution of independent directors across corporations, and institute awards for the best of them on a global basis.

Malcolm Salter has noted that some disasters help trigger deep learning and change. He says, 'Political scientists have the Bay of Pigs; engineers have the *Challenger* disaster; and corporations have Enron.' If corporations ignore the lessons that companies like Enron, WorldCom and Tyco have to offer, we will fail to regain the public trust that is so essential to our long-term success and survival. Corporations that genuinely recognize and embrace the principles of 'good governance' will derive enormous benefits—the availability and lower cost of capital, the ability to attract talent, clients and business partners, improved competitiveness and financial performance, and truly sustainable long-term growth.

Corporate Governance and its Relevance to India

Corporate governance is about a governance model to maximize the shareholder value in a corporation on a sustainable basis while ensuring fairness to all stakeholders—customers, employees, investors, vendor-partners, the government and society at large. It is about raising the trust and confidence of stakeholders in the way the company is run. It is about owners and managers operating as trustees on behalf of every shareholder—large or small. There are three players in the corporate governance game—the shareholders who have invested their money in the corporation; the executive management that runs the business and is responsible to the board of directors; and the board of directors which is elected by the shareholders and is accountable to them. The corporate governance problem, according to economists, is about minimizing agency cost or the cost of managers who manage the corporation on behalf of the shareholders. In other words, the primary problem in corporate governance is to ensure that we do not create an asymmetry of benefits among different players in this game—generally, between the owner-managers or professional managers of a company and its shareholders at large.

Why has the topic of corporate governance gained so much prominence these days? There are several reasons and I will discuss some of them.

C.D. Deshmukh Memorial Lecture, New Delhi, 14 January 2004

Instances of fraud and misconduct have become only too common in the corporate world of late. Inflated revenues, conflicted analysts, boards of directors who fail to perform their duty—the list is endless. The public opinion of CEOs and the senior management has never been lower. In fact, several surveys in the USA show that CEOs are the least trusted people. Unless this community corrects itself and redeems its honour, the very future of capitalism and capital markets is at stake. Unfortunately, this feeling of distrust is not limited to one country but is a discernible pattern in almost every country, including ours. It compromises the future of the sound and vibrant capital markets that are a must for entrepreneurship and job creation to flourish. According to Prof. Balasubramanyam of IIM, Bangalore, the median return of 256 companies in India for the period 1990-98 was –1 per cent. During the same period, the compensation to the top management increased by 50 to 75 per cent on an average. The ratio between the salary of the highest level and the lowest level has moved up from 10:1, prior to economic reforms, to about 100:1 now. As a result of such corporate excesses, today every aspect of corporate behaviour is under scrutiny and there is widespread scepticism about CEOs and their actions. I am reminded of Franklin Roosevelt's words that 'confidence languishes, for it thrives only on honesty, on honour, on the sacredness of obligations, on faithful protection and on unselfish performance; without them it cannot live'. Thanks to the excesses we have seen in the recent past, there has been significant damage to the reputation of several corporations. It is time for us to regain the trust of society.

Thanks to globalization, there is increasing integration of economies around the world through trade and financial flows, as well as movement of people and knowledge across borders. Today, global trade accounts for around 30 per cent of the world GDP. This is four times the share of global trade as a percentage of world GDP in the early 1970s. The developing countries too have grasped the incomparable advantages of globalization. In fact, twenty-four developing countries, with a collective population of 3 billion people, including India, China, Brazil and Mexico, have doubled their ratio of trade to GDP over the past two decades.

Clearly, global capital is free to move wherever it finds a hospitable environment. Therefore, unless a corporation follows the highest degree of transparency and the best principles of corporate governance, it is unlikely to attract world-class investors.

Developed nations have recognized the quality of Indian talent. Our young men and women are now sought after around the world. At the same time, they have become increasingly mobile and are free to work in any country they choose. In addition, they have significant career opportunities to work for reputed multinationals in India. My conversations with youngsters in India reveal that, other things being equal, they want to work for a corporation with a good reputation. An organization that follows good corporate governance standards is better positioned to sustain such a quality reputation and will invariably attract and retain the best and the brightest talent.

The advantages for ethical corporations extend beyond its employees. Thanks to globalization and the information revolution, customers in every corner of the world have access to and are aware of the best products and services produced anywhere. With the entry of highly reputed multinational companies and with the proliferation of the Internet and advanced media channels, the Indian consumer has become very savvy. This has raised customer expectations. They refuse to deal with companies that sell shoddy products, pollute the environment or short-change the investors. They demand that there be transparency in all dealings. They demand fair pricing. In this context, unless we live up to the best examples of customer focus and customer fairness, we cannot enhance or maintain our market share.

Our government has ushered in economic liberalization and taken several steps to reduce friction to business. They have removed licensing and drastically reduced the bureaucratic hurdles that entrepreneurs face. Most importantly, they have reduced taxes from a punishing 97 per cent at one time to a healthy 35 per cent today, with the hope that we will run our businesses ethically and pay our fair share of taxes. It is important for corporations to be fair in our dealings with the government. This entails following every law of the land. Such an approach helps the industry win the trust and confidence of government officials, and encourages governments to respond with more favourable policies for corporations. Otherwise, we run the risk of returning to those unfriendly days of high taxation and heavy bureaucracy.

In today's complex world, no single company can cater to all the needs of consumers, and has to collaborate with the best in the world. Such collaboration with our vendor-partners requires us to meet their expectations in terms of honest dealings and the highest level of transparency and disclosure. It is an accepted fact that well-governed corporations receive better valuations in capital markets than others. Consequently, their cost of debt is likely to be lower. In fact, according to a study conducted by John Kotter and James Heskett of the Harvard Business School over an eleven-year period, companies that cared deeply about their customers, shareholders and employees increased their revenue by 682 per cent compared to 166 per cent for other companies.

I can go on and on about why we need good corporate governance. Let me conclude with one more important reason. We live in a poor country. Over 250 million people in India live in utter poverty. The dogmas and shibboleths of socialism and centralized planning espoused by our leaders during the first forty years of independence have proved to be false. There is now a realization that capitalism with integrity is the only way forward to create jobs and solve the problem of poverty. We, the business leaders, are the evangelists of capitalism with integrity. If the masses are to accept us, we have to become credible and trustworthy, embrace the finest principles of governance in our companies and walk the talk.

There has recently been a flurry of activity all over the world to improve the level of corporate governance. The Sarbanes–Oxley Act in the USA and the prescriptions of the Organization for Economic Cooperation and Development (OECD) are good examples of such efforts outside India. In India, the Confederation of Indian Industry (CII) has been a leader in this area. My friends Rahul Bajaj and Omkar Goswami brought out the first code of corporate governance in India as early as 1995. The Securities and Exchange Board of India (SEBI) has been very active here, and has implemented the recommendations of the Kumar Mangalam Birla Committee. The report of my own committee, appointed by SEBI as a sequel to this, is expected to be implemented soon. All these committees aim to improve governance by enhancing the power and competence of the board, and are working to improve access to information for the shareholders and reduce the risk to corporations arising out of the greed and dishonesty of senior management. I will desist from going into the technicalities of the recommendations, for they are freely available. I will concentrate instead on what we, the corporate leaders, can do to get the best out of these recommendations.

I believe that good corporate governance is a necessity and is no longer a luxury for corporations in contemporary India. Unless a corporation learns to show fairness to all the stakeholders, it will not be successful in the long term. It is time to make traditional values like honesty, integrity, decency and respectability fashionable again.

If you want good corporate governance, you need good leadership. We need men and women who are daring, who can dream big and make sacrifices. Let us remember the words of Henry David Thoreau who said, 'It is truly enough said that a corporation has no conscience. But a corporation of conscientious men is a corporation with a conscience.' We need business leaders with integrity. We need corporate chieftains who are committed to a good value system. They should walk the talk in demonstrating their values and beliefs. Without this, no corporate governance system will ever work. 'We must become the change we want to see in the world,' said Mahatma Gandhi. The best index of success for a corporation is its longevity. The long-term success of a corporation is predicated on maintaining harmonious relations with employees, customers, vendor-partners, the government and society. This will enhance their trust and confidence in us.

Corporations are best run with simple business rules. Simple business rules are easy to understand, easy to follow, and easy to communicate. Besides, no one can cheat others with simple rules. When formulating a business rule, we, at Infosys, ask ourselves if we are being fair to all the constituents and if our conscience will be clear if we implement the rule. Our motto for fairness is guided by our belief that 'the softest pillow is a clear conscience'.

Building trust and confidence requires an environment where there is a premium on transparency, openness, boldness, fairness and justice. We should encourage this. Investors understand that there are cycles in business. They know that there will be boom times and lean times. What they ask of us is that we level with them. They want us to be open and honest in all our dealings with them. The Infosys motto on transparency and disclosure is: 'When in doubt, disclose.'

One area of intense debate has been the compensation structure of the senior management of a corporation. I believe in a compensation structure that is market-driven but fair. We have to look at three important criteria in deciding managerial remuneration—fairness, accountability and transparency. In order to ensure accountability, the compensation should have a fixed component and a variable component. The CEO, other directors and the senior management should swim or sink with the fortunes of the company. The variable component should be much bigger than the fixed component and should be linked to achieving the firm's long-term objectives. This will also avoid manipulation of stock prices for short-term gain. In addition, senior management compensation should be reviewed by the compensation committee of the board consisting entirely of independent directors. The compensation recommended by the compensation committee should be approved by the shareholders.

We should identify errant CEOs and make an example of them. We have to implement severe penalties for any violators of the codes of corporate governance. So far, we have had a soft approach towards white-collar crimes. This must change. We should ensure that there are no five-star prison vacations for such people.

Good governance requires an open environment where anybody, regardless of hierarchy, can express disagreement over what he/she perceives as wrongdoing by the corporate leaders. Consequently, it is our responsibility to create mechanisms where the smallest voice of concern is given adequate hearing.

We have to create a climate of opinion that venerates respect more than wealth. We can do this by instituting awards for good corporate behaviour and giving these awardees better exposure at an international level. It may also be a good idea to publicly rank corporations based on their practice of corporate governance and respectability.

Good corporate governance is about putting the good of the corporation ahead of individual good. It is about being a good corporate citizen. It is about civilized behaviour and about long-term orientation. It is about making life better for the next generation of leaders in the corporation. This is what civilized societies are about, and history has shown that it is civilized societies that have progressed. There is a lesson in this for all of us.

I believe that rules cannot build character. In fact, in the USA, regulators have attempted to legislate for all possible contingencies. As a result, standards have become detailed and lengthy. In 1985, there were roughly 2,300 pages of accounting standards mandated by the Financial Accounting Standards Board (FASB). By 2002, this document had almost doubled to 4,000 pages! Clearly, the absence of rules was never a problem. But you cannot mandate honesty. I recall the words of Russian author Aleksandr Solzhenitsyn that: 'The line separating good and evil passes not between states nor between classes but through the middle of every human heart.' The rule of law can only defeat the perverse mind. It cannot defeat the perversity of the heart.

There is no doubt that the economic reforms that have taken place in India since 1991 have accelerated modernization within our market mechanisms. Today, we have the necessary regulatory framework in place. Major advances such as the establishment of SEBI, reforms in company law and increased efficiency of financial markets have put Indian corporates in a favourable position to seek capital, not only domestically, but also in global capital markets. It is up to us to continue to create more wealth, legally and ethically. To do so, we have to follow the highest standards of corporate governance. While we have made significant progress, we still have a long way to go. Let us remember that big countries like China and Brazil are in fierce competition with us for financial capital. In fact, both these countries are ranked above India in the FDI Confidence Index published by the Conference Board, which recommends that India must continue to improve its corporate governance and financial infrastructure to actually realize its vast potential.

Today, Indian industry has tremendous opportunities for growth. We have made rapid strides in most sectors of our economy—automotive, steel, manufacturing, services, software, biotech and telecom, just to name a few. The inflation rate is well under control. The interest rates are half of what they were a decade ago and our foreign exchange reserves at $100 billion are at their highest ever. Our companies have access to newer and larger markets around the world. At the same time, the world is waking up to India's crucial role as the largest democracy and a dynamic economy. There is a great opportunity for our business leaders to shape the destiny of our nation. We will do well to remember the words of French philosopher Jean-Paul Sartre that we have no destinies other than those we forge ourselves. Surely, we must be concerned about having the right strategy, having the right product, bringing it quickly to market and offering great service. But to build a business that truly achieves greatness and to grow the bottom line consistently over time, one must build a culture that inspires ethical behaviour with all stakeholders. This is the only way Indian industry can leverage the opportunity for growth. Corporate governance has never been more relevant in India than today.

Corporate Governance:
A Practitioner's Viewpoint

Recently, we have seen many instances of fraud and misuse in the corporate world. Elsewhere, we see corporate governance reforms being enacted with a sense of urgency. It is time to act in India as well—we should not be waiting for problems to occur. Let us avoid 'governance by embarrassment' and be proactive. What should be done in India? I will talk about the more important steps that need to be taken, especially from the perspective of corporations and regulatory agencies.

The most important task, in my opinion, is revitalizing the institution of independent directors. The independent directors of a company should be faithful fiduciaries protecting the long-term interests of shareholders while ensuring fairness to employees, investors, customers, regulators, the government of the land and society. Unfortunately, very often, directors are chosen based on friendship and, sadly, pliability. Therefore, it is appropriate to define what we mean by 'independent directors'. To me, an independent director is one who will be objective in board decisions. Generally, this independence stems from stature, competence, integrity, character, upbringing, confidence in oneself, openness and, of course, from not having any material income (other than the director's fee) derived from the company while he/she is on the board. Today, unfortunately,

Ranganathan Memorial Lecture, New Delhi, 27 November 2002

in the majority of cases, independence is only true on paper. This is the case not just in India but all over the world. In India, we have seen many instances of legal counsels being appointed to the boards of the companies they advise. Such actions will not enhance the independence of the board. Such boards will become, as Harvard Business School Professor Myles Mace says, 'decorative and decorous baubles with no real purpose'.

The need of the hour is to strengthen the independence of the board. We have to put in place stringent standards for the independence of directors. The board should adopt global standards for director-independence, and should disclose how each independent director meets these standards. It is desirable to have a comprehensive report showing the names of the company employees or fellow board members who are related to each director on the board. This report should accompany the annual report of all listed companies.

Another important step is to regularly assess the board members for performance. The assessment should focus on issues like competence, preparation, participation and contribution. Ideally, this evaluation should be performed by a third party. Underperforming directors should be allowed to leave at the end of their term in a gentle manner so that they do not lose face.

Rather than being the rubber stamp of a company's management policies, the board should become a true, active partner of the management. For this, independent directors should be trained in their roles and responsibilities. In 1995, I sent out a three-page document on the roles and responsibilities of the independent directors at Infosys when we invited several well-known people to join our board. The unanimous reaction from all these people was that we were one of the few companies in India which clearly defined the role of independent directors, their responsibilities and how they would be compensated. Independent directors should be trained on the business model and risk model of the company, on the governance practices, and the responsibilities of the various committees of the board of the company. For instance, at Infosys board meetings, half the time is dedicated to presentations by executive directors as well as senior management on the strategy and action plans of the company across its different functions. This is done so that our external directors understand the nuances and risks of our business.

The board members should interact frequently with executives to understand operational issues. As part of the board meeting agenda, the independent directors should have a meeting among themselves without the management being present. I am glad to say that Infosys has been practising this for quite some time.

The independent board members should periodically review the performance of the company's CEO, the internal directors and the senior management. This has to be based on clearly defined objective criteria, and these criteria should be known to the CEO and other executive directors well before the start of the evaluation period. Moreover, there should be a clearly laid down procedure for communicating the board's review to the CEO and his/her team of executive directors. Managerial remuneration should be based on such reviews. At Infosys, once a year, executive members of the board and members of the senior management are expected to make presentations on their performance including budgets, targets and achievements. Once a year, we ask the independent members of the board to tell us how they have added value to the company.

There will be occasions when the board disagrees with the management. For example, a few years ago, our management took a certain view on the computation of gratuity under the US GAAP, and the auditors took a different view. The external board members disagreed with us and went with the auditors. This is the kind of independence we must foster in companies because such independence is in the interest of the minority shareholders.

Additionally, senior management compensation should be determined by the board in a manner that is fair to all stakeholders. We have to look at three important criteria in deciding managerial remuneration—fairness, accountability and transparency. Fairness of compensation is determined by how employees and investors react to the compensation of the CEO. Accountability is enhanced by splitting the total compensation into a small fixed component and a large variable component. In other words, the CEO, other executive directors and the senior management should rise or fall with the fortunes of the company. The variable component should be linked to achieving the long-term objectives of the firm. Senior management compensation should be reviewed by the compensation committee of the board consisting of only the independent directors. This should be approved by the shareholders. It is important that no member of the internal management has a say in the compensation of the CEO, the internal board members or the senior management.

The SEBI regulations and the CII code of conduct have been very helpful in enhancing the level of accountability of independent directors. The independent directors should decide voluntarily how they want to contribute to the company. Their performance should be appraised through a peer evaluation process. Ideally, the compensation committee should decide on the compensation of each independent director based on such a performance appraisal. This is a tough job. I do not know of any company that has implemented such a compensation scheme yet.

Another major area that needs reforms is auditing. An audit is the independent examination of financial transactions of any entity to provide assurance to shareholders and other stakeholders that the financial statements are free of material misstatement. Auditors are qualified professionals appointed by the shareholders to report on the reliability of financial statements prepared by the management. Financial markets look to the auditor's report for an independent opinion on the financial and risk situation of a company.

We have to separate such auditing from other services. For a truly independent opinion, the auditing firm should not provide services that are perceived to be materially in conflict with the role of the auditor. These include investigations, consulting advice, subcontracting of operational activities normally undertaken by the management, due diligence on potential acquisitions or investments, advice on deal structuring, designing/implementing IT systems, book-keeping, valuations and executive recruitment. Any departure from this practice should be approved by the audit committee in advance. Further, information on any such exceptions must be disclosed in the company's quarterly and annual reports.

To ensure the integrity of the audit team, it is desirable to rotate auditor partners. The lead audit partner and the audit partner responsible for reviewing a company's audit must be rotated at least once every three to five years. This eliminates the possibility of the lead auditor and the company management getting into the kind of close, cosy relationship that results in lower objectivity in audit opinions. Further, a registered auditor should not audit a company if, during the year preceding the start of the audit, the company's CEO, CFO or chief accounting officer was associated with the auditing firm. It is best that members of the audit teams are prohibited from taking up employment in the audited corporations for at least a year after they have stopped being members of the audit team.

The audit committee should consist of only independent directors. A competent audit committee is essential to effectively oversee the financial accounting and reporting process. Hence, each member of the audit committee must be 'financially literate'. Further, at least one member of the audit committee, preferably the chairman, should be a financial expert—a person who has an understanding of financial statements and accounting rules, and has experience in auditing or being audited.

It is important for companies to have effective internal controls to ensure good corporate governance standards. The annual report should contain the opinion of the audit committee on the measures taken during the year to strengthen internal controls. Right now, in India, this is mandated only for listed companies. We should extend this to include the subsidiaries of public companies as well.

We should also review the rules governing the disclosure of financial statements of a privately-held company, one of whose parents is a listed company. In India, it is currently required that a privately-held company's financial statements be separately disclosed in the annual report of the parent. However, there is a technical problem in doing this. For instance, Infosys has a subsidiary called Yantra in the United States which is venture-funded. The Indian company law requires that we attach the balance sheet and the income statement of Yantra along with that of Infosys. However, the other investors of the company are against this idea since Yantra is a privately-held company. This is a complex issue and should be debated and decided by the accounting profession.

The audit committee should establish procedures for the treatment of complaints received through anonymous submission by employees and whistleblowers. These complaints may be regarding questionable accounting or auditing issues, any harassment to an employee or any unethical practice in the company. The whistleblowers must be protected.

Any related-party transaction should require prior approval by the audit committee, the full board and the shareholders if it is material. Related parties are those that are able to control or exercise significant influence. These include: parent–subsidiary relationships; entities under common control; individuals who, through ownership, have significant influence over the enterprise and close members of their families; and key management personnel.

Accounting standards provide a framework for preparation and presentation of financial statements and assist auditors in forming an opinion on the financial statements. However, today, accounting standards are issued by bodies comprising primarily of accountants. Therefore, accounting standards do not always keep pace with changes in the business environment. Hence, the accounting standards-setting body should include members drawn from the industry, the profession and regulatory bodies. This body should be independently funded.

Currently, an independent oversight of the accounting profession does not exist. Hence, an independent body should be constituted to oversee the functioning of auditors for independence, the quality of audit and professional competence. This body should comprise a majority of non-practising accountants to ensure independent oversight. To avoid any bias, the chairman of this body should not have practised as an accountant during the preceding five years. Auditors of all public companies must register with this body. It should enforce compliance with the laws by auditors and should mandate that auditors must maintain audit working papers for at least seven years.

To ensure the materiality of information, the CEO and CFO of the company should certify annual and quarterly reports. They should certify that the information in the reports fairly presents the financial condition and results of operations of the company, and that all material facts have been disclosed. Further, CEOs and CFOs should certify that they have established internal controls to ensure that all information relating to the operations of the company is freely available to the auditors and the audit committee. They should also certify that they have evaluated the effectiveness of these controls within ninety days prior to the report.

False certifications by the CEO and CFO should be subject to significant criminal penalties (fines and imprisonment, if wilful and knowing). If a company is required to restate its reports due to material non-compliance with the laws, the CEO and CFO must face severe punishment including loss of job and forfeiting bonuses or equity-based compensation received during the twelve months following the filing.

We should take steps to accelerate the disclosure of insider trades. Such trades should be filed within two days of the trade. This accelerated disclosure should be mandated for trades by senior management personnel, by people with reasonable shareholding, or for any trade by an insider.

I believe that investment banks should ensure independence in their research. Otherwise, investors will be hurt. Companies should not have any role, for example, in supervising or compensating analysts. There should be a research blackout period following offerings in which the investment-banking firm has participated as an underwriter or dealer. Analysts' research reports should disclose details of analysts' holdings in the analysed company's securities; compensation received from the company; any relationship with the company or company's personnel; and any compensation received by the analyst out of investment banking fees paid by the company.

At the end of it all, rules cannot be a substitute for character. No external mandate can guarantee that the CEO, the internal members of the board and the senior management will embrace the right values. I recall the words of Lord Macaulay that the measure of a man's real character is what he would do if he knew he would never be found out. This is the ultimate test of ethics. It is extremely important that we focus on this test because we cannot afford to ignore the rights of the small and minority shareholders. These people have invested their savings in our companies. Hence, we should have a mechanism to ensure that their savings are being utilized for the intended purpose. If we cannot ensure this, then the whole movement of corporate governance will fail. This is the responsibility of corporate leaders. Unless we can do this, we cannot claim any success in our profession.

A New Model for Effective Public Governance

Running a large state or a country is much more of a challenge than running an enterprise. I have been involved in running an enterprise for the last twenty years, but I believe some of the lessons I have learnt are applicable to the realm of public governance as well.

Globalization has led to higher foreign trade, an increase in foreign direct investment, and other forms of capital flows. In today's globalized world, economic growth requires every country to create a hospitable environment to attract capital and technology. The quality of public governance in a developing country plays an important role in its ability to leverage the benefits of globalization. Thus, globalization has led to renewed attention to better governance and to a call to reduce corruption in developing countries like India.

Good public governance is first about setting an exciting and worthwhile objective for social progress and then focussing on good execution of that objective. To start with, it is extremely important to have a powerful, exciting vision. Transformational progress happens only with a great vision as it raises the aspirations of people, makes them enthusiastic and energetic, and helps them commit to hard work and sacrifice. Mahatma Gandhi created a powerful vision for independent India, raised the aspirations of our people and got them to make tremendous sacrifices to achieve independence. Similarly, Jawaharlal Nehru created a vision for modern India that enthused

The fifth J.R.D. Tata Memorial Lecture, New Delhi, 1 August 2002 millions of Indians to build steel plants, dams and institutions of higher learning. Similarly, our politicians have to create a powerful vision to achieve economic growth with fairness and equity.

Good leadership is what translates a great vision into productive results through the instrument of effective public governance. Effective public governance has to be championed by inspirational leaders acting as change agents to achieve what appear as impossible goals. Progress requires lots of hard work, commitment, sacrifice and honesty. Trust and confidence in leaders is what will motivate people to make sacrifices in the short term in the hope of betterment in the long term. The best instrument leaders have for creating trust and confidence is walking the talk—demonstrating their belief in sacrifice, commitment, honesty and hard work through action rather than just rhetoric. For instance, it is said that J.R.D. Tata personally inspected the toilets in every Air-India plane in which he travelled. It was this kind of leading by example, of attention to detail, and concern for service that made Air-India under JRD's stewardship one of the premier commercial airlines in the world.

Progress takes time. It is the responsibility of leaders to keep up the enthusiasm of people by demonstrating through personal example that putting the interest of the community first in the short term will indeed lead to individual betterment in the longer term. I have realized that by putting the interest of Infosys ahead of mine in the short term, I have benefited hugely in the long term. For instance, at Infosys, the founders reinvested their after-tax dividends back into the company in the initial years to make the company strong. The result has been considerable wealth for the founders, more than was possible otherwise.

Effective public governance requires a laser focus on the customer. While focus on the customer has been a well-accepted phenomenon in the private sector, public governance systems, thanks to the aftermath of colonial rule, rarely focus on their customers who are the citizens of the country. Accountability to stakeholders has been rarely emphasized in our public institutions since colonial governments focussed primarily on revenue collection and law and order, neither of which depends on how happy the customer is. On the other hand, the survival of a corporation depends on satisfying and exceeding the customer's expectations. Historically, at Infosys, revenues from existing clients have accounted for 85 per cent of our revenues. A key factor behind this is the care we take to deliver on time and within budget while meeting the highest quality standards. Since India has a democratic government elected by its people, it is time that we brought focus on accountability to citizens in our public governance.

Fairness and transparency are very important in public governance. Success in public governance comes from ensuring fairness to every stakeholder—citizens, civil society, the government and the private sector. We, at Infosys, focus on a high level of transparency in every one of our dealings with our stakeholders. This has been an important factor in building trust in us among our stakeholders and has been crucial for our progress.

A strong value system is essential for effective public governance. Every nation is in a global competition to attract strategic resources— human resources and capital. A good value system can be a competitive advantage for governments. A value system is based on fairness and equity in policies, transparency and honesty, avoiding nepotism, abiding by contracts and discharging obligations on time. At Infosys, our value system is reflected in our belief that 'the softest pillow is a clear conscience'.

Accountability is an important factor in creating trust in public governance. Unlike the private sector, accountability is often not the strong point of the public sector. The private sector has the advantage of a self-correcting market mechanism. For example, wastage of valuable resources by a corporation leads to reduced profit which is reflected in the value of the company as perceived by the market. However, in the case of public governance systems, there is no such market mechanism that ensures self-correction. Hence, it is important to incorporate measures to enhance accountability. For instance, in China, officials are held accountable for an annual economic growth of at least 7 per cent. They are also required to continuously improve environmental quality, build better infrastructure and reduce crime levels. They will lose their jobs if they fail to meet these targets. In my opinion, the most pressing need in India is a system of accountability in public governance systems.

It is important to provide a stable, predictable and speedy policy and a good legal environment. In fact, these are two of the vital attributes of a successful economy. We have to decouple political risks, patronages and ideologies from policy formation and implementation. Otherwise, such uncertainties will result in a loss of trust of both citizens and foreigners in our country and create enormous economic overheads for conducting business. Developing economies cannot afford to pay this premium. We must also cut delays and rent-seeking due to bureaucracy and reduce the cost of legal compliance.

We should create regulatory councils consisting of eminent people from various walks of life that will monitor the health and progress of governance initiatives and function as watchdogs. Such councils would operate in a fashion similar to independent directors in publicly-traded companies. It may be worthwhile to pilot new governance systems with a comprehensive package of civil service reforms and governance methodologies in selected areas of the country. After validation, such pilots can be rolled out to the entire country, customizing it to the requirements of each region. Civil servants for these pilots should be chosen carefully and proper incentive structures must be designed for them.

Integrity programmes should be piloted in each department of the state and Central governments. Such integrity programmes would focus on achieving a stated objective in a desired time frame at an optimal cost. An example is the anti-corruption programme. Such programmes must have a short time-line, have key performance indicators and should result in measurable improvement.

Let me re-emphasize that it is important to define clear, measurable objectives, similar to those that exist in the private sector, if we want to succeed in public governance. What cannot be measured cannot be improved. Assessing objectives in this way will greatly help in the success of our public projects. For instance, if we decide to build 1,000 houses of 800 sq. ft at Rs 8 lakh per house within ten months, and monitor performance month by month, we are likely to achieve our target. Even if we slip up on the target, we will at least know why we failed and will avoid such mistakes next time. Unfortunately, no such mechanism exists currently in public governance.

It is important to plan the duration of every public project to be less than a reasonable time limit. Let there be no project of more than two years' duration. A lengthy project should be split up into smaller projects to meet the two-year limit. Performance deliverables should be clearly defined for every project and for every phase of a large project.

The progress of important public projects at the Central and state levels should be monitored using governance scorecards. Once a week, every newspaper and TV channel should carry data on the progress and the money spent (budget vs actual) for the hundred most important projects at the national and state level. Such project-level data should also contain the names of the minister and the secretary in charge. A timely escalation mechanism is also necessary to handle problems and delays that emerge. For instance, at Infosys, any software project that results in a delay beyond 5 per cent of the project's duration gets escalated to the senior management for remedial action. We also have a quarterly operations review where the top management reviews the performance of important projects. Similar mechanisms should be introduced as part of effective public governance procedures.

Elections are expected to act as a check against malpractices by political leaders. However, our political leadership is generally elected on considerations other than merit and performance. The Election Commission should make it compulsory for every party to clearly bring out, in quantifiable terms, their performance during their term in office or in opposition, and the performance credentials of their candidates. Any false data should result in debarring the entire party from elections.

It is very important to create incentives for good governance. Lack of incentives is the reason for the failure of most of our governmental initiatives. A major part of the remuneration of our bureaucrats should be performance-based variable pay. In fact, research shows a negative correlation between the wage levels of bureaucrats and corruption. At Infosys, we have adopted a role-performance-based compensation. An individual's compensation is decided by his or her role in the organization, and his or her relative performance within the role. Most significantly, age plays no part in determining compensation.

The objective of technology is to reduce cost, reduce cycle time, simplify work, improve productivity, improve quality of implementation and enhance customer satisfaction. Who needs these more than the poor? Hence, technology is crucial in delivering basic services to the poor in India. Technology has to be embraced enthusiastically by governments both at the state and federal levels.

One aspect of quality of service is timely delivery. On-time delivery demands that there are no delays in the decision or value addition chain. The best way to eliminate delays is to document the entire workflow of the decision or value addition chain, use technology to automate the workflow, and bring transparency to the whole process. The loan application system at Infosys is a good example of such a system. An employee can apply for a loan on our Intranet, get his or her supervisor to approve it online and get the loan department to disburse money into his or her account—all in one day!

Technology helps democratize information. Let me recall the words of Thomas Jefferson that 'that government is the strongest of which every man feels himself a part'. Technology can literally make this possible. The Internet empowers people by conquering distance and time zones, and by increasing transparency. Democracies need this powerful tool to enhance interaction between governments and citizens. The Internet can also serve as an ombudsman for citizens. For instance, news channels often have online polls on key topical issues of the day, the results of which are broadcast the next day.

Another important use of the Internet is in e-governance which enhances the productivity of citizens in their interaction with the government. Our citizens spend a lot of time interfacing with their government for securing ration cards and driving licences, for land registration and records and for payments of taxes and utility bills. This time can be greatly reduced through e-governance systems.

Technology also has an important role in reducing corruption. Typically, corruption is fuelled by a lack of transparency. The Internet can help in reducing corruption in two ways—by separating the decision-making point from the delivery point of the service, and by improving transparency in workflow and the approval chain. For example, the Regional Transport Offices (RTOs) in Bangalore plan to install closed-circuit cameras which will monitor any agents who act as middlemen. These systems will also record the time duration when officers are not at their seats.

I am very optimistic that our national leaders will act with alacrity to improve the standards in our public governance system so that we can create a fast-growing, equitable and fair economy to make life better for the poorest of the poor.

PART VII

CORPORATE SOCIAL RESPONSIBILITY AND PHILANTHROPY

Compassionate Capitalism

Capitalism is a system based on the principle of individual rights and responsibilities. The bulk of economic activity is organized through private enterprise operating in a free market. Each person survives and flourishes based on his freedom to use his ability. Individuals and companies are allowed to compete for their own economic gain. Market forces determine the prices of goods and services. Such a system is based on the premise of separating the state from the industry. The role of the state is to regulate and protect. Each person has a right to the product of his own work and is driven to action by the opportunity to create wealth. Collectively, we create wealth for society. This results in an efficient and optimal allocation of resources. Adam Smith rightly said that in such a system, 'the private interests and passions of men' are led in the direction 'which is most agreeable to the interest of the whole society'.

In a market system, there are personal incentives for workers to do their jobs well, and for managers to make good decisions. It now seems obvious that a market economy is vastly more productive than one controlled from the centre. The extraordinary level of material prosperity achieved by the capitalist system over the course of the last two hundred years is a matter of historical record. Socialism, on the other hand, is a method of organizing a society in which the

A lecture delivered at the Global Brand Forum, Singapore, 1 December 2003

means of production and distribution of goods are controlled by the state and private ownership is controlled in the interest of the state. It is based on cooperation rather than competition and utilizes centralized planning and distribution. It propounds the idea of equality of income and property. Unfortunately, socialism has only led to the concentration of economic power in unaccountable centralized institutions. Under the socialist doctrine, as is practised by some emerging countries, there is an assumption that a limited amount of wealth exists in the world and must be divided equally among all citizens. This system assumes that life is a zero-sum game. One person's gain under such a system is another's loss. By ignoring the effects of competition, we create, in the words of economist Paul Krugman, 'antiquated factories producing consumer goods of ludicrously low quality'. Obviously, the state occupies a big role for itself in such a system.

If the wealth of the world is equally divided among people throughout the world, there will, of course, be no rich people any more. But everybody will still be poor. You cannot distribute poverty. Socialists often forget that we have to first create wealth in order to distribute it. We have seen how such an economic system of centralized planning leads to 'ordinary citizens in political fetters with low standard of living and little power to control their own destiny', as noted by Milton Friedman. A popular joke on socialism is that in a socialist system there is no unemployment while, at the same time, no one works; no one works, but everyone still gets a salary; and while everyone gets a salary, there is nothing to buy!

Soon after Independence in 1947, India placed its bet on a complex and rigid central planning system. There was extensive public ownership of commercial assets; a complex industrial licensing system; substantial protection against imports; and restrictions on exports. This model clearly proved unsuccessful. During the first thirty years, the per-capita growth rate was barely 1.2 per cent; industrial growth was less than 6 per cent; and India's share of world trade decreased from 2 per cent to around 0.5 per cent. Rather than sharing in prosperity and wealth, people shared in poverty. In 1991, confronted with a drastic economic crisis, India began a sweeping reform process to open its economy to a changing world. The rest, as they say, is history.

'An economy that does not liberalize will slowly die from a sedentary lifestyle,' say Raghuram Rajan and Luigi Zingales in their book *Saving Capitalism from Capitalists*. Free markets and open trade, which capitalism promotes, help create wealth and spread opportunity. The task of the government is to create an environment where it is possible for people to create wealth and jobs legally.

Openness to trade and FDI can provide access to imported inputs, new technology and larger markets. There is clear evidence of the productivity-enhancing effects of trade liberalization. The World Bank estimates an annual gain of $2.8 trillion by 2015 from the elimination of trade barriers on all goods and services. Developing countries would gain to the tune of $1.5 trillion which would lift 320 million people out of poverty.

Countries that have embraced capitalism and let free markets thrive have progressed. The United States, Singapore and much of the developed world are examples of such nations. By leveraging the power of capitalism, the world has surely made tremendous advances. The world GDP has grown six-fold in the last fifty years. We have created tremendous economic capital, albeit for a small part of the planet.

Is capitalism all rosy? Yes, if the state plays its role as a fair, diligent, transparent and accountable regulator of free markets. This has obviously not happened. Let me give a few examples. It is very easy to observe that we have not made significant progress in enhancing social capital in the world—trust, concern for the less fortunate, honesty and fairness. The disparity between the rich and the poor has increased. In fact, World Bank studies show that the gap between rich and poor countries has doubled in the past forty years. The average income in the richest twenty countries is more than thirty-five times higher than that in the poorest twenty. There are 1.2 billion people in this world who live in extreme poverty. About 1 billion people lack access to safe drinking water! I recall the words of Anita Roddick who said, 'People are forced to eke out a bare existence on the margins of the world, denied their fundamental human rights by the fickle voracity of the global business juggernaut.'

We have created a situation where a poor child is ashamed that she cannot afford to buy lunch at school while hundreds of poverty alleviators from multilateral institutions treat themselves to sumptuous five-course meals next door. There is a danger of ignoring the interests of over a billion farmers in the developing world while protecting the interests of 6.5 million farmers in the developed world. There is continued concentration of wealth in the hands of a few, not just in poor countries but also in rich countries like the USA. 'To be poor is hard, but to be poor in America, a land of such wealth, can be intolerable,' says Anita Roddick. In fact, according to a United Nations study, even in the developed world 54 million people live in slums. This number is slated to double in the next thirty years. This is what prompted author and economist David Korten to describe capitalism as 'an extremist ideology that advances the concentration of ownership without limit, to the exclusion of the needs and rights of the many who own virtually nothing'.

In a well-known corporation in the USA, the top managers made millions of dollars in bonuses and stock sales while more than 3,000 employees lost their savings and were fired. It is not uncommon to see CEOs canvas enthusiastically for mergers and acquisitions with promises of a better bottom line. They achieve such bottom lines not by any corporate wizardry but by eliminating a large number of ordinary jobs. In 1980, the average pay for CEOs of America's biggest companies was about forty times that of the average worker. Today, it is about 400 times! No wonder that Alan Greenspan was prompted to talk of the 'infectious greed' among CEOs. What is even more unfortunate is the lack of harsh punishment for these business leaders. I am reminded of what a journalist recently wrote: 'If a guy steals $5,000, he goes to jail for ten years. If he steals $500 million, he appears before Congress and gets called bad names for ten minutes!' Consequently, today, capitalism seems increasingly dysfunctional and alienating. Even for the vast majority in the developed world, it seems to fundamentally conflict with humanity's non-economic values. People have lost confidence in such an economic system. 'While free markets fatten people's wallets, they have made surprisingly few inroads into their hearts and minds,' say Raghuram Rajan and Luigi Zingales.

We have the responsibility to repair this situation. We have to transform the pursuit of 'more' to the fulfilment of 'better for all of us'. While every citizen of the globe has a role to play in this, corporate leaders have to become leaders in this transformation. The need of the hour is to practise compassionate capitalism. We have to create a world where more and more wealth is created while human dignity is enhanced.

Compassionate capitalism is about bringing the power of capitalism to the benefit of large masses. It is about combining the power of mind and heart, the good of capitalism and socialism. The Swedish model that combines private ownership of the means of production with an elaborate welfare system is a good example of this. No wonder then that, during the twentieth century, Sweden developed from one of the poorer countries of Europe into one of the richest, with a literacy rate of almost 100 per cent, an infant mortality rate of 0.3 per cent and an average life expectancy of around eighty years!

The benefits of growth have to be distributed widely. We cannot have a situation where there is economic growth for the strong and deprivation for the weak. The resultant social stress will break the very fabric of our economic system. Decades of progress will be reversed. We must remember the words of Adam Smith who said, 'No society can surely be flourishing and happy of which by far the greater part of the numbers are poor and miserable.' Compassionate capitalism is about fairness, integrity and putting the interest of society ahead of one's own interest. It is about overcoming greed and short-term orientation. It is about creating a community that believes in the concept of 'vasudaiva kutumbam' (the world is one family).

Why do we need compassionate capitalism? We need it for many reasons. First, we have to make capitalism fashionable again in the developed world. Second, we have to make it the most accepted model for growth in developing countries like India and other emerging countries. We want the people and leaders in developing countries to become believers in capitalism as the tool for their emancipation. We have to get millions of entrepreneurs excited about the opportunity to create wealth. We need dreamers who see a fire in every spark and an apple in every seed. The idea of prosperity always starts in the minds of men. They have to believe in an economic system which allows them to prosper. However, we cannot have market freedom without a focus on the conditions required to maintain this. We have to redeem people's faith in capitalism as an economic system which believes in the sanctity of private property, the freedom of contract, the power of free trade and the rule of law. Such a system allows them the freedom to experiment, invent and produce.

If we fail to act today, the poor, who have been alienated from economic and social progress, will lose faith in capitalism. Remember that the legitimacy of our economic system is at risk. We will do well to remember the words of John F. Kennedy who said, 'If a society cannot help the many who are poor, it cannot save the few who are rich.' It is our duty to create a mandate for an ideology that we believe in—one which allows unfettered opportunities to create an upward spiral of wealth and prosperity for everyone. This duty is even more vital for us, the business leaders, who have enjoyed the benefits of this system.

Greedy behaviour from corporate leaders has strengthened public conviction that free markets are tools for the rich to get richer at the expense of the welfare of the general public. The *Economist* says, 'It is a market driven by conflicts of interest, swelled by covert deals and protected by successful lobbying.' Consequently, a large majority of the developing world sees no legitimacy in a system in which they have been proven losers. We have to make the leaders in countries like India who are sceptical about capitalism appreciate its power in solving the problem of poverty.

Now I come to the most important question: How do we practise compassionate capitalism? We, the business leaders, have to take the lead in regaining the trust of society. We have to conduct ourselves more ethically and legally. The people at the vanguard of the capitalist movement have to make themselves more acceptable to those left behind by shunning a vulgarly rich life. Compassionate capitalism is about putting community interest ahead of private interest in the short term and being a good corporate citizen. It is about civilized behaviour and about long-term orientation. It is about making life better for the next generation. This is what civilized societies are about and history has shown that it is such civilized societies that have always progressed.

For this, we have to abide by the value system of the community. A value system is a protocol for behaviour that enhances the confidence, commitment and enthusiasm of people. Our value system enthuses us to follow the finest principles of corporate governance. Corporate governance is about enhancing shareholder value on a sustainable basis while ensuring fairness to all stakeholders— customers, employees, investors, vendor-partners, the government of the land and society at large. The clause 'sustainable basis' is important. For instance, if we look at Enron, it surely did enhance shareholder value by not so acceptable means, but only for a short period. The best index of success of a corporation is its longevity. Business leaders have to remember that corporations cannot succeed in societies that fail.

The goal of every corporation is to create wealth for its shareholders legally and ethically. But the power of wealth is the power to give it away. William Ford Jr said, 'A good company delivers excellent products and services. A great company does all that and strives to make the world a better place.' Corporations have to make a difference to the context through society-oriented and charitable activities.

Business leaders should shun excessive managerial compensation. Managerial remuneration should be based on three principles— fairness with respect to the compensation of other employees; transparency with respect to shareholders and employees; and accountability with respect to linking compensation with corporate performance.

We have to create a climate of opinion which says respect is more important than wealth. We can do this by instituting awards for good corporate behaviour. We should have an internationally recognized ranking of socially-responsible corporations just as the Fortune 500 ranking is based on economic parameters. We should create an equivalent of the Nobel Prize for CEOs of such corporations.

The developed countries that have enjoyed the benefits of the capitalist movement have to ensure that free trade also implies fair trade. For instance, according to the *Economist*, the thirty member countries of the OECD spend more than $330 billion a year on supporting their farmers—both through direct subsidies and through higher prices. Reduce this by 5 per cent and you have enough money to treble the rich world's current donations to fight AIDS. According to Mike Moore, former director general of the World Trade Organization (WTO), in 2001, American cotton producers received $3.4 billion in government subsidies. The beneficiaries were farmers whose net worth averaged about $800,000! The World Bank reckons that removing these barriers would increase incomes of cotton-producing countries in poor Western and Central African countries by $250 million a year. Thus, rich countries should ensure that they do not ignore issues that are crucial to the economic survival of poor countries. Dismantling such unfair protectionism will give a chance to millions of farmers in poor countries and increase trust in capitalism.

We have arrived at a time in our history when we are equipped with the strength of knowledge, the power of globalization and the convenience of technology to accomplish seemingly impossible goals—elimination of poverty, hunger and disease from this world. Let us derive the best out of free markets and open competition and, at the same time, show compassion to the less fortunate in this world. Let us proudly stand up and proclaim, as Anita Roddick has done, 'That's what I want to do to the business world—nurture a revolution in kindness.' Let us make this a time, in David Korten's words, 'filled with hope for a new millennium in which societies will be freed from the concerns of basic survival to pursue new frontiers of social and intellectual advancement'. This is the only way we can continue to grasp the incomparable advantages that capitalism can offer. Let compassionate capitalism flourish.

The Travails of Philanthropy in India

Has India made sufficient progress since Independence? Can we be happy about this progress? Have we kept pace with the rest of the world? Have we achieved progress that is sustainable? Can we dream of an India where poverty, ill-health and ignorance will have vanished?

Let us analyse where India stands today. Our social indicators have improved in the past few decades. The proportion of the population below the poverty line declined from 45 per cent in the early eighties to 26 per cent in 2000; the literacy rate increased from 43 per cent of the population in 1980 to 65 per cent in 2001. However, we still have a long way to go. Around 50 per cent of the population do not have access to essential drugs; 69 per cent still do not have access to adequate sanitation. Life expectancy is only sixty-two years as compared to seventy-seven in the USA. Forty-seven per cent of our children are underweight, as compared to 10 per cent in China. Around 190 out of 100,000 people are afflicted with malaria, as compared to forty in neighbouring Bangladesh. We are ranked 124th on the Human Development Index (out of 173 nations).

Clearly, much needs to be done to improve the condition of the vast majority of our people. I am reminded of the words of George Bernard Shaw that the worst sin towards our fellow creatures is not to hate them, but to be indifferent to them. That is the essence of inhumanity.

Maulana Azad Memorial Lecture, New Delhi, 29 March 2004

There are a number of philanthropic organizations in the country that fight against this inhumanity. In fact, there are over two million NGOs and development groups in India. However, as Harvard professors Michael Porter and Mark Kramer say, 'Concerted effort, through secular charitable foundations, has to go well beyond the gifts of private donors. They should achieve a social impact disproportionate to their spending.' Unfortunately, Indian philanthropic efforts are yet to achieve such a social impact. Let me talk about some of the challenges.

India is a vast geographic area, divided into numerous cultures and languages. Over 700 million Indians live in rural areas. Of these, around 190 million live below the poverty line. In fact, India has the largest number of poor people in the world. In addition, 84 per cent of our illiterate population is in the villages. The diversity and magnitude of the problem create huge challenges.

At the same time, our philanthropic organizations are disorganized and lack effective channels for communication and resource sharing. There is no credible directory of organizations within India; there is no widespread platform to share best practices; and there is no public effort to collect knowledge and insight. The disorganized reporting practices limit our ability to accurately track activities across the nation. The inability to record observations and transfer knowledge limits efficiency. Every information seeker has to independently verify information, usually with multiple visits. I am reminded of an experience at the Infosys Foundation. The Foundation conducts a number of philanthropic activities; starting libraries for village children is a part of this. On one occasion, a man approached the Foundation and attempted to sell his books to it. He claimed to be a close personal friend of the Foundation's chairperson. What he did not realize was that he was talking to the chairperson herself!

A major challenge of philanthropy in India is the misuse of funds leading to lack of credibility. People are worried that the money they donate may not be used properly. Consequently, they tend to be sceptical of philanthropic organizations. Scepticism has led to apathy. We have not yet developed a culture of 'giving'. In a survey of philanthropy in Asian countries, it was found that high-income

Indians give less than their Indonesian, Thai and Filipino counterparts. Indians give only 1.7 per cent of their household income to philanthropic efforts. In comparison, Indonesians give almost 6 per cent. Apathy in solving community matters has held us back from making progress which is otherwise within our reach. We have to remember that fundamental social problems grow out of a lack of commitment to the common good.

For many decades after Independence, Indians believed that social issues relating to public causes were the responsibility of the government alone. Our rigid central-planning system and our 'hangover' from the days of colonial domination contributed to this mindset. Consequently, there was insufficient partnership between philanthropic organizations, the government and private corporations. During the past decade, we have witnessed a slow change in this mindset. We have also witnessed increased activity in corporate philanthropy. For instance, according to a study of Indian companies by IMRB (Indian Market Research Bureau), as many as 83 per cent considered social responsibility as an integral part of their strategy.

Internationally, public–private partnerships involving governments, the private sector and civil society are increasingly recognized as important to tackle social issues—from building health care to bridging the digital divide. The Global Health Alliance, forged by Rotary International, the United Nations, private sector corporations and governments, is an example of such a partnership. Such partnerships help create innovative solutions for society's needs leveraging the expertise of the private sector. The innovation of the Simputer in India is an example of such an innovation. Such partnerships can also ensure a steady flow of income to philanthropic organizations.

Bureaucratic delays are a major cause for concern. In one instance, a philanthropic organization was constructing a hospital for the poor. During the course of the project, it encountered many situations where clearances were required. Rather than initiate speedy clearances, the bureaucrats used red-tapism to delay the project's completion by two years. I recall the words of Robert Schaeberle that we can feed the world if we can ever make red tape nutritional.

Today, India is at the cusp of a revolution in economic growth. As a progressive nation, we have to focus on both the creation of wealth (through entrepreneurship) and the redistribution of at least a part of that wealth (by philanthropy). Philanthropy is part of the implicit social contract that nurtures and revitalizes economic prosperity. Much of the new wealth created has to be given back to the community to nurture future economic growth. This is the only way we can create hope for the large majority of our poor. Robert Kennedy once said, 'Each time a man stands up to improve the lot of others, he sends forth a tiny ripple of hope.' There is no more opportune time for us than now to create a multitude of such ripples.

Today, thanks to liberalization and subsequent economic growth, a large number of Indians have the capacity to contribute. Wealth invested back into society expands opportunity for a larger section of people, and we can thus create an upward spiral of wealth and prosperity. This is at the core of social success in countries like the USA.

In promoting philanthropic activity, we have to focus on both the supply side of philanthropy (donors) as well as the demand side (recipients). On both sides of the equation, many of our voluntary organizations have the capacity to solve problems but have little or no money to implement them. On the other hand, many of those that have the financial resources hardly have time or the focus to sustain programmes that cater to society's demands. How can we ensure increased participation in charitable activities as well as improve the effectiveness of our philanthropic effort? I will talk about some of the steps that we can take.

The need of the hour is to enthuse a large section of our affluent population to become active participants in philanthropy. According to a survey by Independent Sector, a coalition of philanthropic organizations in the USA, over 80 per cent of US households donate to charitable causes; 83 million American adults involve themselves in voluntary activities, representing the equivalent of over 9 million full-time employees at a value of $239 billion. Philanthropy has allowed the USA to tackle many of its social problems. In 2000, American philanthropic contributions accounted for almost 2 per cent of the national income. There are similar signs of increased philanthropic activity in Latin America, Spain and Russia, to name just a few countries.

Contributions from individuals have tremendous potential in India. However, most individuals donate to religious organizations. In fact, this accounts for about 35 per cent of donations made by Indians. Further, a majority of voluntary organizations in India lack the marketing and branding skills and the methodology to tap this very important source of funds. Owing to lack of transparency and accountability, many voluntary organizations suffer from serious crises of credibility. This often deters individuals from contributing to welfare or developmental projects.

The idea of professional foundations in the USA underpins today's philanthropic work there. Indian philanthropic groups should spearhead the evolution of philanthropy from private acts of conscience into a professional field. They should meet their obligations to create value. The need of the hour is to bring entrepreneurial acumen to philanthropy, demanding measurable results and carefully assessing social investments. Use of management ideas and information technology tools to create sound management systems is another aspect of professionalization of philanthropic groups.

Remember that public trust is the singlemost important asset of the philanthropic community. Without it, donors will not give and volunteers will not get involved. This implies accountability to the public and to the charitable intent of the donors. Improved performance also requires lowering the cost of administration and investing in more effective strategies for social change. Programme evaluation, focus on results, and even impact studies to measure the effectiveness of social investments are part of this. Independent Sector in the USA outlines a series of steps the philanthropic and non-profit sector must take to ensure accountability. We need a similar code in India.

Accountability requires a regime of impact measurement. What cannot be measured cannot be improved. Thus, the goal of a measurement programme is superior performance in a chosen area. A philanthropic organization should measure its success by the social impact of its work. This includes tracking various metrics like funds raised, membership growth, people served, expenses, overhead costs and social benefits reaped.

Comprehensive and accurate information about philanthropic organizations must be made accessible in ways that donors and other stakeholders find useful. In India, the information available from many of our philanthropic groups is woefully inadequate for analysing performance. The Internet should be used by small philanthropic groups to disseminate information on performance. Such information will help donors in comparing one organization with another in the same sector or locality. Most importantly, it will ensure that philanthropic organizations operate in a competitive environment to attract funds.

Philanthropic organizations should have a clearly defined and articulated strategy. This requires setting programme objectives and planning for sustainability. Accordingly, they have to focus on a few important areas after making an assessment of their opportunities, strengths and weaknesses. For instance, the Infosys Foundation has decided to focus only on a few areas—learning and education, health care, social rehabilitation, rural uplift and promotion of folk arts.

In India, the Internet has the potential to transform social service initiatives. It can help network social work activities across the country. For instance, it can bring together all organizations working for the same social cause. These may be industries, social organizations, donors etc. An Internet platform could thus bridge the gap between the resources and the needy communities. ResourceLink, promoted by Hewlett Packard, and Aidmatrix, promoted by i2 Technologies, are examples of this. Both pair food suppliers that have surplus food or products for donation with certified charitable organizations that can use these goods. Another example in the global context is networkforgood.org managed by AOL, Yahoo and Cisco Systems. However, the power of the Internet has not yet been harnessed fully in India where philanthropic activities are concerned.

Today, the role of a donor in India is slowly graduating from a 'giver' (of funds) to an investor in social change. However, change cannot be obtained through charity alone. Charity is important and necessary, but it only soothes. We must move from charitable care to developmental assistance. Consequently, we should focus on empowerment and developmental assistance. I am reminded of the twelfth century Jewish philosopher Maimonides who said, 'Give a man a fish and you feed him for a day. Teach a man to fish and you feed him for a lifetime.'

Providing microcredit in rural areas is an instance of this philosophy. I believe that this has tremendous potential to provide scalable solutions for tackling rural poverty. We can also leverage technology for microfinance. For instance, Hewlett Packard is now testing a Remote Transactioning System (RTS) which will serve to create virtual branches of Micro Finance Institutions (MFIs) in remote villages.

Philanthropy and volunteerism have long been an integral part of Indian society. The concept of *daana* goes back to the Vedic period. We must now regain those days of social activism. This battle must be fought with all our resources, collectively and in partnership. Let us remember the words of Ralph Waldo Emerson who said, 'To know that even one life has breathed easier because you have lived; this is to have succeeded.'

We, the privileged few, who have enjoyed the fruits of India's growth, hold the future. If we fail to act today, we are at the risk of endangering the well-being of generations to come. I am reminded of a quote by Dietrich Bonhoeffer that action springs not from thought, but from a readiness for responsibility. I am confident that people from all sectors—government, civil society and business—will take responsible action in this regard. This is the only way we can overcome the travails of philanthropy in India.

PART VIII

ENTREPRENEURSHIP

Reflections of an Entrepreneur

Many of my conversations with young management graduates lead to questions about the pleasures, opportunities and travails of entrepreneurship. I will reflect here on some of the lessons that I have learned from founding Infosys with a team of talented colleagues and managing it for the last twenty years. While this experiment was conducted in a faraway, less market-oriented India, I believe that the fundamental lessons I have learned have broader applicability.

My mind goes back to a sultry, fateful morning in July 1981, and a meeting with the six other founders of Infosys. The seven of us had forsaken—at least as it then appeared to our friends and families—safe and promising corporate careers. We were huddled together in a small room in Bombay in the hope of creating a brighter future for ourselves, for Indian society and, perhaps, we dreamed, even for the world. Confidence, commitment, passion, hope, energy, enthusiasm and the capacity for hard work were available in plenty. However, money was in short supply. We struggled to put together a princely sum of $250 as our initial seed capital. We were helped in this by our ever-enthusiastic bankers—our generous wives! Our enthusiasm can be expressed in the words of Eleanor Roosevelt who said, 'The future belongs to those who believe in the beauty of their dreams.' We knew our dream had to be based on a lofty vision, something larger than

Commencement Lecture, Wharton School of Business, Philadelphia, 20 May 2001 ourselves. Our vision was and is: to be a globally respected software corporation providing best-of-breed end-to-end business solutions leveraging technology and employing best-in-class professionals. I have realized, over the years, that a powerful vision expressed as a simple sentence, capturing the core of our values and aspirations, enthuses generation after generation of employees in the company. The beauty of such a simple yet powerful vision is that it is easy to understand, to communicate, to share and to move towards.

We built Infosys on three key concepts: the criticality of customized software in creating competitive advantage for a corporation, globalization and professionalization of the entrepreneurial venture. Every successful company is built on an idea that is taken seriously in the marketplace. For this, an idea has to achieve one or more of the following: improve customer satisfaction, reduce cost, reduce cycle time, improve productivity, increase customer base and improve the comfort level of customers. Strategy, an important building block of success, is all about becoming unique in a marketplace. This requires that every corporation build this uniqueness into its business rules and models. These rules and models become embedded in the information systems of the company. Thus, there was, is and will be considerable opportunity in creating customized software.

While we had a good idea, the market for the idea did not exist in India at the time. Therefore, we had to embrace globalization. When we founded the company, we knew that India, with its vast pool of English-speaking, analytically strong technical talent and the excellent work ethic among its professionals, had essential ingredients for global success in customized software development. Our idea was to produce software in India for clients in the G-7 countries. Our approach, while distinctive, was far from unique; companies in industries such as textiles and semiconductors were following similar strategies.

Since the co-founders had been professionals before we started Infosys, we wanted to build a company of professionals, for professionals and run by professionals. Accordingly, it was our belief that the first duty of a corporation is to uphold the respect and dignity of the individual. Right from day one, we eschewed any transaction that created an asymmetry of benefits between the founder-employees and other employees. Our core corporate assets walk out every evening, mentally and physically tired. It is our duty to make sure that these assets return well rested, energetic and enthusiastic the next morning. Our respect for our professionals can be summed up in our belief that the market capitalization of Infosys becomes zero after working hours end at 5 p.m., no matter what it was during the day.

A strong team is essential for every successful entrepreneurial experiment to succeed. Such a team brings together a set of complementary skills, expertise and experience. Today, the venture capitalists backing entrepreneurs help create such teams by connecting them with key talent networks. However, in those days, we did not have any venture capitalists in India. We ourselves had to bring together people who had some experience in human resources, finance, strategy, technology, project management, software development, and sales and marketing. In addition to complementary skills, it is essential that the team operates on a common value system and maintains the dignity and respect of every individual in every transaction. The motto for workplace interactions at Infosys has always been: 'You can disagree with me as long as you are not disagreeable.'

During the initial days, we faced tremendous challenges attempting to do business in India. It took us a year to obtain a telephone connection, two years to get a licence to import a computer and fifteen days to get foreign currency for travel abroad. Thus, the first ten years of our marathon seemed interminable and frustrating. Although we managed to keep our heads above water, we were floundering. However, the positive aspect of these years was that we learned to plough through adversity and, I hope, became better managers and better human beings as a result. The fuel that kept us going was our passion to make a difference. Even today, I believe that our passion is more important than our finances.

Louis Pasteur once said, 'Chance favours the prepared mind.' As we were struggling along, the Indian economic reforms of 1991 came as a heaven-sent opportunity for us at Infosys. These watershed reforms—likened by some to the winning of an economic freedom on the same lines as the securing of political freedom from British rule in 1947—changed the Indian business context from one of state-centred control orientation to a free, open market orientation, at least for hi-tech companies. We, at Infosys, leveraged the positives of liberalization and the opening up of the Indian economy—and have never looked back since. In fact, I take quiet pride in how Infosys has become a shining example of all the good that came out of India's economic reforms. The lesson from the Indian experience is a clear clarion call for all who are willing to listen: free trade can bring great benefits to society.

I will elaborate on some key lessons that we have learned from managing Infosys over the last twenty years. I believe that most of these lessons, while rooted in the Infosys experience, are valid in start-ups, as well as in large corporations, all over the world.

The great American civil rights leader Dr Martin Luther King Jr once remarked, 'The ultimate measure of a man is not where he stands in moments of comfort, but where he stands at times of challenge and controversy.' A company's value system is the guiding light in its hours of darkness, confusion and self-doubt, and when it is faced with a moral dilemma. A value system builds confidence, provides peace of mind, and enhances energy and enthusiasm during trials and tribulations. The importance you attach to your value system is reflected in the cost you are willing to incur for your beliefs and convictions. The more profound one's commitment to a value system, the greater is the cost one is willing to incur to defend the value system. At Infosys, we have had several instances when our values were severely tested. These events occurred in our dealings not only in India but also all over the world, including the USA. In every incident, we were firm and stood by our values because we knew that taking short cuts that compromised our ethics would be suicidal for us. This was what bound the team together. Our value system at Infosys can be captured in one sentence: 'The softest pillow is a clear conscience.' We try constantly to live up to this standard. We only act in ways that will let us sleep peacefully every night.

Every company has to recognize its strategic resources and ensure their long-term supply. In our case, human intellect, technology and processes are the three key strategic resources. We operate in a domain where customer preferences and technology change rapidly and business models, paradigms and rules quickly become obsolete. The only constant for us is change. These days, the world moves so fast that often the person who says that something cannot be done is proved wrong by another person who is already doing it. Our success at Infosys depends on our ability to recognize, learn and assimilate these changes quickly, and in bringing business value to our customers by leveraging the assimilated knowledge. Learnability is critical for us. We define learnability as the ability to extract generic inferences from specific instances and to use them in new, unstructured situations. Our company has always placed a premium on recruiting people with a high learnability quotient. In fact, the implicit belief at Infosys is that each person should surround himself or herself with much smarter people. Such an environment creates competition and confidence, and leads to energy and enthusiasm. We provide these people with up-to-date technology and a strong foundation in processes. Infosys's longevity will depend on how well we continue to build on our people resources. The biggest challenge for a knowledge company like Infosys is to recruit, enable, empower and retain the best and the brightest talent. We realized long ago that we had to make a compelling value proposition to our employees, much the same as we did for our customers.

Openness to new ideas, meritocracy, speed, imagination and excellence in execution are the five time-invariant and context-invariant attributes of a successful corporation. In fact, speed in imagination is the most critical success factor. Never before in history has imagination played a more significant role than it does today. As the power of incumbency keeps diminishing, the importance of imagination keeps increasing. The future winners will be those firms that escape the gravitational pull of the past on the fuel of innovation. The task of the CEO is to ensure that the corporation embraces and uses these five attributes in every aspect of its operation. This implies that every corporation has to create incentives for people to be innovative at all times. The best incentive for innovation is proactive obsolescence by wide dissemination. Such a proactive step helps a corporation to be in control of obsolescence, and remain a leader in its field. Obsolescence of a firm's innovations by its competitors will generally take it by surprise and find the firm unprepared. Such unprepared corporations are the poster children of missed opportunities and will not survive.

We have realized over the years that solutions to most of our problems lie within ourselves. Rationalizing failure is simply a sign of weakness. The easiest way to escape from accountability is to blame reality. It renders people and nations apathetic and justifies inaction. Leaders, on the other hand, transform reality from what it is to what they want it to be.

The main fuel of achievement comes from aspirations that are higher than the status quo. Leadership is all about raising the aspirations of followers. It is about making people believe in themselves; it is about making them confident; and it is about making people achieve miracles. Leadership is about dreaming the impossible and helping followers achieve them. Such lofty aspirations build great firms, great countries and great civilizations.

The best form of leadership is leadership by example. In a knowledge company whose core competencies include human intellect and learning through a process of observation, data collection, analysis and conclusion, leaders have to walk the talk. Any dissonance between rhetoric and action by leaders will hasten the loss of credibility. Leaders will do well to heed the words of Mahatma Gandhi who said, 'You must be the change you wish to see in the world.'

In this global age, given the path-breaking impact of the Internet on business practices, leaders in the business world can come from anywhere. Competition is global, all the more so in the world of digital products and services. The best ideas or business models will dominate, regardless of their national origins. It is in this competitive global regime that the best hopes and aspirations of India rest. It goes without saying that many challenges lie ahead, but I am sanguine about the future role that India, and other human-resource-rich countries such as China, will play in the global knowledge economy.

A well-run corporation embraces and practises a sound

Predictability–Sustainability–Profitability–De-risking model. We call this the PSPD model at Infosys. A good forecasting system for sales, based on data gathered from the trenches, ensures predictability (although predictability of costs is also needed to have predictable profit streams). Sustainability is achieved by energetic and motivated sales people who pound the pavement and make sales happen; by production people ensuring that quality products are delivered to the customer on time; and by billing and collecting on time. Every enterprise must focus on high profitability in order to strengthen the corporation and to ensure the best returns for its shareholders. Indeed, the long-term success of a corporation depends on having a model that scales up profitably. Finally, the corporation must have a good de-risking approach that recognizes, measures and mitigates risk along every dimension. The Degree of Affordable Risk (DAR) is a composite measure of the risk threshold of a corporation. Every corporation must measure its DAR, constantly improve its DAR and operate within the limits of its DAR.

Having emphasized the importance of de-risking, I must hasten to add that I do not, even for a moment, want to dissuade you from taking risks. Take risks you must, but take carefully thought out risks. We know that ships are safest in the harbour. But they are not meant to be there—the best ships are destined to ply the wide oceans and brave the stormy, heavy seas, before returning to the welcome safety of the port.

Another lesson that is anchored in the Infosys experience concerns governance. Corporate governance is focussed on maximizing shareholder value while ensuring fairness to all the stakeholders—customers, investors, employees, vendor-partners, the government of the land and society at large. In these days of free-flowing global capital, the ability to attract capital requires that corporations adhere to the best global standards of corporate governance. Studies have shown a significant correlation between the standards of corporate governance of a firm and its cost of capital. The foundation of our corporate governance philosophy at Infosys is the belief that it is better to lose a billion dollars than to act in ways that make one lose a night's sleep.

We also believe that it is a good practice to under-promise and over-deliver. Further, it is best to deliver the bad news to the stakeholders proactively and at the earliest. This creates goodwill with all the stakeholders. They fully understand that there inevitably will be ups and downs in every business. What they value, however, is for the management to level with them at all times.

Quick progress comes in an environment that respects competence, where there is healthy competition and where there are no prejudices. Infoscions, the name by which we call all our employees, have a sense of respect for our competitors, a healthy sense of paranoia that keeps us on our toes and a sense of humility about what we have achieved. We remember that success is, generally, ephemeral. We remember that we are only as good as the results of our last quarter. We fully believe that we are running a marathon, not a sprint; and our strategies and policies reflect that.

One of my strongest beliefs is that corporations have the important responsibility of contributing to society. While, on average, tremendous progress has been made in enhancing the economic well-being of people, the chasm between the haves and the have-nots of the world has unfortunately widened, especially in the developing world. No corporation can sustain its progress unless it makes a difference to its context. In the end, unless we can wipe the tears from the eyes of every poor man, woman and child on this planet, I do not think any dream is a worthy one.

Let me now share a few words of personal advice based on my experiences. First, I want to emphasize the importance of being trustworthy in all your dealings. It is on such foundations that great organizations are created. Second, fear is natural but do not let your actions be governed by it. Just as fear may sometimes be the hidden voice of your intuition alerting you to what your rational mind may not yet have seen, it is sometimes also an invitation to explore a new part of yourself and the world. Third, a supportive family is the bedrock upon which satisfying lives and careers are built. Create a support system for yourself with people who will rejoice in your success and be there for you. With this rock-like support behind you, you can endure almost anything in your career. Fourth, learn how to manage yourself, especially your feelings, in a way that respects the dignity of others and yourself. I have found it helpful to separate the merits and demerits of a decision from the feelings accompanying it. At Infosys we call this 'being transaction-oriented'. Finally, live your life and lead your career in a way that makes a difference to your society.

I want to close with an incident that is vividly etched in my mind. Some of you might remember an acclaimed series of interviews that the highly talented Bill Moyers did with Joseph Campbell, the great American mythologist and folklorist, some years ago. Deep into a profound discussion about life, Bill Moyers leaned over and asked Joseph Campbell, 'Joe, I am sure you have thought about this question. Why are we here on the Earth? What is the path for one to follow?' Joseph Campbell smiled and said, 'Yes, I have thought about it and the only answer I have found is this: Follow your bliss. All else will follow.' I urge you to do the same: Choose a worthy dream for yourself. Go after it confidently. Create a life that you will be proud of in the years to come. But always, without fail, ensure that you follow your bliss.

On Entrepreneurship

It is only recently that there has been some acceptance, in India, of the idea that the creation of wealth is necessary to solve the debilitating problem of poverty. Mahatma Gandhi's dream was to wipe the tears from the eyes of every poor person in the country. In my opinion, fulfilling this dream requires a consensus among all political parties on the following tenets:

  i. The only way we can solve the problem of poverty is by creating jobs with disposable incomes and new wealth legally and ethically, not by redistributing existing wealth.

  ii. There are only a few people who can lead the task of the creation of wealth, just as there are only a few good surgeons, professors and lawyers.

  iii. These people are human beings and they need incentives to create wealth.

  iv. The task of the government is not to create jobs and wealth but to create an environment where these leaders are enthused to create more and more jobs and wealth.

There are two kinds of wealth creators—those that add to existing wealth passed on to them by the previous generation of wealth creators and those that create wealth from scratch. I belong to the latter category and have very little idea of the former. Hence,

The fourteenth Anantharamakrishnan Memorial Lecture, Chennai, 8 February 1999

I will talk a little bit about creating wealth from scratch. Entrepreneurship refers to such creation of corporate wealth as leveraging ideas and sweat equity. In such cases, the lack of adequate finance forces an entrepreneur to take a path hitherto untrodden and create a niche for himself or herself. These entrepreneurs take advantage of the opportunities for innovation in markets with nothing more—especially in the initial stages of the enterprise—than new ideas and sweat equity. The software industry worldwide is full of such successful entrepreneurs. Rapid advances in technology and the consequent productivity gains have opened great market opportunities for innovation and thus ensured a steady stream of entrepreneurs in the American software industry. Whether it is Bill Gates of Microsoft or Larry Ellison of Oracle, the common factors are: a powerful idea, innovation, a brilliant vision, a well-thought-out strategy and flawless execution.

I have studied entrepreneurship in the Indian software industry for over twenty years and have come to some conclusions. During 1979–81, ten to twelve entrepreneurs (professionals) started software companies operating in the domestic and export markets. As of today, only one or two of them have survived, succeeded and been consistently among the top five Indian software export houses. A case study of these ten to twelve companies is a great education. We can draw certain conclusions from these case studies and can define some criteria for success. The physiology of successful companies and the pathology of unsuccessful companies bring out the following criteria for success.

Shared vision
The founders of the company must articulate a clear vision of what they want their company to be in the long run. This vision must be something that provides for a clearly definable synergy between the corporate objectives of the enterprise and personal aspirations of the entrepreneurs and the professionals within the enterprise.

A marketable idea
Unless you have an idea whose value to the customer can be expressed in a simple sentence, not a compound or complex sentence, there is

no point in proceeding further. Your product or service must provide one or more of the following benefits for its users that is better than the existing alternatives: reduced cost, reduced cycle time, improved productivity, improved comfort or enhanced customer base. Most failures are due to the negligence of this cardinal principle. If you are lucky, your idea may create a discontinuity in the market by providing value that no product did in the past. Netscape, computers, the television and automobiles are good examples of such discontinuities in ideas. The market must also be ready to accept and pay for your idea, else your idea will fail. Thus, timing is very important.

A sound strategy and an implementable action plan

Strategy is about making oneself unique in the marketplace. A strategic plan that clearly brings out the competitive advantages of the idea of the entrepreneurs, masks the weaknesses of the entrepreneurs, is realistic and ensures sustainability, is needed. A realistic action plan that has the required resources is needed to put this strategy into action.

A layer of competent management

The bane of most entrepreneurs is that they are primarily idea people or technocrats and hardly understand managerial issues in building an enterprise. Indeed, I have come across entrepreneurs who cannot read a balance sheet and can hardly distinguish between a term loan and working capital. They have a healthy contempt for anything other than technical challenges. Such an attitude is a sure recipe for unmitigated disaster. A successful enterprise will bring together complementary skills in ideas, technology and management. Success in an enterprise requires a good understanding of human motivation, finance, leadership, technology, production, quality and a host of other skills.

A shared value system

The initial years of a start-up are full of sacrifice, difficulties and challenges. There is more darkness than light during these years which are full of dilemmas, conflicts, hard work, deferred gratification and hope. This is where you need a common set of protocols and norms of behaviour among the members of the team. When you realize that your team members follow the agreed set of protocols, you are full of confidence, hope and enthusiasm in the future of the enterprise. You are willing to make sacrifices since you are confident that other members will not be taking advantage of them. The temptation to bend your own set of do's and don'ts is very compelling but the ability to stand firm in the face of an adverse situation is what separates the men from the boys. I have seen many an enterprise flounder because the entrepreneurs could not embrace a shared value system.

Professionalism

I have seen several budding entrepreneurs criticize their employers and do exactly what they criticized them for when they start their own company. Professionalism is drawing a clear line between personal and company resources; treating all your colleagues with respect and dignity; being issue-based and not personality-based; establishing and following person-independent rules and procedures in the company; and showing integrity and honesty in all transactions with your customers, colleagues, vendor-partners, the government and society.

Separating control from management

Indeed, if there is one critical issue for succeeding in entrepreneurship, it is the ability to separate control from management. In the USA, any entrepreneur will know that his venture capitalist will put in a management structure independent of his shareholding in the company. You, as the entrepreneur, will be asked to perform the role best suited to the organization's needs. We all know the story of Steve Jobs and how he brought in John Sculley to head Apple when he realized the need for professional leadership. You must recognize your strengths and contribute to the organization only in that role. Just because you have a certain stake in the company does not make you the boss, and it does not make you omniscient or omnipotent so far as the affairs of the company are concerned.

The spirit of sacrifice

Nothing can ever be built unless there is some sacrifice at least in the initial period. Most entrepreneurs fall prey to the trappings of the so-called 'industrialist syndrome', spending money on silly luxuries during the formative years and ending up jeopardizing the long-term interests of the enterprise. In fact, deferred gratification is a strategic tool for transforming a start-up into a large organization.

Pride in the creation of wealth

I have met several entrepreneurs who are very apologetic about the creation of wealth. For heaven's sake, there is absolutely nothing wrong in creating wealth by legal and ethical means. Do not ever confuse creation of wealth with charity. First you create wealth efficiently, and only then can you donate your share of the profit to any charity.

Ideology, intellectual arrogance and the enterprise

I have seen several instances where my entrepreneur friends have destroyed their enterprise just because they went on an ill-founded ideology trip. For example, one of my good friends felt that his company must produce compilers and word processors in India and compete with Microsoft and Borland, even though it was clear to everybody but him that such a strategy was absolutely unwise and disastrous. His whole argument was that we, Indians, are second to none and that we should prove to the world that we can produce system software better than anybody else. Obviously, he did not succeed as much as his superb intellect should have enabled him to.

R & D and the bread-and-butter stream

It is a truism in any business that the bread-and-butter stream of your enterprise pays for all costs including R & D. A smart enterprise derives its revenues from a bread-and-butter revenue stream, pays for the operational costs and uses a small percentage of this revenue (usually 5 to 10 per cent) to conduct R & D in promising new areas. Some of these new areas will, in the future, become bread-and-butter streams for the enterprise. I have known a couple of entrepreneurs who tried to derive a large part of their revenues from R & D and, I am sad to say, got into serious trouble.

Leadership by example

In enterprises dominated by white collar and knowledge professionals, you must lead by example. Today's professional has global level skills and opportunities, and is aware of it. Any discrepancy between what you preach and what you practise will be easily analysed by your younger colleagues and will create dissonance.

Finance

Money is extremely important to run a start-up since you have to pay salaries and bills. But it is not the most difficult resource to get. If you have a good idea, put together a good team and instil a good value system, the venture capitalists will chase you.

Let me close by saying that openness to new ideas, meritocracy, speed, imagination and excellence in execution are the five attributes of any successful entrepreneur. Those who leverage these attributes will survive and succeed in the coming decades of intense competition.

PART IX

GLOBALIZATION

Do We Need a Flat World?

Thomas Friedman first used the term 'flat world' to popularize the power of globalization. A flat world is a world that allows globalization to flourish. Globalization is about sourcing capital from where it is cheapest, sourcing talent from where it is best available, producing where it is most efficient and selling where the markets are, without being constrained by national boundaries. Globalization is nothing new. Nayan Chanda notes in his recent book *Bound Together* that globalization is a process of ever-growing interconnectedness and interdependence that began thousands of years ago and continues to this day with increasing speed and ease.

Globalization provides the opportunity for every nation to offer the best value-for-money products and services in the global bazaar without being restricted by bureaucracy, political hindrance or xenophobia. It provides a corporation with an opportunity to hire the best talent in the world, and to list on the best stock exchanges of the world. A globalized corporation is different from a multinational corporation (MNC). An MNC generally starts a subsidiary in a country to produce and sell in that country alone. A globalized corporation, on the other hand, produces its products for the entire world in a country or a region where it is cheapest to produce. In a typical globalized corporation, product development takes place where

The first Michael Dell Lecture, University of Texas, Austin, 15 November 2007

human talent and innovation are best; production takes place in factories situated in countries where it is most cost-effective to produce; and sales take place in countries with high disposable incomes.

However, we are far from the ideal globalized world. Pankaj Ghemawat, professor of strategy at the Harvard Business School, argues that a domestic focus is still the primary focus in most sectors of the economy even after a century of attempts at globalization. He shows that international telephone calls are still just 3 per cent of the total call volume, foreign direct investment is less than 3 per cent of the total direct investment, and international tourists account for less than 10 per cent of the total tourist traffic. He concludes that we are still a long way from being a borderless world.

My own view is that globalization has indeed advanced significantly in industries where a corporation from a country or a region has a distinctive, monetizable competitive advantage to offer in the global market. Examples abound. The computer industry, investment banking, the hospitality industry and the education sector are all clear instances of the prominent market share that the USA has in the global bazaar thanks to the distinctive competitive advantages and brand positions built up by US companies and universities in these sectors.

Let me give you a couple of examples of globalized operations leveraging the power of a flat world. Reebok and Niké are good examples of such corporations. During the early eighties these pioneers of modern sports shoes realized the huge market potential for such shoes in advanced markets, and the tremendous cost efficiency, quality and productivity of labour in countries like Taiwan and South Korea. They hired brilliant designers in the USA and Europe to design cutting-edge sports shoes, got them produced in Asian countries, hired brand experts and star brand ambassadors from G-7 countries to create powerful brands, and registered huge sales. The result was a huge gain for customers since they got world-class shoes at a fraction of the prevailing prices.

A second example is my own company, Infosys. In 1981, we realized that the demand for software in the developed world would skyrocket, thanks to falling hardware prices and the availability of inexpensive software engines that support robust online transaction processing on minicomputers and super-minicomputers. At the same time, we saw a tremendous shortage of skills in the developed world. Additionally, almost every prospect told us about the cost and time overruns in most software projects and their desire to bring engineering discipline to software development. Being in India, we found a large supply pool of technically trained talent with an excellent work ethic available at very competitive costs. This led to the creation of the Global Delivery Model, a model that is based on collaborative software development. In this model, about 20 to 25 per cent of the work involving heavy customer interaction is delivered by our people at or near customer premises while 75 to 80 per cent of the effort with little or no customer interaction is delivered from scalable, talent-rich, technology-based, process-driven and cost-competitive development centres in countries like India and China. This model has resulted in the delivery of superior quality software at a fraction of the prevailing prices. Most importantly, over 95 per cent of such projects were completed on time and within budgets against the then-prevailing average of only 45 per cent of projects. This was a true win for our customers.

One aspect of globalization that has received a great deal of attention is outsourcing, the globalization of services delivered from abroad. There have been several passionate arguments for and against outsourcing. Theory as well as data shows that outsourcing benefits a nation and its people, and that it is not the cause of wage declines or job losses. Economists Paul Krugman and Robert Lawrence have argued that increased trade does not impact real income and that low-wage US workers do not suffer due to foreign trade and competition. According to David Ricardo, even if a country could produce everything more efficiently than another country, it would reap gains from specializing in what it is best at producing and trading with other nations. The Heckscher–Ohlin theorem notes that a capital-abundant country will export capital-intensive goods while a labour-abundant country will export labour-intensive goods. In fact, research by McKinsey shows that US corporations and their investors actually benefit from outsourcing their IT services to India.

What are the benefits of a flat world? Is it a panacea for the ills of world trade as made out by the proponents of globalization, or is it all bad as made out by several journalists, special interest groups and human rights organizations? Let me cover a few benefits first, then talk about some concerns and finally discuss how we can overcome some of these concerns.

First, a flat world is clearly a powerful platform for leveraging the global intelligentsia towards enhancing the innovation power of corporations everywhere. India and China, thanks to their huge population and their focus on higher technical education, have become reservoirs of technical talent. Every year, China produces 600,000 engineers while India produces 450,000. In comparison, the USA produces 70,000 engineers a year. Several global corporations have consequently realized the importance of sourcing this global talent. For example, General Electric (GE) has set up an R & D laboratory, the largest of its kind outside the USA, in Bangalore; over 1,000 GE researchers work on leading-edge solutions out of this facility. Microsoft has established R & D facilities in China and India. Indian units of US firms like Cisco Systems, GE, IBM, Intel, Motorola and Texas Instruments filed over 1,000 patents in the year 2004 alone. Manufacturing firms like Ford and Boeing see India as critical for their global supply chain and R & D. There is a vast pool of highly educated talent in several emerging countries that can add value to the giant corporations of the USA and the West.

Second, the demographics of the West will result in a large number of old people and retirees in the next twenty-five years. As a result, there is likely to be a shortfall of labour even for basic services. For example, the share of the US population of people aged sixty-five and older is projected to increase from 10.7 per cent in 2003 to almost 14 per cent in 2015. Currently, the baby boomers alone represent around 27 per cent of the total US population and account for nearly half of US consumer expenditure. Additionally, the retirees would require services with very efficient cost structures since their post-retirement disposable incomes will be low. Countries like India, which have a demographic advantage, can provide many such services—accounting, legal services, tax advice, travel and hotel bookings, medical appointments and medical analysis—remotely, at a fraction of the cost in the USA.

Third, globalization enhances the competitiveness of corporations. In a competitive market like the USA, corporations are forced to continually improve their efficiency, trim their costs and reduce their product prices to obtain larger market shares. This is possible only if corporations can leverage the power of the flat world by moving some of their functions to less expensive regions. Such competitive positioning requires reduction of cycle times and improvement of productivity. One way of achieving these reductions and improvements is to use the power of the 'twenty-four-hour-workday' by combining the prime time of the USA with the prime time of countries like India and China which are at the other end of the world and have abundant skilled professionals. Such a move also enhances the profits of US corporations so that they can employ more US labour, pay them better compensation and invest more in R & D. Thus, it is a win-win-win proposition for the corporation, the local labour force and the countries involved in the trade.

Fourth, globalization helps a nation overcome its supply challenges. Thanks to the tremendous focus on innovation in developed markets, there is considerable demand for qualified professionals in the USA. The USA has always been at the forefront of innovation, thanks to its world-beating talent. However, there is a huge shortage of professionals in most engineering areas in general, and in computer science in particular. The enrolment of students in computer science in the USA, I am told, has gone down from 52,196 in 2001 to 48,046 in 2005. Interestingly, over 40 per cent of the enrolled students are from abroad, particularly from India and China. Asian students, in fact, account for over 44 per cent of the total student visas in the USA. Data shows that the USA has benefited from such immigration—a World Bank study noted that a 10 per cent rise in the number of skilled immigrants as a share of the US labour force tends to increase future patent applications by 0.8 per cent and university patent grants by 1.3 per cent. Several well-known corporate leaders in the USA have repeatedly said that the country must have favourable immigration policies to enable local corporations, particularly technology firms, to retain foreign students to be able to maintain and enhance their competitive capabilities.

Given that the living conditions in these talent-supplying countries are improving and their opportunities for research are increasing, it is likely that many of these well-qualified people will return to their native lands. If US corporations have to leverage their expertise, it is necessary to outsource some of the advanced work to these countries.

Fifth, globalization expands the market geographically. Most corporations with traditional products like food, clothing and automobiles have found that the markets in developed nations have matured and growth rates are low. Hence, they have started focussing on emerging markets. The opportunities offered by the flat world have enhanced the purchasing power in these countries, making these markets important. For example, India and China are some of the fastest growing markets for the auto and airline industries. A recent report by PriceWaterhouseCoopers notes that the BRIC countries—Brazil, Russia, India and China—will account for more than 40 per cent of the forecast for global light vehicle assembly increases and represent 52 per cent of the industry's forecast for global capacity expansion during 2005–10. Thus, providing outsourcing opportunities to these countries in some sectors will open up huge opportunities for corporations in developed countries like the USA in other areas. This again is a win-win proposition.

Sixth, the flat world paradigm is sine qua non for a peaceful world. It is generally agreed that most of the anger, violence and terrorism that we see today is due to the huge economic divide that exists between the haves and the have-nots. A sure way to reduce this divide is to focus on bringing the poorer world into the mainstream by making them trade partners so that it is a win-win proposition for both. A world concentrating on improving the quality of life through international trade is likely to be a peaceful world. Thanks to the multilateral trading system, ideological blocks get weakened. Once trade becomes the focus of the relationship between two countries, any geo-political differences are likely to be resolved peacefully, since no politician will be ready to lose trade and bring down the economic well-being of his/her people.

Having covered the benefits from the flat world phenomenon, let me now address some of the concerns expressed in the USA about the flat world.

Clearly, the first concern is about the loss of some jobs in the short term. Critics argue that globalization favours outsourcing and an increase in immigration, both of which result in job losses and lower wages. These are clearly important views. Robert Feenstra and Gordon Hanson have examined the impact of outsourcing of labour-intensive components on US manufacturing firms. They concluded that outsourcing raised the real wages of US workers. Take the case of immigration. Philippe Legrain in his recent book *Immigrants* notes that flexible advanced economies can absorb large numbers of immigrants without any cost to native workers if the inflows are reasonably predictable and with only a short-term cost to them if they are unexpected. Legrain looks at how cities like London, New York and Toronto have benefited from the diversity of immigrants. Quoting several studies, Legrain also concludes that the influx of immigrants does little or no harm to the wages or employment prospects of native workers.

My view is that short-term job losses are inevitable if we want to create new opportunities for a larger number of people in the medium term and to provide better value-for-money for a large number of consumers. Let me give you an example. A few years ago, I was asked by a journalist in Australia about my views on the loss of jobs in Australia. I took the example of India and demonstrated how the entry of multinationals had benefited consumers in a big way, even though there was some loss of jobs in the short term. I said that I would any day accept benefit to a vast majority of people at the cost of a small number of jobs which is likely to get redistributed over a short period of time. Let me elaborate this with a few examples.

In my house, my old, wonderful Indian refrigerator has been replaced by a gleaming new one from a South Korean company. This might have led to some loss of jobs in India since many components for the new refrigerator are imported from South Korea. However, when South Korean and Western firms like Samsung, LG, Electrolux and Whirlpool started manufacturing in India and sourcing components locally, they created more jobs than the jobs that were lost earlier.

I use a Toyota car to get to my office. India had just a few car manufacturing firms prior to the entry of companies like Toyota, Honda, Ford, GM, Suzuki and Hyundai. Prior to the entry of these auto majors from abroad, consumers had very little choice in cars and the quality of cars in India was very poor. When the global auto majors started expanding in India, the Indian players reported massive losses and some of them were even forced to shut down. This resulted in job losses. Meanwhile, the entry of global majors expanded the car market and India is now among the fastest growing car markets in the world. This has resulted in a boom in the auto component industry creating huge employment opportunities in this sector.

The story is the same in the case of electronic equipment and the computer hardware industry. I use a Dell computer in the office. We too had our computer manufacturers, not very efficient, but they had created lots of jobs. These jobs were lost since most of the computers and laptops are imported into India today. Currently, firms like Flextronics, Dell and Nokia have their manufacturing locations in India creating thousands of new jobs in India. While India lost about 3 to 4 million jobs due to the closure of the old and inefficient domestic companies, the country has created at least three times the number of such jobs, thanks to these new multinational companies. More importantly, we have seen keener competition in the market, prices have come down, and consumers have benefited immensely. Thus, while 3 to 4 million jobs were lost in the short term, the country has seen benefits for 300 to 400 million consumers. However, we must provide new opportunities to those people who became unemployed. Fortunately, this too has happened. A recent OECD report notes that India adds over 11 million jobs every year, thanks to globalization.

In the case of the USA, the job market has adjusted itself positively. In a recent speech, Federal Reserve Board Chairman Ben S. Bernanke noted that a 'positive churn' in the US job market has resulted in higher-paying jobs. According to him, over the past decade, nearly 16 million private sector jobs have been eliminated each year in the USA, while more than 17 million jobs are being created every year. Another study by Prof. Lori Kletzer corroborates this. Kletzer examined three types of manufacturing industries by classifying them into low, medium and high import competing, based on the change in the import share during 1979–94. Across the three groups of industries, about two-thirds of the people who were displaced earlier were reemployed within two years, with about half of that group ending up with jobs that paid roughly as much or more than their previous jobs.

The second concern is the possible lowering of the quality of life of people in developed countries as a result of globalization and outsourcing. Let us look at the data on the per-capita GDP of the USA itself. According to a recent paper published by the Economic Policy Institute, US trade with China has eliminated production that could have supported 2,166,000 US jobs during the period 1997–2006. However, during the same period, the per-capita GDP of USA increased from $31,011 in 1997 to about $43,500 in 2006. This has happened because US corporations have used innovation to move up the value chain and created new products and services which other countries have not been able to do. The USA has been able to export several high-end and innovative products with higher productivity or higher revenue per person. In comparison, the sales revenue per employee of products exported out of China or India is low. The USA has always been the leader in this and will continue to move up the chain in terms of higher sales per employee.

What is the solution to the temporary loss of jobs in the USA brought about by the flat world? Even famous economists like Paul Samuelson have warned about the potential job losses that will come from it. To stem this, people who are entering the workforce must first be well equipped to manage changing demands. To make this happen, they must be provided industry-oriented education and training. Second, the existing skill levels of the labour force must be improved. I understand that the Trade Adjustment Programme, which looks at offering up to thirty months of job training, income support and health insurance support, is already looking into this.

It is best to remember the words of Jagdish Bhagwati, a well-known free-market economist, who has argued that the USA will always maintain its supremacy in global trade and will retain its prosperity if it continues its focus on higher education, innovation and merit-based immigration policy to attract the best and the brightest. He notes that the USA is a reasonably flexible, dynamic and innovative society and that the twists and turns of the US economy will produce higher-wage jobs.

Finally, let me reiterate that we need a flat world because it spreads the American beliefs in free trade to the rest of the world; it benefits consumers from all over the globe; it helps create a world with better opportunities for everyone; and, finally, it brings global trade into focus, shunning terrorism and creating a more peaceful world. As a great admirer of the USA, I am extremely optimistic that the country will continue to be the unquestioned leader in prosperity in this flat world through its scientific and technological innovation.

Making Globalization Work for India

Today, we live in a world where every nation that has something to contribute can improve the lives of not just its own people but of people throughout the globe—the rich and the poor, the powerful and the weak, the educated and the not-so-educated. Never before in the last two hundred years did the developing countries have an opportunity to take their share of the limelight as they do today. In fact, currently, more than half of the world's GDP, measured at purchasing power parity, is generated by developing countries. Air travellers in the USA going from La Guardia airport to Ithaca are flying Embraer aircraft from Brazil; well-known Wall Street companies are running heartbeat systems designed by Indian software engineers; Indian companies and the Indian operations of companies like Intel, Cisco and Texas Instruments filed over a thousand patent applications with the US patent office in the year 2004 alone; and sophisticated electronic gadgets like iPods, manufactured in China, have filled the shelves of Best Buy in the USA. These are all good examples of global integration and the contribution of the developing world to the global economy.

What is globalization? I will define it at two levels. At the macro level, it is about frictionless flow of capital, services, goods and labour across the globe. It is also about global sharing of ideas, knowledge and culture. It is about creating a shared concern and plan for global

The fourth Nani Palkhivala Lecture, Mumbai, 15 January 2007

issues like poverty, AIDS and the environment. Thomas Friedman calls such a world a 'flat world' while I call it a 'globalized world'. At the microeconomic or firm level, it is about sourcing capital from where it is cheapest, sourcing talent from where it is best available, producing where it is most efficient and selling where the markets are, without being constrained by national boundaries. Infosys, IBM and Niké are all good examples of globalization at the firm level.

Joseph Stiglitz, the Nobel Laureate economist, is an expert on globalization. I have read and learnt much from his three books on this topic: *Globalization and Its Discontents*, *The Roaring Nineties* and *Making Globalization Work*. His arguments about fair trade, patents, the 'resource curse', the burden of debt, reforming the global reserve system, the democratic deficit in multilateral institutions, and saving the planet, are all well thought out, and are supported by data. His work is an extraordinary addition to any discussion on globalization. Being a humanist, Stiglitz is sympathetic to the position of developing nations, examines the deficiencies and ills in the perspectives of developed nations and multilateral institutions towards globalization, and argues for reforms. Other economists like Jagdish Bhagwati, Jeffrey Sachs and Paul Krugman have also done seminal work in this area. I have neither the competence nor the inclination to engage in debate with these distinguished experts. I will look only at globalization today, primarily from the perspective of what we, in India, have to do to bring its benefits towards alleviating the poverty of the larger masses. I will dwell on what we have to learn from the successes of globalization in China, the East Asian countries and Mexico. I also believe that performance brings recognition, recognition brings respect, and respect brings power. Hence, I will focus on creating a culture of speed, performance and excellence in our public institutions, and the role of leadership in doing so.

I must make clear a few of my beliefs before proceeding further, since the very basis of my arguments stands on these beliefs. First of all, I believe in capitalism. Having sympathized with, studied and experienced socialism and communism, I am convinced that we have to give compassionate capitalism a fair chance if we have to solve the problem of poverty. After all, capitalism is about creating an environment of equal and fair chance to every citizen to improve his or her life economically through hard work, enterprise and initiative. Compassionate capitalism is about pursuing capitalism while keeping the interest of society in every decision we take to further our own interest.

I believe in democracy. As Winston Churchill said, democracy may not be the best form of government, but the alternatives are worse. Democracy is about achieving the collective aspirations of a nation and not that of a few vested interests. Democracy mandates openness for discussion and debate and generally brings out the best ideas. Democracies provide the most effective platform for addressing the basic needs of every citizen—education, health care, shelter and nutrition. A democratic setup creates equal opportunities for everyone to better his or her life. It also averts disasters, as eloquently argued by the Nobel Laureate economist Amartya Sen.

I believe in Max Weber's philosophy. His essay on the Protestant work ethic and the spirit of capitalism is a favourite of mine. Having observed the Indian society in action and seeing the slow progress we have made in alleviating poverty, I believe that work culture, discipline, integrity and honesty play an important part in the rational pursuit of economic gain and, consequently, in eradicating poverty. I also believe that these attributes can be influenced by leadership in corporations, communities and nations. I will talk about the issues of creating a culture of performance, the role of leadership, leveraging the power of democracy to win in the globalized world and enhancing the accountability of bureaucracy.

Let me now discuss why we have to embrace globalization and integrate better with global markets. The primary objective of every nation is to ensure prosperity, harmony, peace and joy for all its citizens. Harmony, peace and joy come only if abject poverty is eradicated and prosperity is ensured. Let us remember Jawaharlal Nehru, who said, 'We have to fight poverty as stoutly and as bravely as we fight any enemy who invades our country. We can build our nation only when we build our people and make them happy and contented.' I believe that the only way we can eradicate poverty in India is by creating jobs with disposable incomes. This is a massive task. Several estimates put the number of unemployed in India at around 250 to 300 million. Every year, we are adding about 15 to 20 million new job seekers to this massive figure. This problem is exacerbated when we realize that about 70 per cent of these youngsters—aged between eighteen and twenty-five—are illiterate or barely literate. As against this, the country has been able to generate hardly 2 to 3 million jobs a year. It means we are moving towards a grave situation which may soon become explosive. Let me add another dimension to this problem. About 92 per cent of the jobs are in the unorganized sector where the salaries are low and benefits are non-existent. There is a third dimension too. About 65 per cent of the population or about 650 million Indians are in rural areas and their primary livelihood is from agriculture and related services, which just add 26 per cent to the GDP. In other words, 650 million people add just Rs 800,000 crore ($200 billion) to the GDP every year, or a mere Rs 13,200 ($300) per person per annum. This is less than Rs 40 a day. Even by Indian standards, this is not sufficient to keep body and soul together. Thus, we have two gigantic problems— generating employment for 15 to 20 million new entrants in the job market every year and enhancing the per-capita income for the vast majority of 650 million Indians employed in agriculture and related sectors.

It is evident that the latter problem can only be solved by one or more of three initiatives—increasing the prices of agricultural commodities, improving the growth rate in agriculture, and moving people from agriculture to some other sector. Increasing the prices of agricultural commodities massively is not feasible in view of the low global prices of food items and the impact of such an increase on the large number of poor people in the country.

The growth rate in agriculture has gone down from 3.2 per cent in pre-1985 India to about 1.9 per cent during the current decade, making life worse for rural folk. The production of rice and wheat, the two staple food items for Indians, has declined or remained constant between 1999 and 2005 at around 85 and 75 million tons respectively. If the population grows at 2 per cent per annum in rural areas and the agricultural sector grows at 2.5 per cent per annum, the per-capita GDP in agriculture will remain the same even ten years from now. If our economy continues to grow at the current rate of 8 per cent over the next ten years and the agriculture sector grows at 2.5 per cent during the same period, then, in 2017, agriculture will contribute to just 16 per cent of our GDP as against the current 26 per cent. To get to the same per-capita GDP from agriculture as the national per-capita GDP, at the current 8 per cent growth rate, by 2017, we have to move a whopping 100 to 120 million people from agriculture to other sectors (assuming there are four to five family members per earning member). So, we have to move at least 10 to 12 million people a year from agriculture to other sectors for the next ten years. Add to this the problem of 15 to 20 million youngsters joining the job-seeker category every year. Then you see a whopping 25 to 30 million people who have to be employed in either new jobs or better-earning jobs.

Which sectors can provide opportunity for these people? Services sectors like software, BPO and financial services can employ well-educated youngsters and create opportunities for at best a million job seekers a year. Remember that a large percentage of these 25 to 30 million people are illiterate or semi-literate. China has understood this problem well and has focussed on low-tech manufacturing jobs. It has been able to create about 150 million jobs in the low-tech manufacturing sector over the last eleven years. This is some sort of a record. If we have to solve the problem of poverty in India during our lifetime, we have to perform better than China. At the same time, we have to continue to focus on high-tech, high per-capita jobs since that is our forte.

Such an initiative calls for focussing on exports, since domestic consumption is likely to be low due to low disposable incomes. Most progressive developing countries like China, Brazil, Mexico and the East Asian countries have a contribution of more than 30 per cent of GDP from exports. On the other hand, we are still at less than 15 per cent. We have to ensure that exports contribute to 30 to 40 per cent of our GDP. To achieve this, we have to focus on products that advanced nations need. We have to become the factory of the world like China has become. We should create a supportive environment for foreign firms to invest in 100 per cent export-oriented units so that these units produce world-class products at low prices. We have to enhance our interactions with global markets and integrate ourselves better with people from other markets. After all, this is what globalization is all about.

This is a tall order, but I believe we can succeed if we show courage. We have to leverage our strengths—our democratic setup, the rule of law, our English-speaking technical talent, our demographic structure, our vast uncultivated land and natural resources—to bring about equitable growth for both rural and urban folk. For example, only 34 per cent of arable land is irrigated in India while 44 per cent of arable land is irrigated in China. Interestingly, India has more arable land than China.

We have to enhance and use the country's arable land. At the same time, we have to accept urbanization and make living in cities bearable. If we have to become a factory of the world, it is inevitable that we welcome a large number of foreigners to live amongst us and create an environment that they feel comfortable in. Doing this in rural areas requires much greater investment and time. We should try converting a village into a modern livable place with good connectivity, like the Pais have done in Manipal, and upgrade a few of our urban areas. We must accept that urbanization is inevitable and should not fight it.

Now, let me come to a few major mindset transformations we need to bring about to make globalization work for India.

i.   First, we have to stop arguing on -isms and philosophy. As Nani Palkhivala once said, 'Poverty is cruel, but curable. The only known cure is economic pragmatism instead of woolly ideology.' Let us focus on moving ahead with the creation of jobs. We have to become open-minded to learn from people and nations that have developed earlier and faster than us. To be open-minded, we have to become humble. We have to become more facts-and-data-oriented in our discussions. My interactions with many foreigners tell me that Indians are low on humility. This nation has had a reputation for arrogance from time immemorial. We become defensive pretty quickly in any conversation and start defending failures like our huge population and our bureaucracy. The tragedy is that we do nothing to address these apparent weaknesses, if they are indeed weaknesses. For example, we have completely given up on controlling population ever since Indira Gandhi lost the election in 1977 after aggressively propagating family planning.

ii. We have to stop using democracy as an excuse for failure. Discussing democracy as a liability impresses no one. Let us remember that most developed nations are democracies. Even in India, Nehru and his team leveraged the power of democracy to achieve so much during their term in office by creating a sound infrastructure for economic progress—land reforms, five steel plants, the Bhakra Nangal dam, the Atomic Energy Commission, institutes of higher learning, and much more. While discussions and debates on democracy are needed, our leaders have to accept that this system is better than any alternative.

iii. To achieve fast progress, all political parties have to be on the same page on the big issues. To do this, we have to embrace intellectual integrity in discussions. Our politicians say one thing when they are in government and the exact opposite when they are in the opposition. Integrity of thought requires education and data orientation. We have to train the majority of our political leadership to understand the nuances of the modern world, rudimentary economics, development theory, entrepreneurship, prerequisites for succeeding in the global economy and cross-cultural negotiations. Instead of becoming emotional on issues, we should use data to come to conclusions.

iv. We have to embrace speed if we have to succeed in today's globalized world. The speed of decision-making in government has to improve on a daily basis so that we can catch up with countries like China. I can cite many instances where decisions have been pending for over a decade: building a power plant for Bangalore has been pending for over twenty years; creating a fast track for Japanese and German businessmen which Prime Minister Rajiv Gandhi announced in 1987 has been pending for nineteen years; and even a minor request like providing a 240-page passport to frequent travellers in the software industry has been pending for over eight years!

v.   We have to become a reliable nation. One constant complaint against India by foreigners is that our government is very unreliable. We make promises and do not keep them. We renege on our commitments and contracts. We announce policies and do not implement them for years. The decisions of our ministers get hijacked by legal inanities and bureaucracy. Investors cannot make firm business plans based on government pronouncements.

vi. Our leaders have to straddle both worlds—the urban and the rural, the educated and the not-so-well-educated, the rich and the poor. They must understand how jobs can be created and encourage such creation. They should not take sides. They should not play a zero-sum game. For example, the software industry in Bangalore has been pilloried for just asking for better roads to commute to the offices. It is ironic that the leaders who espouse the cause of rural India sit in urban India and condemn those that create jobs there. Our leaders have to lead by example and become examples of Mahatma Gandhi's prescription: 'We must be the change we want to see in others.'

vii. The elite and their vested interests have played havoc with the future of the poor in this country. For example, while the rich and the powerful send their children to English-medium schools, we have denied the same benefit to the poor. Every year, I get requests from dozens of cleaning women, drivers, peons and clerks who want to admit their children to English-medium schools. They too want their children to become software engineers, bankers, lawyers, civil servants and journalists. My umpteen requests to successive chief ministers in Karnataka in this regard have fallen on deaf ears or resulted in ineffective band-aid solutions. Let there be no doubt that we will regret this in the future when countries like China become proficient in English and nullify the advantage that Nehru created for us.

viii.   We have to improve the quality of education in both primary and higher education. As Aristotle said 2,300 years ago, the foundation of every state rests on the education of its youth. Despite our boasting, Indian universities and educational institutions rarely figure in global rankings. China, on the other hand, has done a remarkable job in this area. I agree with Joseph Stiglitz that the main difference between China and India is not democracy but the lack of India's focus on education and health care. We must liberalize the education sector like we liberalized the industrial sector in 1991. All institutions of higher learning have to become completely autonomous. There should be greater interaction with well-known universities abroad. Syllabi will have to be revised rapidly to keep pace with changes in the world. Rote learning, the bane of the Indian higher education system, has to give way to a problem-solving orientation. Our current attitude to education reminds me of what Mark Twain said, 'In the first place, God made idiots. That was for practice. Then he made school boards.'

ix.   Another major reason for our slow progress is our bureaucracy which has little accountability and no incentive to perform. Most of the delays in execution have very little to do with our political systems. It is due to the lack of attention to speed and excellence in execution. There is hardly any training, planning and preparedness of the bureaucracy to handle growth. Bringing economic pragmatism to government decision-making seems alien to us. When I talk of government, I am reminded of Chester Bowles who said, 'After two years in Washington, I often long for the realism and sincerity of Hollywood!' There is no linkage between performance and reward in our governments. Hence, most projects are delayed inordinately. The mindset is administrative and in favour of maintaining the status quo. It should become managerial, which is about progress based on completing tasks on time, within budgeted cost and to the satisfaction of the customers. The days of the generalist revenue-collector type of administrators are over. Today, you need specialists who will have to spend all their time in one function, learning and constantly upgrading their skills. They should be trained to become managers.

x. If there is one skill that most of our bureaucrats must learn, it is project management. We have to get to a higher level of project performance. This can be done if, at the start of the term of each new government, about fifty major projects in each department are identified with budgets for time, quality and cost. The senior officers must be given a contract of ten years as secretaries, and continue for this period, no matter which government is in power. Continuation of the tenure of a bureaucrat every year must depend only on how well he or she has performed. It must become compulsory for every TV channel, newspaper and Internet website to publish the progress of each project on an annual basis with the names of the minister and the senior bureaucrats involved. The progress must be certified by a citizen committee consisting of highly respected people from various walks of life. The bureaucrats must have a small fixed salary and a large variable salary which will depend on the progress of the projects handled. This is the best way to bring accountability to the bureaucracy and politicians.

xi. Our bureaucrats have to learn to stand up for their beliefs and values rather than be subdued by their 'respect' for their superiors—political and otherwise. It is wise to remember Bernard Shaw's words, 'Some people have so much respect for their superiors that they have none left for themselves.'

xii. The Right to Information Act (RTI) is a wonderful instrument to bring transparency to our governments. Our governments must strengthen this act and not allow vested interests to weaken it.

xiii. Talking about transparency, I must say that technology and systems should play a mandatory role in governance if we want to improve accountability and transparency. First, every activity in the government, including routine ones, should be designed as projects and project management software must be used to monitor their progress. Second, it is necessary to use workflow software for every decision-making process. Such software will ensure that these processes are divided into steps, and each step can be assigned both a completion time target and the person responsible to complete the step can be identified. Thus, any delay in the progress of a project or a decision can be pinpointed to the individual who might be sitting on the decision. Also, all the paperwork regarding that step and the previous steps can be seen by anybody on the net! Thus, for every decision, there will be full transparency and accountability since the person, the duration for which he or she is sitting on the decision and the reason for the delay will be known to every citizen.

xiv. We should encourage the growth of business by reducing friction to business and not by tax incentives. Let us remember that Nani Palkhivala often said, 'To every economic policy and legislation we must apply the acid test—how far will it bend the talent, energy and time of our people to fruitful ends and how far will it dissipate them in coping with legal inanities and a bumbling bureaucracy.' We should abolish all tax incentives for exports above a low threshold of Rs 10 crore of profit and tax exemption on dividends above a low threshold of Rs 1 lakh, and plough that money into rural education, mid-day meal schemes and rural health care. If need be, we should not hesitate to raise both corporate and personal tax rates to 50 per cent of the income, as long as we install a mechanism to ensure that the money is used properly.

xv. We retain the mindset of the enslaved and of victims even six decades after Independence. We view every foreigner with suspicion. This has to stop. A classic example of such a mindset is our going back on the announced policy of 74 per cent foreign ownership in the telecom industry. The excuse offered is security. Frankly, nobody has been able to explain to me how foreign ownership of 74 per cent in telecom companies affects the security of the country. The question of having network control centres outside India is another issue that is being resisted. Here, too, we must understand that India is still a small market in data traffic. Having network control centres in India at this stage is simply not viable, though it will surely happen in the future. In any case, we can insist that the government will take control of these facilities in India should there be a warlike emergency. Insisting that the CEO of telecom companies with foreign investment must be an Indian is another irrational requirement. Today, a CEO is just the first among several leaders in a corporation. He/she cannot do much without cooperation from the senior management of the company. In any case, a good regulator, an independent board and a robust whistleblower policy will prevent the CEO from misusing any powers. We have to learn from the example of nations that have made tremendous progress in this area.

xvi.   We have to accept new business models and not give in to vested interests. The software industry has been discussing, with the Ministry of Telecommunications, the need to provide IP-driven voice network connectivity through private user groups for over ten years now. Such a facility helps our project managers attend to our customers in a different time zone from home during night hours. The tragedy is that we have been paying for the bandwidth and are not able to use it because of the government's refusal. This makes us non-competitive in the market and forces our employees to spend sixteen hours in the office from 8 a.m. to midnight. This affects the employees' health, family life and morale. Continuing with this policy will, in all likelihood, kill this industry in a few years.

xvii. We must involve the private sector and create public–private partnerships (PPPs) to enhance the efficiency of the government. The government brings focus on the public good while the private sector brings focus on efficiency, effectiveness and accountability. Unfortunately, Indira Gandhi's experiment of bringing private sector experts to the government was given up by her successors. Similarly, S.M. Krishna's experiment in creating the Bangalore Agenda Task Force, a unique PPP, was disbanded by his successors. These experiments must be persisted with.

xviii. Finally, any progress requires discipline. I do not know of any developed country or a country which aims to become developed that has not adhered to strict discipline. Unfortunately, in our country, discipline is given the least importance. This has to change if we want to create a large number of jobs to eradicate poverty through globalization.

All these are doable. I am an optimist and take solace from Winston Churchill's words, 'A pessimist sees difficulty in every opportunity; an optimist sees opportunity in every difficulty.' None of my suggestions involve rocket science. However, they do require courage which is the first attribute of a great leader. They require a mindset that is ready to sacrifice personal interest and the interest of this generation so that our future generations are better off. I know that we can pull it off. We just have to make tough decisions. That is all.

Transforming Emerging Economies and Leaving Behind Legacies

I will focus here on the role of future business leaders in transforming emerging economies (EEs) and leaving behind legacies while running successful businesses and making profits. I will use my experience as a businessperson in India and China as well as ideas from three wonderful books: *The Fortune at the Bottom of the Pyramid* by C.K. Prahalad, *The 86% Solution* by Vijay Mahajan and Kamini Banga, and *We Are Like That Only* by Rama Bijapurkar.

What are emerging economies? They form 86 per cent of the world's population spanning across the 150 nations that have a per-capita gross national product (GNP) of less than $10,000. These are markets that were, till recently, ignored by most MNCs or explored unsuccessfully using methods that worked in developed markets. However, these markets offer a major growth opportunity for MNCs whose growth rates in traditional developed nation markets have slowed down.

There are many reasons why emerging economies should be on the top of the agenda for businesses today. First, EEs have been growing fast. Several indicators show that emerging economies are gaining dominance in the world economy. Since 2005, the combined GDP of emerging markets (measured at purchasing power parity)

'View from the Top', a lecture delivered at the Graduate School of Business, Stanford University, 15 October 2007

has accounted for more than half the total world GDP. According to the *Economist*, their share of world exports has jumped to 43 per cent in 2006 from 20 per cent in 1970. EEs consume over half the world's energy and have accounted for four-fifths of the growth in oil demand in the past five years. They also hold almost three-quarters of the world's foreign exchange reserves. China with an average annual growth rate of over 10 per cent in the last fifteen years and India with over 7 per cent average annual growth rate during the last ten years are just two examples. Domestic markets in the EEs are growing faster than ever. For example, the retail sector in China has been growing at 15 per cent for the last twenty years. China is already the largest mobile telephone market in the world with over 400 million subscribers and the mobile telephone market in India is growing at the rate of 8 million new subscribers each month. The fast moving consumer goods (FMCG) market in India is worth around $10 billion and is growing at around 7 per cent. China adds 33 million personal computers a year while India adds 8.5 million a year. I can go on and on with such data. The message is clear: there is a fortune to be made in these markets, in general, and from the poorest segment of these societies, called the bottom of the pyramid, in particular.

Second, the world has moved from viewing emerging economies as perennial recipients of aid from rich countries to viewing them as sourcing zones, manufacturing hubs and markets by creating a platform for these economies to participate in the world market. These advantages create jobs and eradicate poverty. In other words, there is a consensus that creating a level playing environment leads to sustainable economic prosperity as against providing economic aid to the EEs. This has happened due to globalization which I define as the paradigm that helps corporations source capital from where it is cheapest; source talent from where it is best available; produce where it is most efficient; and sell where the markets are, without being constrained by national boundaries. Such a world, which Thomas Friedman calls a 'flat world', has created a huge opportunity for companies in the developed world to operate efficiently. China's success as the factory of the world and India's emergence as the software development centre of the world are good examples of this paradigm.

Third, a significant percentage (as much as 65 to 70 per cent) of the population of these EEs lives on an income of just about $2 a day. What is interesting is that these poor people are value-conscious consumers who will buy products and services as long as they get value for money. While per-consumer revenue and profits may be low, their large volumes will, indeed, add up to a tidy sum of profit. The performance of several corporations like Nokia and Unilever has proved that there is definitely money to be made at the bottom of the pyramid. So far, the EEs have mostly been out of the radar screen of most MNCs who were used to Western business models. The challenge is to bring in their consumers by enabling dignity and choice through markets, as C.K. Prahalad says.

Fourth, the growth rates of companies in several sectors like food, personal care, automobiles, banking and retail in the developed world are flattening. These companies are looking at the emerging markets in Asia and Latin America for maintaining their growth rates and margins. Open any magazine and you will see that the contribution of Asia is increasing steadily in the revenue and profit profile of several well-known corporations. For example, India and China are some of the fastest-growing markets for the automobile and airline industries. A recent report by PriceWaterhouseCoopers notes that the BRIC countries—India, Brazil, Russia and China—will account for more than 40 per cent of the forecast for global light vehicle assembly increases, and represent 52 per cent of the industry's forecast for global capacity expansion during 2005–10.

Fifth, most of the anger, violence and terrorism that we see around us today is due to the huge economic divide that exists between the haves and the have-nots. A sure way of reducing this divide is to focus on bringing the poorer world into the mainstream by making them trade partners so that it is a win-win proposition. A world concentrating on improving the quality of life through international trade is likely to be a peaceful world.

There is yet another reason why we should be concerned about emerging countries and their markets. Plato in his celebrated book *Republic* elevates the role of rulers through his concept of guardians or philosopher-kings who are above warriors, merchants and farmers.

Similarly, several Hindu scriptures dated as early as 2,000 BC provide evidence that in ancient India philosophers were assigned roles higher than the roles assigned to kings, warriors, merchants and farmers. To me, in these days of globalization and cross-border trade, the highly-educated youth are, indeed, the philosophers who have a responsibility to transcend the boundaries of nations and races and become global healers. They have to use the power of corporate wealth to create opportunities to better the lives of the poor around the world and simultaneously make profits for corporations.

What are the political and social characteristics of these emerging nations?

First, the political leadership in most emerging countries is sceptical about foreigners and foreign corporations due to a history of colonization or due to cases of exploitation by MNCs. Second, most such nations have large rural populations. In emerging economies with a democratic setup, the electoral energy, therefore, lies with the rural masses with low income and low literacy while the economic energy lies in urban areas where economic progress takes place. Hence, leaders have to tread carefully and not play a zero-sum game in allocating funds to urban areas to improve industrial competitiveness. Third, local business lobbies tend to prevent foreign competition from entering the market since they are not confident of competing with foreign corporations on cost, innovation, quality and customer satisfaction. It is very important that their fears are allayed. Fourth, a few cases of unintended malicious acts like patenting basmati rice or turmeric, grown in India for over 5,000 years, create doubts about the intentions of foreign corporations. It is very important to create trust in these markets. Finally, it is important to remember that the bureaucracies in these economies are very rigid; transparency is low; and corruption incidents higher than in developed nations.

Generally, these economies were either colonized or were under despots or under communism. In other words, capitalism was not practised there till recently. Barring exceptions, most of them have understood that the Fabian socialist model has not succeeded in solving the problem of poverty. Centralized planning and control in economic policies have played a big role in retarding the progress of such economies. The bureaucracy is rigid and mistakes the interest of the government for the interest of the people. As Hernando De Soto has pointed out, these economies are most often asset-rich but capital-poor since there is no speedy and efficient legal system to guarantee property rights. For example, in most of these countries, it is said that 95 per cent of the landowners do not have legal titles to their land. These nations have realized rather recently (during the seventies, eighties and nineties) that the only way poverty can be eradicated is by creating more and more jobs with higher and higher disposable incomes, and that entrepreneurship is the only way to create more jobs. Their citizens have also realized that it is not the responsibility of the government to create these jobs but to create an environment that has the least friction and the highest incentives for entrepreneurship. In other words, there is growing appreciation of free markets in these countries.

What do we mean by transforming EEs?

i.   It is about ensuring that every child has access to decent education, health care, nutrition and shelter by providing these at appropriate prices.

ii. It is about ensuring that every individual is free to better his or her life by leveraging his or her competency.

iii. As C.K. Prahalad says, it is about believing in the power of free markets to enable dignity and choice through markets and creating a large number of productive jobs in a win-win manner.

What does it take to transform these economies and possibly leave legacies behind?

i.   First, you have to accept that these are viable markets. What they need is innovation in business models, product design, pricing, financing, production, marketing and selling. We have to move from the era of aid to enabling the poor by serving them through appropriate products at appropriate prices and market mechanisms—a win-win solution.

ii. Accept that EEs are not the way developed markets were in their infancy. Thanks to the increased impact of globalization and technology, we live in an interconnected global village. As could be seen in the recent launch of the iPhone, a product released in the USA today is seen on the net instantaneously across the world, its features discussed in detail, its weaknesses analysed threadbare, and its value proposition talked about ad nauseam. Hence, the traditional thinking of MNCs that they can release an outdated product in emerging markets has to go. For example, when a leading European car manufacturer launched an outdated model in India, the product was rejected outright. We have to eschew value arrogance and desist from assuming what worked in the developed markets in the past will work in developing markets now.

Rama Bijapurkar talks about how Kellogg's efforts to position their breakfast cereal as nutritious and fat free was not a great success in south India since idli, a popular breakfast item there, is nutritious and fat free as well, and Indian children do not like to eat cold stuff in the morning. On the other hand, according to Bijapurkar, if Kellogg had branded it as the best nourishment for the tired child returning from school in the evening, it would have taken off better.

iii. Leverage the non-formal segment of the market to grow your revenues by creating innovative mechanisms to provide credit access to the poor. Francisco Zambrano and his team at CEMEX realized that the informal segment accounted for almost 40 per cent of the cement market in Mexico. This market is about $1 billion strong and is likely grow at 10 to 15 per cent a year. They came out with the concept of 'Patrimonio Hoy' (Savings/Property Today) to provide an affordable, savings-based payment system spread over an acceptable period of time without hurting the other basic needs of the poor.

Casas Bahia is another wonderful example of how one can run a profitable business by addressing the needs of the bottom of the pyramid in Brazil, which has a purchasing capacity of over $150 billion. It created innovative credit analysis and financing schemes, and leveraged the power of information technology to reduce the cost of its operations. Casas Bahia delivers and installs electronic appliances in the homes of customers in favelas or shanty towns. The firm has, through this model, built a business of over $1.5 billion.

iv. Enhance the efficiency and reduce the cost of your business operations by enabling the poor to become part of the supply chain. Hindustan Unilever (HUL), a subsidiary of Unilever in India, has fostered entrepreneurship among rural women through their 'Shakti Amma' (Empowered Women) project by enrolling village women as retailers of their products in rural India, by creating a loyalty programme to attract customers, and by a powerful incentive programme to energize retailers. HUL has a vision to enrol 100 million bottom-of-the-pyramid rural clients in 100,000 villages through 10,000 Shakti Ammas in India. HUL has grown from a $500 million enterprise in 1995 to around $3 billion today.

v. Create products to suit the purse of the bottom-of-the-pyramid customer. Realizing that buying a Rs 50 ($1.25) shampoo bottle will be difficult for bottom-of-the-pyramid customers, HUL introduced small sachets that contain just enough shampoo for one-time use and sold it at Re 1 (2.5 cents). This market is growing at a healthy pace. Even if 20 per cent of the population in India uses this shampoo every day, it will result in a market of $1.5 billion annually.

Similarly, Reliance Communications brought about a mobile revolution in India by pricing its handsets at an incredibly low price of $12 and making the cost of calls Rs 1.50 (3.75 cents) per call anywhere in the country. No wonder the Indian mobile market is growing at the rate of 8 million new subscribers per month. Today, Reliance Communications is a very profitable company with revenues of over $4 billion and a market capitalization of over $30 billion. ICICI Bank, the largest private sector bank in India, has also launched a massive technology-based microfinance programme to reap profits from the power of banking to rural masses in India.

vi. Create an export agenda in the portfolio of products. Give priority to exports in your business profile so that the country can become stronger in global markets. In EEs, such export revenues will make you an important and respected player in the local community. To do this, focus on excellence in your products and services. This way, you will also serve the local market better.

vii. Focus on developing world-class leadership in these markets. Create a leadership programme in your company so that you can produce world-class leaders in the local company who can add value to your global operations. This will help your corporation and also raise the self-esteem of your employees and the country. To do this, raise the aspirations of your people and encourage them to dream big. Create an open culture. Benchmark your operations with the best global firms. Focus on the five context-invariant attributes of successful corporations—openness to new ideas and cultures, meritocracy, speed, imagination and excellence in execution. HUL and Citibank have done a wonderful job in developing a cadre of globally-valued managers from India.

viii. Demonstrate values through leading by example. Most EEs have hierarchical cultures. The best way to obtain compliance in such a context is through leadership by example. Demonstrate this through commitment, hard work, simplicity and a focus on excellence.

ix. Add value to society. This means taking part in non-political and non-controversial activities like industry associations, educational activities and societal activities. Create a foundation to address the problems of the poorest of the poor by donating a part of the profits. Exhort your professionals to spend at least a small part of their free time in making a difference to society. Desist from using products and services that destroy the environment.

x. Align your interest with the country's interest. In every decision you make, ask if it makes your company and the country better. If in doubt, choose the country, since your company cannot succeed unless the country succeeds. Such a policy is a sure way of creating profitable and enduring businesses in EEs. Unilever is a wonderful example of this principle.

xi.   Leave a lasting legacy. To create such a legacy, just ask yourself this question often: 'What can we do so that people will miss us if we disappear tomorrow?' and act accordingly.

I can go on giving examples of how you can make profits by addressing the needs of the 4 billion people at the bottom of the pyramid in EEs. As I have said before, this is possible through innovation in product design, pricing, financing, production, marketing and selling. By believing in the power of markets and innovation, you will bring profits to your corporations and the dignity of choice to consumers at the bottom of the pyramid. Most importantly, as a firm believer in the power of free markets, I urge you to demonstrate to the sceptics the efficacy of free markets in eradicating poverty.

PART X

INFOSYS

The Importance of Respect for a Corporation

It was the latter part of May 1981 when the seven founders of Infosys met at my apartment in Bombay to decide on the objectives for the company. The conversation ranged from becoming the software company with the highest revenue in India to becoming the company with the highest profits and the highest market capitalization. Finally, after a four-hour passionate debate based on data and facts—in what was to become the Infosys norm—we decided to strive to become India's most respected software services company. Our logic was that striving for respect ensured that we would not short-change our customers; we would be fair and open with our colleagues; transparent and accountable with our investors; fair with our vendor-partners; would not violate any law of the land wherever we operated; and would create goodwill in society. Indeed, these are the foundations for our value system CLIFE (Customer focus, Leadership by example, Integrity and transparency, Fairness, and Excellence in execution). Our vision was and is to become a globally respected corporation providing best-of-breed, end-to-end business solutions leveraging technology and employing best-in-class professionals.

Why has Infosys been cited as the best-respected company more often than any other company in India in the last decade? It is clearly due to our steadfast commitment to our values. We emphasize the importance of seeking respect from our stakeholders from the very

Published in *Businessworld*, 3 September 2007

first day new Infoscions walk into our Global Education Centre in the Mysore campus. I learnt pretty early in my career that the best way to make my colleagues return to our offices happy and enthusiastic every morning is to make Infosys more and more respectable. Every time I address a new batch as part of the orientation, I tell them that I can guarantee them only three things at Infosys. First, their respect and dignity will be maintained and enhanced in every transaction. Second, the company will always conduct itself in a fair and ethical manner so that they will never have to hang their heads in shame in front of their loved ones and friends. Third, they will be able to learn three times more than in any other environment. Youngsters like this because they are idealistic, respect from peers and family matter to them most, and they place a high premium on learning.

I am glad that Infosys has lived up to its promises so far. We ensure that we put the interest of the customer first in everything we do. The customer champions within the company fiercely defend the interest of the customer in every action of ours. Let me demonstrate this philosophy with an example. In July 1996, we had signed a project contract with a customer in Canada. The customer champion had promised to start the project on a certain Monday. Our project team was to leave India for Canada on the previous Friday. However, there was a delay in obtaining visas from the Canadian High Commission in New Delhi. It became apparent by Wednesday that the team would not be able to travel to Canada on Friday. Our customer champion insisted that we had to start the project on the next Monday, or the client MIS director would look bad in front of his people. Hence, a decision was taken to inform the client MIS director that he could start the first phase of the project on Monday with a vendor of his choice and that we would defray the difference between our price and the cost to the customer.

As great admirers of Mahatma Gandhi, Infoscions believe that the best instrument for creating trust in our people is through leadership by example and walking the talk. Whether it is coming to the office early, working hard, sacrificing financial and material comfort to reduce costs, or focussing on excellence in execution, the managers at Infosys always lead from the front.

Integrity is the life blood of our existence as Infoscions. We can excuse incompetence but not lack of integrity. One of the most difficult decisions we have taken was choosing integrity over talent in the case of an extraordinary individual we let go several years ago. Integrity is predicated upon our belief that we must always live by our word. That is why the phrase 'under-promise, over-deliver' is a much-revered adage at Infosys.

Investors understand that every business will have its ups and downs. What they want the management to do is to bring them the bad news proactively and early. This is why transparency becomes very important. Our belief in transparency is driven by our desire to disclose when in doubt. Infosys has always believed in bringing any possible bad news voluntarily to its investors. I can recount several examples. Bringing the news of the loss of business from our biggest client, our losses due to investments in the secondary stock market, forecasting a slower growth in 2001, and admitting, early enough, the possible financial liability in a harassment case are a few of these.

Fairness is the foundation on which all happy and sustained relationships are built. The best instrument for ensuring fairness is using data and facts to decide on every transaction. My discussions with younger colleagues tell me that they are willing to accept an adverse decision as long as we go through a fair and due process, use data and facts to arrive at a transparent decision, and provide full opportunity to the affected individual to present his or her data. That is why we believe in the adage, 'In God we trust, everybody else must bring data to the table.'

Excellence in execution is extremely important since brands are built on product or service experience. No rhetoric will convince a customer as much as delivering more than you promised. We believe that our actions speak the loudest and that they create trust in every stakeholder. Hence, the focus at Infosys is on execution rather than words. That is why, even today, we spend most of our time in enhancing the quality of recruitment, training and project execution. Every week, we receive reports on how clean our security gates are, since they are the first touch points of our stakeholders. Another important aspect of excellence in execution is the speed of response to requests, suggestions and grievances from our stakeholders, particularly fellow Infoscions. Every mail that we receive is responded to within twenty-four hours with a suitable action initiated, if not completed.

In the end, respect comes from creating trust and confidence in every transaction with your stakeholders. Let us remember that performance brings trust and confidence, trust and confidence bring respect, respect brings recognition and recognition brings power. This is the mantra at Infosys.

The Journey So Far

What does one say to a set of people who dreamt lofty dreams and made tremendous sacrifices to realize those dreams? What does one say to people who believed that their aspirations were their possibilities? I can only say thank you, and well done. Get ready now for the longer marathon. It starts today.

This journey has been a mosaic of courage, confidence, dreams, hope, integrity, irreverence for the traditional, a quest for excellence and pluralism. My mind goes back to literally thousands of images of the past that have exhilarated me. All great journeys are a continuum towards a vision. We started ours by believing that 'we will be a globally-respected corporation'.

When I decided to leave PCS to start my own enterprise, the first person I spoke to was N.S. Raghavan (NSR), who was to take over from me at PCS. How can I forget that day when NSR provided the initial vote of confidence in me by deciding to toil with me, rather than have a well-paid, safe job? Not many people in the world would have had the courage of our first customer, Donn Liles, who terminated his own operations at Bombay to work with us.

I vividly remember that day in 1982 when we were short of money for the maintenance allowance to be sent to my six colleagues in the USA. It took less than a minute for Sudha, my wife, to decide

A lecture delivered on the occasion of Infosys's Billion Dollar Day celebrations, Bangalore, 13 April 2006

to pawn her jewellery to raise the money. It is hard to forget young Kris and Nandan, on the verge of their marriages, taking confident decisions to forsake their steady jobs to plunge into Infosys.

I still remember the childlike enthusiasm of Mohan and Bala who often came running into my room, announcing that they had created yet another record in financial reporting. GRN was solid as a rock in every challenging situation. It is not easy to have the courage of a Sharad or a Prahlad or a Hema who chose a fledgling Infosys in preference to cushy and safe options.

I cannot count the number of times this organization has turned to Dinesh to recover from a seemingly impossible project situation. Who can forget Phaneesh, Srinath, Basab, Girish, Preeti and Pravin's cool handling of the most demanding customers? There can be only one Shibu and I am glad he is with Infosys. People say that programmers cannot be poets. Ashok disproved this by writing programs that were elegant poems.

I cannot forget the joy on the happy faces of hundreds of young Infoscions and petit Infoscions as they walked the streets of our campuses across the country. I still remember the camaraderie among hundreds of Infoscions from diverse backgrounds during the first Samavesh. I cannot forget the pride on the faces of the winners of the very first awards for excellence. I still rejoice at the moment when I came to know that we employed Infoscions of more than thirty nationalities. I rejoice at every moment I have spent with our independent directors.

I would like to thank the families of the founding members who went through tremendous sacrifice so that we could build a strong Infosys. My sincere thanks also to every Infoscion and ex-Infoscion, and their families, for their sacrifices in making this dream possible, and holding us steady as we scaled various challenges.

I would like to make special mention of a few people outside Infosys without whose help we could not have come this far: K.S.N. Murthy, the then chairman of the Karnataka State Small Scale Industries Development Corporation (KSSIDC) and former chief secretary of Karnataka, who sanctioned a huge loan in record time with the help of an extraordinary individual, late Rudradev; B.S.

Patil, the then MD of the Karnataka State Financial Corporation (KSFC) and a former chief secretary, who was an active and enthusiastic partner of KSSIDC in this loan; N. Vittal, the then Secretary, Department of Electronics at the Centre, Late Shri Varadan, the first director of Software Technology Park, Bangalore, and his successor, B.V. Naidu, who demonstrated that India is not short of industry-friendly bureaucrats.

This company would not have come this far but for the extraordinary support shown by our first major domestic customer—Mico. I thank Mr Vikram Bhat, Mr Venkatarajan and Mr Rajiv Lal; these are extraordinary men who put faith in people with lots of integrity, dedication and commitment but little money.

What are Infosys's contributions to India? Our greatest contribution is raising the confidence of young entrepreneurs in this country. We have shown that innovation is possible in India and that we can benchmark on a global scale; that it is possible to do business and create wealth legally and ethically; that sharing of wealth in a never-before manner is possible; that predictability, sustainability, profitability and de-risking are the cornerstones of corporate success; that openness to new ideas, meritocracy, speed, imagination and excellence in execution are essential ingredients for creating value; that people with passion and the will to learn can face any challenge and perform in a global environment; that one must do what is right for a new future, not what is traditionally acceptable; that each individual is a pioneer, a trendsetter who can change the course for the better; and that the context is an opportunity for progress and not a constraint.

Amongst you are the founders of the next generation Infosys. The next journey has begun. Ably led by Nandan, Kris and a great team, you will surely succeed.

All I can say is: be original, daring, different and unreasonable. Work hard, have good values, put the interest of the country in every deed of yours and make this country the best place in the world.

On Reaching Adulthood

It is a matter of great pride to see your child grow up, embrace a good value system, seek high aspirations and achieve more than you ever thought was possible. Infosys is one such child—a child that has made all of us proud not by its achievements alone, but just as much by its humility, grace, value system and courtesy.

There are two sets of people I want to thank on this occasion. First, of course, are the Infoscions and ex-Infoscions. They embraced high aspirations, and a great value system, and proved that 'a plausible impossibility is better than a convincing possibility'.

But their dreams, their aspirations and their hard work would have all come to naught if it were not for a set of extraordinary people with equally high aspirations, courage, dreams and, perhaps, even nobler objectives. In fact, these people carried the hopes and dreams of millions of Indians, and worked against all odds to make what seemed impossible, possible. I am referring of course to the late prime minister Shri P.V. Narasimha Rao, the current prime minister Dr Manmohan Singh, Shri P. Chidambaram and Shri Montek Singh Ahluwalia, the architects of the 1991 economic reforms.

Infosys is a shining example of the success of economic reforms. It is a company that has created more than 55,000 high quality, high disposable-income jobs, contributed more than $2 billion a year to

---

A lecture delivered on the occasion of Infosys's twenty-fifth anniversary celebrations, Mysore, 30 July 2006

India's exports, raised the image of India by conducting business legally and ethically and by earning many laurels abroad.

Let the critics of India's economic reforms realize, by our example, that there is no alternative to the creation of jobs to solve the problem of poverty. Let them understand from our example that there is no alternative to high aspirations, courage, confidence and excellence in execution in competing with the global best to leave behind a better society for our children.

Several images pass through my mind today, one after the other. Waiting at the entrance to the Reserve Bank of India month after month with my good friend Anil Bhatkal, and some times with Sudha and little Akshata, for four to six hours, to obtain part of our own hard-earned dollars to support my six other founders, is an experience that I cannot forget and cannot wish on anyone else.

When in 1992, the young librarian at Infosys, asked by our first head of E & R about a library book, referred to me—the borrower—as 'the gentleman that sits at the entrance', I knew our job had been done in demolishing hierarchy. When the first telephone was installed in the house of P. Bala who was in charge of the computer centre, and not in the house of the CEO, I knew we had created a customer-focussed organization.

When we spent 1.5 times of our revenue in 1992 to start India's first campus, I knew we had started on a journey of worthy dreams. When we politely refused General Electric's unreasonable conditions in 1995 and walked away from their business though they contributed to 25 per cent of our revenues and 8 per cent of our profits, I knew we had built a courageous and principled organization.

When Ramachandrappa, an attendant, told me recently about the fabulous house he has built, I knew our experiment in the democratization of wealth had achieved success and indeed served a great purpose. When Infosys Foundation financed and fulfilled the dream of higher education of the bright but poor Hanumanthappa, belonging to a disadvantaged community, I knew our hearts were in the right place. When I stood up in front of 1,500 investors and accepted that we had erred in investing some of our free cash flow in the secondary market and lost it, I knew we had fulfilled our pledge to be transparent with our investors.

I can go on and on. But what is important is to remember that we have bigger challenges and rewards ahead of us. I will not be there when all of these are achieved. But remember that aspirations, courage, principles, innovation and relentless focus on execution will carry you to greater success.